D0082954

John Milton is one of the seventeenth century's most highly regarded poets: a worthy heir to the ancient poets Homer and Virgil, it has been argued, and yet also a key figure in the politics and social debate of his own age.

This guide to Milton's extraordinary work offers:

- an accessible introduction to the contexts and many interpretations of his texts, from publication to the present
- an introduction to key critical texts and perspectives on Milton's life and work, situated within a broader critical history
- cross-references between sections of the guide, in order to suggest links between texts, contexts and criticism
- suggestions for further reading.

Part of the *Routledge Guides to Literature* series, this volume is essential reading for all those beginning detailed study of Milton and seeking not only a guide to his works, but a way through the wealth of contextual and critical material that surrounds them.

Richard Bradford is Professor of English at the University of Ulster at Coleraine

Routledge Guides to Literature*

Editorial Advisory Board: Richard Bradford (University of Ulster at Coleraine), Jan Jedrzejewski (University of Ulster at Coleraine), Duncan Wu (St Catherine's College, University of Oxford)

Routledge Guides to Literature offer clear introductions to the most widely studied authors and literary texts.

Each book engages with texts, contexts and criticism, highlighting the range of critical views and contextual factors that need to be taken into consideration in advanced studies of literary works. The series encourages informed but independent readings of texts by ranging as widely as possible across the contextual and critical issues relevant to the works examined and highlighting areas of debate as well as those of critical consensus. Alongside general guides to texts and authors, the series includes 'sourcebooks', which allow access to reprinted contextual and critical materials as well as annotated extracts of primary text.

Available in this series

Geoffrey Chaucer by Gillian Rudd
Ben Jonson by James Loxley
William Shakespeare's The Merchant of Venice: A Sourcebook edited by S. P. Cerasano
William Shakespeare's King Lear: A Sourcebook edited by Grace Ioppolo
William Shakespeare's Othello: A Sourcebook edited by Andrew Hadfield
John Milton by Richard Bradford
Alexander Pope by Paul Baines
Mary Wollstonecrafts's A Vindication of the Rights of Women: A Sourcebook edited by Adriana Craciun
Jane Austen's Emma: A Sourcebook edited by Paula Byrne
Mary Shelley's Frankenstein: A Sourcebook edited by Timothy Morton
The Poems of John Keats: A Sourcebook edited by John Strachan
Charles Dickens's David Copperfield: A Sourcebook edited by Richard J. Dunn
Charles Dickens's Bleak house: A Sourcebook edited by Janice M. Allan
Herman Melvilles's Moby-Dick: A Sourcebook edited by Michael J. Davey
Harriet Beecher Stowe's Uncle Tom's Cabin: A Sourcebook edited by Debra J. Rosenthal
Walt Whitman's A Song of Myself: A Sourcebook and Critical Edition edited by Ezra Greenspan
Robert Browning by Stefan Hawlin
Henrik Ibsen's Hedda Gabler: A Sourcebook edited by Christopher Innes
Thomas Hardy by Geoffrey Harvey

* Some books in this series were originally published in the Routledge Literary Sourcebooks series edited by Duncan Wu, or the Complete Critical Guide to English Literature series, edited by Richard Bradford and Jan Jedrzejewski.

John Milton

Richard Bradford

Routledge
Taylor & Francis Group

LONDON AND NEW YORK

First published 2001
by Routledge
2 Park Square, Milton Park, Abingdon, Oxon, OX14 4RN

Simultaneously published in the USA and Canada
by Routledge
711 Third Ave, New York NY 10017

*Routledge is an imprint of the Taylor & Francis
Group, an informa business*

© 2001 Richard Bradford

This volume was first published as
The Complete Critical Guide to john Milton

Typeset in Schneidler by
HWA Text and Data Management, Tunbridge Wells

*British Library Cataloguing in Publication
Data*
A catalogue record for this book is available from the British
Library

Library of Congress Cataloging in Publication Data
A catalogue record for this book has been requested

ISBN 978-0-415-20243-5 (hbk)
ISBN 978-0-415-20244-2 (pbk)

To Helen and Gerard Burns
And Amy, Cork's Eve

CONTENTS

CONTENTS

ACKNOWLEDGEMENTS

Thanks are due to the Art, Design and Humanities Faculty of the University of Ulster for providing me with the time to complete this Guide. Even more are due to Dr. Jan Jedrzejewski for reading it and advising on it. Talia Rodgers has offered much encouragement and her colleague at Routledge, Liz Thompson, has done tireless and heroic work on the preparation of the final draft. Beth Holmes and Rosemary Savage of the University of Ulster have provided invaluable help. Amy Burns has shown generous tolerance.

ABBREVIATIONS AND REFERENCING

Throughout the book, references to the works of Milton are taken from the following texts and abbreviated as shown:

TP   *The Poems*, eds J. Carey and A. Fowler (London: Longman, 1968)
CPW *The Complete Prose Works of John Milton*, ed. D.M. Wolfe (New Haven: Yale University Press, 1953–82)
WJM *The Works of John Milton*, ed. F.A. Patterson (New York: Columbia University Press, 1931–40)

For the poetry, all references are to line numbers. For the prose works, all references are to page numbers. Where *CPW* or *WJM* are followed by a Roman numeral, e.g. *CPW III*, the reference includes a volume number.

For all other references, the Harvard system is used; full details of items cited can be found in the bibliography.

Cross-referencing between sections is one of the features of this series. Cross-references to relevant page numbers appear in bold type and square brackets: **[28]**.

INTRODUCTION

The three-part format of this guide is largely self-explanatory. A brief biography of Milton, his life and times, is followed by a middle section in which each of his poems is examined in detail. The third part considers the critical controversies and questions addressed by Milton's critics from the seventeenth century to the present day.

More important than the separate functions of each section are their mutual relationships, and here John Milton almost demands this Guide's triple perspective. Few, if any, major British writers have been so closely involved with the crucial issues and events of their time. If Milton had never written a poem his vast number of pamphlets and tracts of the 1640s and 1650s and his role in the post-war Cromwellian government would have earned him a place in surveys of seventeenth century British history. But he did, of course, write many poems, one of which, *Paradise Lost*, remains as the only serious British contender for equal ranking with the epics of Virgil and Homer. Readers and critics of Milton have speculated constantly on how the different dimensions of his life and work intersect. This Guide will not offer final answers to the questions raised by such speculations, but it will, for the first time in a single book, provide the reader with a map and a set of directions so that they can follow with confidence their own enquiries and reach their own conclusions.

For example, it has often been suggested that the picture of Satan and his defeated compatriots offered in Books I and II of *Paradise Lost* is a political allegory. Perhaps Milton expected his reader to find parallels between the denizens of hell and another more recent group of failed rebels: by 1667, when *Paradise Lost* was published, the Cromwellian experiment in republican government was a recent memory. A survey of what actually happens in Books I and II is available in Part II of this Guide, which will address the reader to the question of political allegory. To properly consider the question the reader will need a clear perception of what the Civil War and its aftermath involved, particularly for Milton: a detailed account of this will be provided in Part I. The reader will also want to know how literary critics have dealt with the same questions and what conclusions they have reached. Part III will deal with this. Throughout the Guide bracketed references will assist the reader in their pursuit of such contentious issues, directing them to the relevant parts of each section.

The principal benefit for the reader of this triple perspective on Milton is that it strikes a unique balance between the provision of information and explanation. The fact that Milton's first wife left him in 1642 and that the following year he published *The Doctrine and Discipline of Divorce* is beyond dispute. The dispute to which these events contribute also involves Milton's representation of gender in his poems: was he a misogynist and, if so, how did personal experience contribute to his state of mind? This question has divided modern feminist critics. The reader must make their own decision and the Guide will assist them in this by pointing them to relevant features of Milton's life and work and engaging them with the consequent critical debates. In doing so it will provide the reader with a uniquely multidimensional framework against which they can test their own responses and inclinations, and will better enable them to organise their thinking without imposing upon them a final conclusion. That is up to you: read on.

PART I

LIFE AND CONTEXTS

(a) INTRODUCTION

This section is a brief biography of Milton, involving the political, religious and cultural contexts of his life, which also includes discussions of his prose pamphlets and essays. The poems will be mentioned here but dealt with in more detail and exclusively in Part 2. Full publication details of the three biographies referred to in this section as 'Phillips' (1694), 'Parker' (1968) and 'Wilson' (1983) can be found in the bibliography. These and other biographies of Milton are discussed in 'Further Reading' at the end of this section.

(b) BREAD STREET 1608–1625

The family into which John Milton was born on Friday, 9 December 1608 exemplified the mutations and uncertainties of England at the beginning of the seventeenth century.

His paternal grandfather, Richard, had been a yeoman and worked a farm near Stanton St. John, a village about four miles north of Oxford. Richard had initially occupied a position in the social hierarchy only just above that of the medieval serf but by means still undisclosed, probably a good marriage, he acquired an estate that in 1577 was recorded as providing the considerable income of £500 per year.

Milton never in print made reference to his grandfather, which is not entirely surprising given that Richard's public allegiance to Roman Catholicism earned him excommunication from the Elizabethan Church of England in 1582 and in 1601 fines amounting to £120. Religious difference caused a feud between Richard and his son John, Milton's father. It is known that John senior attended Christ Church, Oxford sometime during the 1570s, although there is no record of whether he did so as a chorister or a student: he did not receive a degree. In any event it is likely that in Oxford John witnessed the disputations that attended the new theology of Protestantism, then in England barely fifty years old. One day after John had returned to the family home Richard discovered his son in his room reading that symbolic testament to Anglicanism, the Bible in English. Quarrels between father and son intensified, with the eventual result that in the early 1580s John was disinherited and left Oxfordshire for London, never to return, nor as far as is known to communicate again with Richard.

Nothing is known of how John, then in his early twenties (b. 1562) kept himself when he first arrived in London, but in 1583 or thereabouts he was taken on as an apprentice by James Colbron, a scrivener, and by 1590 had become a successful and independent member of that profession. Scriveners combined the functions of contract lawyer, accountant, financial adviser, money lender and debt collector. They had serviced the guilds and middle ranking professional classes of the metropolis since the early Middle Ages and by the turn of the sixteenth century they had become, perhaps more than any other profession, the financial beneficiaries of the growing status of London as one of the major trading and seafaring capitals of Europe. John Milton senior did well. By 1600 he felt financially secure enough to court Sara Jeffrey, from a comfortably off family of merchant tailors, whom he married within a year. The marital home would be a five storey house in Bread Street, near Cheapside, a region favoured by wealthy, upwardly mobile traders and merchants. Their first child died before it could be baptised in May 1601 but a few years later a daughter, christened Anne, survived. Their son, John, was baptised in All Hallows parish church, Bread Street on 20 December 1608.

Milton was the child of what in modern parlance is called the professional middle classes, the bourgeoisie. John senior planned for his son a conventional route to success via the educational channels that had been denied to himself. When Milton was ten his father hired for him a private tutor called Thomas Young, a graduate of St. Andrews University. Two years later John was admitted to St. Paul's School, an esteemed institution adjacent to the Cathedral and only a few minutes walk from Bread Street. Five years after that, aged 16, he would matriculate as an undergraduate at Christ's College, Cambridge, and enjoy the decent status of a 'lesser pensioner', meaning that his father was wealthy enough to pay for modest privileges and accommodation in college.

The influence of these years upon John Milton the writer is a matter of speculation but what we know of them is more than suggestive of their effect. Milton during the later seventeenth century was to become the most esteemed and controversial living poet in England, and *Paradise Lost* would remain as the poem in English most deserving of the title of epic. His status and reputation were sustained partly by his mastery of language and verse form, but only partly. In his writing he addressed himself to fundamental issues – our relationship with God, our origins, our condition as a species and our fate. These are recurrent features of all Renaissance verse, but Milton had a special, almost unique perspective upon them. He was born into the cauldron of tensions and divisions that characterised English society in the sixteenth and seventeenth centuries, a state which began with Henry VIII's break from the Roman

Catholic Church in 1534 and which would reach its apocalyptic climax in the Civil War of the 1640s. Milton not only observed these events, he was a participant in them. He served the republican cause as its most eminent pamphleteer and polemicist during the Civil War years and he would become Latin Secretary – an office not unlike the modern post of a foreign minister – for the victorious Cromwellian government. No other major English writer has been so closely involved with the intellectual and political shaping of their age. His early years had trained him well for his role and to properly appreciate the nature of this involvement we should have a clear perception of the world – essentially England and Europe – into which Milton was born.

(c) RELIGIOUS AND POLITICAL CONTEXTS

In 1517 Martin Luther, an Augustinian monk, fixed on a church door in Wittenberg his 'theses' against the corrupt 'indulgences' of the Roman Catholic church. He initiated the Reformation, but it was John Calvin, a Geneva theologian, who created the most radical branch of Protestant theology. His *Institutions of Christian Religion* (1535) became the benchmark for division. In it he proposed a complex theological, indeed philosophical, thesis. Essentially Calvinism was founded upon the tenet of predestination, which holds that God has in advance 'elected' those who will be rewarded with eternal, heavenly existence. Human beings enter life in a state of sinfulness, carrying the burden of Adam and Eve's Fall. Therefore we are offered the possibility of redemption, but God has already decided which of us will choose the path to redemption or damnation.

Calvinists maintained that the difficult and some would argue paradoxical tenet that (a), we must by our actions redeem ourselves, while (b), the redeemed have been preselected by God, troubles us because the original sin of Adam and Eve condemned the human race to a state of punitive detachment from God's wisdom: we must accept even that which we cannot properly understand. Consequently, Calvinists argued that the ceremonial rituals of the Roman Church were self indulgent, even decadent, distractions from an attainment even of a limited knowledge of our God-willed condition and fate.

In its early years the English Reformation, particularly during the reign of Henry VIII, was less a theological than a political rebellion; the Protestant monarch rather than the Catholic Pope became the acknowledged head of the Church, with all the financial, ideological and legislative benefits carried by that role. The practises of the Church itself were largely unaltered by Henry's 1534 Act of Settlement but gradually, through the sixteenth century, more and more Anglicans become apologists and campaigners for what they perceived to be true Protestantism. Influenced by Calvinism they acquired the collective title of 'Puritans'; they sought to purify the Church of England of its Roman practises and beliefs. As a result there was conflict, evidenced respectively in the reigns of Henry's son Edward VI (1547–53) and daughter Mary I (1553–58). Edward, the so-called boy-King, was pro-Calvinist. He instituted the persecution and execution of Catholics and licensed the radical *Book of Common Prayer* (1549) which, for the first time ever, offered scripture in vernacular English, an act of independence from predominantly Latinate Roman doctrine. Mary, his sister, went to the other extreme, married Philip II of Spain, a fanatical anti-Protestant, reinstituted Roman Catholicism as the state religion and persecuted radical Protestants. Bishop Latimer and Archbishop of Canterbury Cranmer, both Anglicans with Calvinist sympathies, were burnt at the stake. The reign of Elizabeth I (1558–1603) restored a degree of compromise. Officially an independent Church of England was returned to but Elizabeth was obliged to play off against each other the interests of different forces within a divided nation, which she did with tactical brilliance.

Significantly, the Elizabethan period also involved the emergence of England as a major financial centre. The defeat of the Spanish Armada in 1588 was more than a military/religious victory. English sea power, along with its Dutch counterpart, became the instrument for early colonialism. The West Indies, America, the Indian subcontinent became predominantly English trading centres. The East India Company (referring to the region now comprising the states of India, Sri Lanka, Pakistan and Bangladesh) was founded in 1600, and the 'Company' part of its title reflects the rapidly changing economic condition of London in the later sixteenth century. The establishment of a company whose profits are distributed among shareholders and which is in itself a speculative enterprise was an inaugural feature of modern capitalism. London was at the turn of the sixteenth century alive with companies, and this environment provided Milton's father with a very profitable profession as, in modern terms, an accountant and stockbroker.

These economic transformations were closely related to the ongoing state of religious conflicts, in that what we now call the middle classes, the traders and entrepreneurs of the period, were predominantly Protestant and Calvinist. And there were a number of reasons for this.

Roman Catholicism was an element of the feudal, hierarchical systems of medieval Europe and, particularly in England, a new class was emerging, managed by enterprise and endeavour rather than birthright. Calvinism did not explicitly incorporate a political philosophy but its conception of man's relationship with God found a sympathetic secular counterpart in the state of mind of the latent middle classes. Calvin emphasised that the elect was an assembly of individuals, unlike the institution of the Church with its self-sustaining hierarchies and oppressive conventions. There seemed for many middle class Protestants to be an obvious parallel between their unsteady relationship with the monarchical, aristocratic structures of the medieval state and with the similarly reactionary characteristics of the old Church, in both its Roman and High Anglican manifestations. But even among Calvinist orientated Protestants there were divisions, caused principally by the notion of predestination. If the elect had already been chosen by God then matters such as conscience in determining an individual's choice between virtuous or sinful acts were at once irrelevant and self contradictory. The writings of the sixteenth-century Dutch theologian Jacobus Arminius inspired the most divisive feature of Calvinism. Arminius held that the tenet of predestination was flawed – God might well be aware of the choices which would be made by human beings between virtuous and sinful acts but such acts were on our part deliberate. Even though God knew in advance who the elect would be, we, because of our post-lapsarian gift of free will, could still choose our destiny.

The parallels between these vast and complex historical determinants and Milton's life and beliefs are by no means straightforward but some connections should be considered.

Arminianist theology did not become the foundation for a particular religious sect or political grouping; rather, it indicates the inherent tensions within the broad spectrum of Protestantism and late Renaissance intellectual life. On the one hand Calvinism replaced attendance to Papal doctrine with an empiricist reading of scripture, while at the same time its findings appeared to impose restrictions upon interpretive freedom and the fundamental notion of the believer as a self-determining individual – Arminius engaged with the latter and these doctrinal divisions would be reenacted within the religious-political fabric of England during the Civil War and its aftermath. Milton's relationship with Arminianism is important because it operates as an index to his position within and dealings with the complex factionalism of English political and religious life. For example, the term Independents is applied to a large number of prominent individuals of the Parliamentarian cause, Cromwell included. Independency advocated an early version of the modern concept of freedom of the individual, arguing that within the institution of the Protestant Church certain particulars of belief should be left to the scrutiny and choice of the individual worshipper. Independency could be regarded as an enactment of Arminianist doctrine, in that both emphasise the importance of choice and self determination in individual's dealings with religious practice. This went against the regimen of the Presbyterian Church, one of the most powerful and influential elements of the Parliamentarian cause. Presbyterianism, originating mainly in Scotland, was organised Calvinism. As an institution it was radical – it rejected the hierarchical Anglican structure of bishops for example – yet authoritarian in that it imposed upon members of its congregation theological ordinances just as unbending as those of the Catholics. As we shall see, the conflicts between Presbyterianism, organised religion, and the Independents were continuous during the late-1640s and early-1650s, when the victorious Parliamentarians were restructuring the civic, political and religious fabric of England.

Milton, in his early years, sometimes allied himself with aspects of the Calvinist-Presbyterian cause – this was the most emphatically anti-Catholic grouping in Britain – but as he began to establish his reputation as a pamphleteer on religious and political issues, and eventually became a civil servant in the Cromwellian republic, he shifted his allegiance to the Independents, the advocates of theological individualism, free speech and free will. Sometimes Milton would attack Arminianism (see *Areopagitica*, *WJM*: 313) **[29–30]**, not so much as a doctrine in its own right but because it had occasionally, and paradoxically, been adopted by Royalist High Anglicans often as a wedge to further divide the factional constituency of radical Protestantism: William Laud, Charles I's notoriously conservative Archbishop of Canterbury, was an advocate. Like many codes of belief, religious and secular, which treat the relation between the conscience of the individual and institutionalised structure in a dialectical, potentially ambiguous manner Arminianism was attractive to otherwise radically opposed parties. In essence, however, it promoted free choice and individualism, and for this reason in much of his later writing Milton supported it (see 'The Ready and Easy Way to Establish a free Commonwealth', 1660, *WJM*: 366 and *Of True Religion...*, 1673, *WJM*: 168). His two most radical and controversial works, the prose tract *De Doctrina Christiana* and the poem *Paradise Lost* are treated by all commentators as sympathetic to Arminianism: the latter foregrounds the tension between free will and doctrinal obligation by situating it in the lives, thoughts and actions of the two original human beings.

It is certain that even as a child Milton would have become aware of the tensions and polarities of belief that informed all aspects of English politics and religious affiliation. Young, his pre-school tutor, had come to London in the wake of James I's succession to the English throne and would in 1620 take up the post of Pastor of the English church in Hamburg. Young's life in Scotland and his move to Hamburg reflected his Calvinist convictions, and his pupil's lessons in Greek, Latin and Hebrew were supplemented with exchanges on contemporary religion. Richard Stock, the rector of Milton's parish church, All Hallows, was a Puritan whose Sunday sermons regularly involved the lambasting of Jesuits as the army of Satan and the Pope as their general. The high master of St. Paul's School, Alexander Gill, the surmaster, William Sound and under usher, Alexander Gill Junior all belonged to the more radical wing of the Church of England, and while St. Paul's was famous for its emphasis upon classical literature as the bedrock of learning, the writings of Virgil, Cicero, Horace, Homer and Juvenal would have been examined through the lens of contemporaneous religious doctrine. At St. Paul's Milton met Charles Diodati, a boy of his own age who would remain one of his closest friends, and Diodati would have informed him of his family history; of how his father, a physician, had first been exiled from his native Italy because of his Protestantism, had lived for a while in Geneva, the home of Calvinism, and then moved north to practise his profession in a city, London, where his religious beliefs would be sympathetically treated; of his uncle Giovanni who had stayed in Geneva to become an influential and controversial theologian, of the Calvinist persuasion.

There is no record of how the young Milton responded to his early encounters with the prevailing conflicts of the period, but if the writings of the adult are an extension of the inclinations of the child he did not submit to indoctrination. He would throughout his life remain a radical Protestant, but Milton's radicalism was of the non-peremptory, undogmatic kind. The features of Protestantism that corresponded most with his temperament were the concepts of individualism and free will, God's generous allocation to his fallen species of the opportunity to speculate on the nature of absolute truth before accepting a pre-formed actuality. And one might speculate on how his own enthusiasm for poetry played a part in this.

At St. Paul's an attainment of competence in Greek and Latin was regarded as of equal importance as a pupil's mastery of his native

English, and a knowledge of the poetic conventions of all three languages was ranked almost as highly as a command of their grammar. Pupils were asked to write poems, not as vehicles for expressive creativity but as exercises of self-discipline; a practical awareness of metre and figurative devices inculcated a greater understanding of linguistic operations per se. This ranking of poetry as an intrinsic feature of language, rather than as a self conscious excursion from its ordinary uses, reflects its broader status within Renaissance culture. Gill senior was a quintessential Renaissance schoolteacher in that he treated Greek, Latin and English as living languages whose interrelationships were mutually productive. He informed his pupils of the relative qualities of contemporary English poets, of how they had adapted, transformed and extended the precedents set by their classical precursors: Edmund Spenser was 'our Homer', Philip Sidney was the English Anacreon, Samuel Daniel the modern Lucan and John Harington the Elizabethan Martial (Shakespeare as a playwright was in Gill's opinion a little too populist for serious scrutiny, having surrendered the discipline of rhyming for the more demotic ease of blank verse (see Parker 1968: 14)).

For Milton in his early teens poetry had already become an active constituent of all discourse. At school he was expected to know its conventions, regulations and idiosyncrasies with the same confidence that attended his parsing of a sentence in Latin. At home poetry was treated as a necessary feature of the civilised household. His father, despite lacking a formal education, was an enthusiastic poeticist. He was a close friend of John Lane, an editor and publisher of poetry and himself a poet, albeit of questionable competence. Milton senior set a number of psalms to music and contributed poems to several of Lane's collections (see Parker 1968: 16). Milton's father's verse combines disarming sincerity and embarrassing ineptitude. There is no record of Milton's opinions upon his father's poems but one is tempted to wonder if they encouraged an early attendance to stylistic probity. Milton himself certainly wrote verse during this period. Undated epigrams on the Gunpowder plot survive, along with exercises in Latin elegiac verse, but they could have been produced by anyone; Milton the poet would not find his individual voice, at least in English, until he was in his twenties.

(d) CAMBRIDGE

Milton, just sixteen, arrived in Christ's College, Cambridge on 12 February 1625 and he matriculated – was formally admitted to the

University – on 9 April. His friend Diodati had gone up to Oxford two years earlier and it is likely that the Miltons chose Cambridge because of its reputation as generally more sympathetic to the cause of radical Protestantism. University dons were mostly clergymen, but if Milton had expected to join a community which addressed itself to the theological and political controversies of the day he was to be very disappointed. His Cambridge experiences, of which in any event there are few reliable records, can best be described as dull. He made no close friends there; the curriculum, unchanged for several hundred years, involved the standard retinue of rhetoric, logic and ethics, with a smattering of Greek and mathematics (Latin was the language of instruction); disputations and speculation were frowned upon, and inculcation preferred. If the move from school to university anticipated the expectation of a shift from regimentation to intellectual challenge, this for Milton seemed to have gone into reverse. St. Paul's had offered a far more stimulating, unorthodox environment than his new home.

The only notable event of Milton's early years at university occurred during the spring term of 1626. Milton's younger brother Christopher would many years later tell of how John had, after disagreements with his tutor William Chappell, 'received some unkindness'. Speculative biographers subsequently assumed that this had meant that he had been 'sent down' from the university as a punishment for insubordination. There is no record of this and such assumptions are based upon a poem in Latin by Milton himself called 'Elegia prima ad Carolum Diodatum' ('Elegy I to Charles Diodati') which is a versified letter to his friend – they corresponded regularly and always in Latin – which includes references to his college rooms as 'forbidden', and to his 'exile' and 'banishment'. It could just as plausibly have been the case that these terms referred to the fact that during this period a plague was spreading through London and other urban centres, Cambridge included, and that Milton, like many other undergraduates, had chosen to 'exile' himself to the safer environment of the country.

The myth generated by the poem is of less significance than the fact that it is in Latin. Apart from a few revisions of psalms the only poems in English by Milton before he received his Bachelor of Arts degree in 1629 were 'On the Death of An Infant Dying of a Cough' and 'At a Vacation Exercise in College'. Both are skilled and competent pieces of work, yet as the latter suggests they read more as exercises than as confident poetic statements. The 'Elegia' to Diodati on the other hand is a precocious, masterly blend of technical refinement and candid informality. Latin seemed to be the medium in which the teenage Milton felt most comfortable. It was the principal language of intellectual and theological debate, reliable and established; while English, like England, appeared to incorporate unease and uncertainty.

In February 1626 Charles I was crowned at Westminster Abbey. His predecessor James I (crowned 1604) had attempted to maintain Elizabeth's balance between religious radicalism and conservatism and with a degree of success. But for various reasons – including the fact that James had previously been King of Scotland and had brought with him to London many Calvinist advocates of Scottish Presbyterianism – division still existed in England. Little was known of Charles' intentions but it soon became evident to those close to the centre of power that the new monarch lacked the intellectual and tactical acumen of his two predecessors and that the traditionalist rather than the Puritan wing of the Church of England was gaining ground. For example, it would have been customary for the Dean of Westminster, John Williams, to have officiated at the Coronation but Williams was known to sympathise with the more radical elements of Anglicanism. He was mysteriously absent, his place being taken by William Laud, then Bishop of Bath and Wells, who favoured the practice of Catholic rites and who would eventually become Archbishop of Canterbury and fervent supporter of the Royalist cause during the Civil War.

One might assume that Milton the young student would remain largely detached from, if not entirely ignorant of, such occurrences, but there is evidence that he maintained an informed awareness of contemporary religious and political developments. Indeed, during 1626 Cambridge itself became the stage for a series of events which reflected the ongoing tensions of London. Two candidates stood for the post of Chancellor of the University; George Villier, Duke of Buckingham, enjoyed the explicit support of the king, while Thomas Howard, Earl of Berkshire, was promoted by the House of Commons. Effectively it was High Anglicanism versus Puritanism. Chancellors were elected by fellows of colleges and Buckingham won by a very slight majority. The Commons, suspecting intrigue and vote rigging by Royalist elements, demanded the suspension of Buckingham; Charles, in response, prorogued Parliament on 26 June. It was as though the early scenes of the Civil War were being rehearsed in the Halls of Academe.

Milton would have witnessed these events – the election was the subject of public debate throughout the university – and while there is no record of his opinions a Latin poem written a few months later in early 1627, as a letter to his ex tutor Thomas Young, shows that he knew and thought a great deal about closely related matters. In 'Elegia Quarta' he presents Hamburg, where Young was still Pastor of the English Church, as a city under siege by the Pro-Catholic armies of the ongoing Thirty Years War (in military terms it was not, but its reputation as a centre for Lutheran Protestantism offered evidence to its symbolic status as a bastion) and he addresses Young as a tragic exemplar of the true religion who, like many others, has been forced to flee to the solidly Protestant enclaves of Europe or New England.

In April 1629 Milton was awarded his Bachelor of Arts degree. He had, in a number of ways, grown up. After the mysterious episode with Chappell he had been allocated a new tutor, Nathanial Tovey, had worked hard and acquired a degree which was the equivalent, in modern classification, of a borderline first. He decided to stay on and do a Master's degree. How exactly Milton responded to this new atmosphere is a matter for speculation; what is known is that on Christmas Day 1629 he began what would be his first significant poem in English, 'On the Morning of Christ's Nativity'. Poems celebrating holy days were a customary feature of Renaissance culture, but what is striking about this one is a sense of intellectual presence which carries it beyond standard expectations of a respectful poeticisation of the birth of Christ. He virtually challenges the reader to engage with the gigantic complexity of the event [61–3]. It set a precedent for verse that would follow, and introduced Milton as a figure for whom poetry, while attending to its aesthetic obligations, was a vehicle for contention, exposition and ratiocination.

(e) LITERARY CONTEXT

The political and theological issues of Milton's early years would play their part in subsequent writing and thinking, but what of contemporary poetry?

In 1621 John Donne, then aged 49, became Dean of St. Paul's and Milton as a pupil at the Cathedral school would have heard him preach. Donne's verse would not appear in print until 1633, shortly after his death, but manuscript copies were in circulation among poetry enthusiasts of the day and it is almost certain that these would have passed through the Bread Street household. It is therefore both intriguing and puzzling that Donne and his work feature neither in Milton's writings nor in records of his opinions.

Twentieth-century consensus esteems Donne as the archetype of a school of writing, predominant in England during the early seventeenth century and known as Metaphysical Poetry. Samuel Johnson in his *Lives of the Poets* (1779) offered a concise description of the Metaphysical's technique; in their verse 'heterogeneous ideas are yoked by violence together'. Johnson was referring, albeit disapprovingly, to the so-called conceit, a metaphor which emphasises and frequently does not attempt to resolve the paradoxical relationship between two ideas, perceptions or states of mind. T.S. Eliot in a 1921 essay on the Metaphysicals offered a single line from Donne's 'The Relic' as an example of this technique: 'A bracelet of bright hair about the bone'. The bone referred to is the wrist of a man's skeleton, uncovered many years after burial but still bearing the thread of a woman's hair as a token of his endless love for her. In eight words Donne has compressed a catalogue of opposing concepts: life as temporary versus love as timeless; physical decay versus imperishable beauty; a decorative token versus eternal commitment etc.

Other poets of the period whose work involved the frequent use of the adventurous conceit were George Herbert (1593–1633) and Andrew Marvell (1621–78). As these dates indicate several of the writers who would later be classified as belonging to the Metaphysical School were near contemporaries of Milton – indeed Marvell would become his colleague and close friend. As a young man, when evolving his own opinions on English poetry, Milton would have been aware of the writing of the first generation of the Metaphysicals, particularly that of Donne and Herbert (Herbert, incidentally, was University Orator during Milton's first few years at Cambridge), but we know practically nothing of what he thought of it. Parker, Milton's biographer, writes that 'London was not so large that a young poet found it impossible to meet the masters of his art if he desired to do so. Milton, unfortunately, left us no account of such meetings.' (1968: 61)

A number of questions are raised by Milton's apparent reluctance to address himself to contemporary verse. Did he, as a classicist, regard the Greek and Latin poets as innately superior to their English-language counterparts? If so, why did he also begin to write verse in English? Another possibility is suggested by the thesis and indeed the title of a book by the modern critic Harold Bloom, *The Anxiety of Influence* (1973), in which Bloom argues that many aspiring poets are so convinced of their own uniqueness that they set about detaching themselves from the reputations of both their precursors and their contemporaries. The only occasion on which Milton did refer in print to another major English poet was in a short poem called 'On Shakespeare', written in Cambridge in 1630 and printed in 1632 among prefatory material to the Shakespeare Second Folio **[64–5]**. Shakespeare had been dead for fourteen years when Milton wrote the poem and it was already becoming evident that his enduring genius would outstrip his contemporaneous popularity. Milton's poem is at once diligently respectful and unnerving, in that he addressed it not so much to Shakespeare the man as to his work which, he implies, is of far more significance than his living presence.

There is one couplet which is particularly unsettling:

> Then thou our fancy of itself bereaving,
> Dost make us marble with too much conceiving

Milton seems here to be, with polite ambiguity, suggesting that the influence of Shakespeare, or at least his work, could be counter-productive. The 'conceit', the extravagant metaphor, was part of early seventeenth-century parlance and Milton implies that 'too much conceiving' (making too many conceits) will consign poets to the past ('make us marble') rather than cause them to endure via their work. Is he suggesting that Shakespeare's massive skill with figurative language has become both his monument and, more sadly, the self-indulgent inheritance of his successors, the Metaphysicals?

It is evident from Milton's early poetry that he was as confident and skilled in his use of figurative devices as any of his contemporaries, but it is equally clear that unlike most of the Metaphysicals he used language, poetic language, as a means of logically addressing the uncertainties of life, unlocking them; not as an experiment but as a harsh confrontation with the relation between language and knowledge.

Two poems written in 1631, during Milton's final year at Cambridge, attest to his growing perception of poetry as a vehicle for both creative and intellectual endeavour. 'L'Allegro' and 'Il Penseroso' are poetic versions of the academic debating exercise where one person displays his skill as a rhetorician by arguing the relative values of two opposing, sometimes antithetical, ideas or propositions. Milton was required to do this as part of his Masters degree and the two poems are based upon his engagement with the question of 'Whether Day or Night is More Excellent'. The principal criterion for success in the academic exercise involved the extent to which equanimity and balance could be achieved between the opposing perspectives, and Milton's poetic celebration of the various joys, benefits and opportunities of daytime and nighttime experience attempts a similar exercise in symmetry. There is, however, a slight but detectable sense of empathy and commitment in 'Il Penseroso' (the night poem), while 'L'Allegro' (day) is more of an exercise in allegiance [66–9]. In short, Milton discloses himself to be more innately predisposed to a state of mind which is removed from the distractions of unreflecting pleasure – he prefers night to day.

17

(f) REFLECTION

After seven years at Cambridge (1625–32) there were several career paths open to Milton. In 1631 his younger brother Christopher had been admitted to the Inner Temple in London to study for the profession of lawyer, but it had been assumed that John would make use of his considerable academic achievements and enter the more respectable sphere of the Church. Instead he chose an existence that some might regard as self-indulgent. He would spend the next seven years reading, thinking, writing and travelling.

In the autumn of 1631 Milton's father retired from business, gave up the house in Bread Street and moved to Hammersmith, now part of Greater London but then a quiet country village some seven miles from the City. Less than a year later his son took up residence with him to begin what amounted to an extended period of self-education. As he would later reflect, 'At my father's house in the country, to which he had gone to pass his old age, I gave myself up with the most complete leisure to reading through the Greek and Latin writers; with the proviso, however, that I occasionally exchanged the country for the town, for the sake of buying books or of learning something new in mathematics or music, in which I then delighted' (*WJM*, VIII: 120). Again, there is a sense here of Milton attending at once to the orthodoxies of intellectual endeavour, particularly classical learning, while calculatedly removing himself from the demands and opportunities of the contemporary world. He seemed set upon an objective, but the exact nature of this and the manner of its realisation remained undisclosed. There were, however, indications.

Close to the Milton house was the estate of Harefield, presided over by Alice, Countess of Derby. Milton was introduced to the household by Henry Lawes, a composer and musician, who had been a friend of his father's since the Bread Street days. Lawes, at the time, was music teacher to the Countess's grandchildren. Milton's attachment to the household is celebrated in his 1633 poem 'Arcades', where the Duchess is presented as the matriarch of a rural paradise in which the arts flourish (Countess Derby, then aged 72, had been a well known patron of poets and playwrights, Spenser included). In June 1631 the Earl of Bridgewater, the Countess's son-in-law, was appointed Lord Lieutenant of Wales, and Lawes and Milton decided to collaborate in the writing of a masque (a dramatic entertainment involving verse, music, dancing and scenic effect) to celebrate this. 'A Masque Presented at Ludlow Castle', later to be known as *Comus*, **[72–4]** was first performed in

September 1634 in the grounds of Ludlow Castle, one of Bridgewater's official residences. Lawes wrote the music for the song parts, and the words, sung and spoken, were Milton's. Three of the parts would be played by Bridgewater's children, who, as Law's pupils, had been well prepared for the demands of acting and singing.

The uncomplicated plot centres upon the kidnapping by the epony-mous Comus, a semi-human demonic presence, of The Lady (played by the 15-year-old Lady Alice), whom he then attempts to seduce. It is a fairy story involving a conflict between Virtue and Vice; the former triumphs and a joyous, idyllic mood prevails. *Comus* was designed as the centrepiece for an evening of dancing and restrained conviviality; it was intended to reflect for its audience, and its participants, a collective feeling of familial order and optimism. (The Lady is eventually rescued by her two brothers, played by Lady Alice's brothers, John and Thomas). Milton, who was responsible for the script and the direction of the plot, wraps a moral fable in light and decorative poetic dress, but at the same time, particularly during the verbal struggle between Comus and the Lady, he inscribes a more disturbing subtext – something that would have resonated for the adult, informed members of the audience. Three years earlier, in 1631, Countess Derby's other son-in-law, Lord Castlehaven, had been at the centre of a trial which, if tabloid newspapers had existed at the time, would have become the newsprint scandal of the decade. Castlehaven was a bisexual, a paedophile and a sadist. He obliged a number of his male servants to have sex with him and on several occasions forced one of them, called Skipwith, to rape Castlehaven's twelve-year-old stepdaughter Elizabeth, at which he was both spectator and participant. Castlehaven was found guilty and executed in May 1631. The family would have recognised the parallels – an adult, demonic figure of aristocratic bearing attempts to satiate himself with a virgin child. Comus, unlike Castlehaven, fails, but there was an implied postscript. Castlehaven was a Roman Catholic and an enthusiastic supporter of Charles I. In 1632 a Protestant, William Prynne, published a pamphlet called *Histriomastix* in which he cites Castlehaven as the worst exemplar of his religious creed. Prynne argued that the grand ceremonialism of the Roman Church encouraged the most sinful, lewd, pernicious aspects of our fallen condition.

It is evident that Milton, even when creating a night of entertain-ment, was aware of another duty as a poetic authority, someone who would cause his audience in the midst of their enjoyment to stop and think. He had not, while still in his early twenties, attempted to claim for himself the role of the modern epic poet, but thirty years later he would. One should in this regard note that the exchange between

Comus and the Lady appears in several ways to be a rehearsal for Eve's encounter with Satan in *Paradise Lost* **[112–14]**.

Apart from writing masques, what was Milton doing during this period of largely self-enclosed study? In 1637 he wrote to his friend Charles Diodati that he had become particularly concerned with history. He knew well the Greek and Roman theorists of philosophy and politics, but he was equally intrigued by the ways in which classical maxims of government had been variously cited and disintegrated by the warring factions of Europe through the dark ages and during the later medieval period. He had begun to feel that the so-called purer times of early Christianity were to some extent a myth, and was becoming more convinced that the real opportunity for Christian contentment and equilibrium was more recent. He summarised Church history as 'after many a tedious age, the long deferred but much more wonderful and happy reformation ... in these latter days' (*WJM*, III: 326). He was aware also that in England the forces of conservative Anglo-Catholicism had gained control of the religious and secular mechanisms of the state. William Laud had embarked upon a systematic purgation of the English Church of its Puritan clerics. He declared open war against parish ministers who publicly went against the now established notions of traditional Church discipline and theology, employing church wardens as informers under oath and prosecuting dissenting clergymen.

In 1635 Milton's father had moved from Hammersmith to a grander house in the village of Horton a few miles further west. Milton had moved with the family and continued with his regime of private study, but in 1636–37 the balanced equilibrium of his detached existence would be unsettled. His father, five years retired, was visited by summonses and law suits relating to share dealings with clients of a decade earlier. These would be settled but they reminded his son that the world was something that one was obliged to experience as well as observe. On 3 April 1637 his mother died, an event which brought the family together and united them in a sense of loss. The year, to Milton, would have seemed characterised by transitions and terminations. In January he had attended the funeral of the Countess of Derby, effectively his patroness. William Sound, one of his St. Paul's teachers, died a month after that, and during August London mourned the passing of a figure who seemed, to many, to be the last remaining representative of a literary generation: Ben Jonson was buried in Westminster Abbey on 6 August. In the same month Milton heard of the death at sea of one of his near contemporaries from Cambridge, Edward King, who had, following graduation, been elected to a Fellowship at Christ's College:

King also was a poet. Whether Milton and King had been close friends or passing acquaintances would become a contentious point for Milton's biographers because it was not so much King's short life and tragic death that has caused him to be remembered to this day but a poem by Milton on both called 'Lycidas' **[74–9]**. The piece was commissioned by John Alsop, a Fellow of Christ's, as part of the collection of commemorative verses entitled *Obsequies for Edward King, lost at sea* .... The other twelve verses have largely been forgotten but 'Lycidas' became a literary event in its own right and is, after *Paradise Lost*, Milton's most complex, puzzling and intensely scrutinised poem. It is, ostensibly and as required, a memorial to King, but its real subject is its author. It has frequently been compared with a piece of music, not because it was intended for song but as a consequence of its curious and unpredictable shifts in tone, subject and perspective. Some found this to be an anticipation of changing harmonies of the symphony (Nicholson 1964: 105), but in truth it bears a closer resemblance to the radical, modernist literary technique of constantly altering the style and the perceived speaking presence of the text. King's death is its starting point but thereafter it takes us through reflections on the nature of poetry, the complexities of religious belief, and political and theological conflict, all of which are interwoven with intimations of something terrible and apocalyptic about to happen. The question of why Milton produced such a strange piece of work can best be addressed by looking at his world as he would have perceived it at the end of 1637 when the poem was written.

He had become aware that his programme of self absorbed reading and study must soon end (see 'Letter to a Friend', *CPW*, I: 319), but he was not certain of what would follow it. Briefly, he took rooms at the Inns of Court, presumably with thoughts of following his brother into the legal profession; but he stayed there only for a few weeks. It is likely that his studies of the history of the civilised world had reached a natural conclusion. He now confronted the present day and what he saw caused him to think again about his role, his duty. As a poet, in 'Lycidas', he presents the reader with a vision of uncertainty, possibly catastrophe, and although there are few specific references to contemporaneous events these would have been on his mind. The co-dictatorship of Laud and Charles I was in open conflict with radical Protestantism. In June 1637 three distinguished clerics of the latter persuasion had been flogged, had their ears cut off and were publicly humiliated in central London. The tensions between the London based Anglo-Catholic hierarchy and their pro-Calvinist counterparts in Scotland had moved beyond theological debate and would, in 1639, spill over into military conflicts – brief and inconclusive but anticipatory of the Civil War.

What did Milton do? He chose to go abroad, to Europe. This decision might appear as a strategy of avoidance, but it was quite the opposite. The intellectual, political, religious divisions of England had their origins further south. Calvinism, Catholicism, the Renaissance fabric of intellectual and aesthetic radicalism were rooted elsewhere. Milton, in order to become fully aware of what he could contribute to the condition of his homeland first needed to encounter its influences.

(g) EUROPE

Milton went first to France, then to Italy and finally to Geneva before returning to London in 1639. His locations were cautiously selected in that in late 1637 he corresponded with Sir Henry Wotton, retired diplomat and then Provost of Eton College, on where and how he might encounter the best embodiments of European culture and religious doctrine (see Wilson 1983: 70–1). In May 1638 he sailed, with one servant, for France and soon after spent time in Paris where he met Hugo Grotius, Dutchman, diplomat, poet and theologian, who was at the time promoting an alliance of states, principally England, Denmark, Holland and Sweden, which would form itself into a Pan-Protestant league. Nothing came of Grotius's scheme and nothing is known of Milton's views on it. After this he sailed from Nice to Genoa.

Italy, for Milton, involved refractions and exaggerations of his life in England. He had already become something of a polymath, an archetypal Renaissance man, and now he found himself in the crucible of the Renaissance. The Renaissance itself (derived from the Latin 'renascenta' or 'rebirth') essentially involved the rediscovery of Greek and Roman culture, to be studied for its own sake rather than merely as an adjunct to the authority of the Church, and it enhanced a massive expansion of indigenous European art and thinking. It began in the mid-fifteenth century and its impact was felt first in Italy, Spain, France, Holland and Germany: its influence upon independence of mind and consequently upon the Reformation in at least three of these countries is still a matter for scholarly contention. The English Renaissance was the latest, beginning in the early sixteenth century and marked by the explosion of literary talent during the reign of Elizabeth. The sense of England as a relative newcomer to Renaissance culture would have been in Milton's mind as he set sail for France, as would a sense of the English Reformation as a token of its arrival.

In Rome, Naples and Florence he attended concerts, viewed private collections of pictures and sculpture and marvelled at the assembly of gothic, neo-classical and baroque styles that made these cities in themselves works of art. He stayed with Giovanni Manso, arguably the most eminent Italian poet of the age. Manso had known Tasso and Marini, Italy's finest sixteenth-century writers whose English equivalents would have been, respectively, Spenser and Donne. More significantly Manso, Tasso and Marini were part of a lineage which originated in the fourteenth century with Petrarch. They were the embodiments and inheritors of the essential Renaissance. (Before his visit to Italy Milton had become intimately familiar with the works of Dante Aligheri (1265–1321) whose *Divine Comedy* was the only major Christian epic prior to *Paradise Lost*.) Surprisingly, given Milton's age and slightness of works in print, his own reputation went before him. He was received in the houses of the nobility and in private academies as a figure of coming greatness. During March 1639, for example, he was invited on two occasions to give readings of his Latin and English poems in the celebrated Svogliati Academy in Florence.

Italy projected him into an idyll of cosmopolitan art and at the same time offered him a perverse vision of religious authoritarianism. Practically all of his hosts were Catholics – he even stayed for a while in the Palace of Cardinal Berberini, the Pope's nephew – and in general it seemed that a shared reverence for European culture transcended religious difference – Milton's Protestant views were as well known as his poetry. Yet all of this was underpinned by a latent sense of repression. Milton was particularly distressed by his meeting with a legendary presence, the astronomer Galileo, who by Papal decree had effectively become a prisoner in his own rooms in Florence. Galileo the disinterested empiricist had observed the universe and reported facts which went against religious orthodoxy. Six years later during the English Civil War Milton, in *Areopagitica*, recalled the meeting with Galileo, 'grown old a prisoner to the Inquisition, for thinking otherwise than the Franciscan and Dominican licensers thought'. This might seem a predictably anti-Catholic comment but elsewhere in the same document Milton notes, with retrospective irony, that his Italian acquaintances had frequently expressed an admiration for England as the paragon of multi-denominational tolerance and free speech. He knew better.

He went from Italy to Geneva, from the home of Catholicism to the hub of radical Protestantism; there he spent time with Giovanni Diodati, an eminent Calvinist theologian and uncle of his friend Charles. Milton was with Giovanni when he was informed by letter from England of Charles's untimely death. Milton left no record of how this news affected him; none was necessary. Charles had been his closest friend and most intimate confidante. Whether his sense of tragic loss coalesced, however obliquely, with his other perceptions of England is a matter for speculation. What is known is that while in Italy he had been informed of the so-called Bishops' War, an inconclusive conflict which had arisen out of Charles I's and Laud's attempts to force the Scots to accept Episcopal liturgy. In Geneva he learnt of how a related but potentially more devastating conflict was brewing between the King and Parliament. Milton, before 1639, would have perceived for himself a multiplicity of destinies, as poet, philosopher, and commentator upon his age. Suddenly he found that these honourable but somewhat unfocussed commitments were becoming specified. His country would soon be at war with itself. He went home.

(h) CIVIL WAR AND EARLY POLITICAL WRITING

The English Civil War was never officially declared by either side; understandably, given that both thought themselves to be the true representatives of the same nation. The first major, and indecisive, battle between the Royalist and Parliamentarian forces was fought at Edgehill in South Warwickshire in October 1642, but a conflict in various forms had been taking place for more than two years before that. The Scots had established a National Covenant in 1638, which was a religious assembly committed to the resistance of Charles's and Laud's doctrine and policies but bore a disturbing resemblance to an alternative seat of government. The consequent skirmishes between Scots and Royalist detachments were inconclusive but Charles was set upon the defeat of the rebellious northerners and in 1639 called an English Parliament to raise money for a second onslaught. The Commons refused and when in November 1640 he tried again they went further and embarked upon a policy of active resistance. They tried and executed his first minister, the Earl of Strafford, and Archbishop Laud was arrested and sent to the Tower where he would remain until his own execution in 1645. The imprisoned Puritan critics of the Royalist government were released, the King was compelled to abolish the Prerogative Courts, through which he had persecuted dissenters, and was obliged to accept a Bill which perpetuated the present Parliament until such time as it chose to dissolve itself. Finally, when asked to relinquish to Parliament his control of the permanent army, he refused and attempted with his private guard to take physical control of Parliament and arrest its most prominent arbiters as they sat in session. He failed, riots ensued and the King fled from London in 1641 to Oxford, which for the next five years would become the Royalist capital and headquarters for military operations.

This was the London to which Milton had returned in 1639, and it was a disturbing place. Families were becoming divided; old friends, colleagues and neighbours were separated by choice and affiliation. By 1641–42 many supporters of the Royalist cause had left the city; it seemed like a besieged encampment. Milton would have witnessed the mixture of terror and resolve which beset the city when Charles, after Edgehill, in November 1642, tried and almost succeeded in retaking it from the Parliamentarians. He would have seen the results of this successful defence, as suspected Royalist conspirators were hanged before the doors of their own houses. Some of them he would have known. He knew certainly that his own brother, Christopher, then in Reading, was a supporter of the Royalist cause.

Witness to all of this he most certainly was, but not participant. In 1639, deciding not to return to his father's rural home in Horton, he had taken a house in Aldersgate Street, London, and there set up a private academy for the young sons of the aspiring middle classes (Edward Phillips, his nephew and eventually his biographer, was one of his first pupils). The enterprise might have been inspired by his experience of the similar university-style institutions run by the intellectuals of Florence, but its purpose was more pragmatic. He still received income from his father's investments, but he wanted a degree of independence and a base in London. From here, particularly during the decade of the 1640s when the Civil War was tearing the country apart, he shifted his affiliation away from poetry and toward political-theological thinking.

The pamphlet, the short treatise published separately and usually without hard covers, had risen to prominence during the later part of the Elizabethan period. In the 1590s a series of anonymous pamphlets published under the pen-name of Martin Marprelate caused enormous controversy by publicly urging the government to purge the Church of its corrupt bishops and establish a Presbyterian structure. The authorities were so alarmed that they commissioned writers such as Thomas Nashe and John Lyly to reply on their behalf. Pamphleteering was effectively the beginning of journalism; opinionated free speech in print. Elizabeth's government recognised its dangerous potential and imposed severe restrictions on the press. These became even more stringent during the reign of Charles I but after the departure of the King from London pamphleteering was reborn as the public forum for practically every controversy of immediate relevance, politics and religion being the core issues. Milton became one of the most prolific pamphleteers of the age. Generally he supported the Parliamentarian cause but he was by no means its uncritical apologist. His pamphlets of the 1640s are marked by their projection of unsettled contemporary issues into the practical sphere of how and with what results the country would be governed after the War, the implied assumption being that the Parliamentarians would be the victors.

One of the first, *Of Reformation. Touching Church Discipline* (1641), addresses itself to the major issues that had divided the Church of England between the High Church and the opposing Puritan/Presbyterian factions, particularly the existence and status of Bishops within the Church hierarchy – and on this Milton sided with the Puritans. More significantly, the pamphlet offers, in the manner of a modern feature article on contemporary politics, a survey of the state of the Reformation. In Milton's view, Protestantism had become an ineffectual shadow of its earlier, inspired manifestation, so fraught with division that it now lacked direction or purpose. He does not specify a solution but rather implies that once the present conflict is settled (like many others he took the optimistic view that the war would be over within a year) reason will prevail and Church will cooperate with government in a purposive relationship. The mood of *Of Reformation* drifts between the impertinent, the speculative and the naïve. Its title indicates its central hypothesis, the idealised vision of England after the Civil War which he foresees as populated by individuals like himself, willing and able to stand outside organised religion and government: 'tis not the common law nor the civil, but piety and justice that are our foundresses; they stoop not, neither change colour, for Aristocracy, Democracy or Monarchy,' (*WJM*, III: 69). This thesis sums up the somewhat unfocussed idealism of the Parliamentarian Independents: guaranteed freedom of religious thought will in itself guarantee some kind of civic idyll; personal morality, instructed by biblical codes, will supplant the factionalism and corruption of previous relations between Church, government and the individual. When we compare this with his later prose writings, when he moved closer to the victorious Cromwellian ascendancy, we find that pragmatism usurped idealism, not completely but sufficient to suggest that for Milton the Civil War was a horribly educative process. Here we should look forward to *Paradise Lost*. Milton, in the early years of the Civil War, perceived the conflict as propitiate to the best that could be hoped for by fallen man. The consequences of the Fall would not be rescinded but human beings could organise themselves in a way that both accommodated and improved upon the future shown to Adam by the angel Michael. When it is shown to him in Books XI and XII of *Paradise Lost* the optimism is far more subdued: by then Milton himself had experienced the dissolution of the Parliamentarian ideal.

In *The Reason of Church Government*, published a year later in 1642, he continues with the same theme, but there is a striking section in the second book of this in which the subject becomes himself, his past, his family, his beliefs and his reputation throughout the continent as a poet. It reads sometimes like a piece of egotistical self promotion, but its purpose, albeit more implied than clearly stated, is to offer his achievements so far as a mere rehearsal for a greater task. What exactly this would be is implied also. For the reader of the pamphlet it might appear that he is introducing himself as an authority, a spokesman, commentator and promulgator of ideas that would inform the governance and condition of the new England. (One should note that his first three pamphlets were anonymous while this, his fourth, was published under his own name.) Perhaps his presentation of himself as a poet with a duty carried a private resonance because among Milton's manuscript papers would later be discovered plans and early drafts for a dramatic poem, provisionally entitled *Adam Unparadised*, on which he was working during the time of the pamphlets. This would explain the Fall and the subsequent condition of mankind, and it was of course the prototype for *Paradise Lost*.

The *Reason of Church Government* is a curious document. Certainly within it Milton celebrates his own status as a poet, but he also rationalises and contextualises this role.

> For although a poet soaring in the high region of his fancies with his garland and singing robes about him might without apology speak more of himself than I mean to do, yet for me sitting here in the cool element of prose ...

He is contrasting the imaginative, unworldly realm of verse with the 'cool' specifics of prose, and initiating himself as a prose writer, someone who will engage with the practicalities of life. He does so and he imagines the England that will emerge from the ongoing conflict,

> because the spirit of man cannot demean itself lively in this body without some recreating intermission of labour and serious things, it were happy for the commonwealth if our magistrates, as in those famous governments of old, would take into their care ... the managing of our public sports and festival pastimes, that they

might be ... such as may inure and harden our bodies by martial exercises to all warlike skill and performance, and may civilise, adorn, and make discreet our minds by the learned and affable meeting of frequent academics, and the procurement of wise and artful recitations sweetened with eloquent and graceful enticements to the love and practice of justice, temperance, and fortitude, instructing and bettering the notion at all opportunities ... Whether this may not be, not only in pulpits, but after other persuasive method, at set and solemn panegyrise, in theatres, porches, or what other place or way may win most upon the people to receive at once both recreation and instruction, let them in authority consult.

(*WJM*, III: 239–40)

This vision was partly inspired by his visit to Florence but in a broader sense he is imagining England as a Christian, Protestant recreation of the Athenian and Roman states: worship, labour, sport, the intellect, the conditions of daily life will be incorporated and attuned. Again we should compare this with his prose writings of the late-1640s, when he had become an active member of the new republic, and note that the speculative idyll is replaced by conditional pragmatism.

The pamphlets introduced Milton to a new discourse. He had at Cambridge refined his skills as a rhetorician and now he was adapting these largely oral exercises to print and prose. He could be a combative and uncharitably polemic writer. He often suffered fools – that is opponents – ungladly and his acerbic, aggressive tendencies become harshly evident in his *Animadversions upon a Remonstrant's Defence against Smectymnuus* (1641). 'Smectymnuus', as everyone knew, was an assembly of the initials of five Presbyterian clergymen who were involved in an ongoing public debate by pamphlet with Bishop Joseph Hall, a Laudian divine, on Protestant theology and ecclesiastical practice. (One of the former was Thomas Young, TY, Milton's childhood tutor with whom he had remained in contact). Irrespective of the theological content of *Animadversions* what is most striking is its author's ability to blend scholastic authority with bombast and ridicule.

One of his most intriguing pamphlets is *Of Education* (1644). It was composed as an open letter to Samuel Hartlib, a response to his book *A Reformation of Schools* (1642). Milton saw education as a practical means of repairing man's relationship with God, but his pamphlet also involved a civic ideal. It is radical, revolutionary, in its formulation of an education system which would unite the country and bring together all of its citizens within a fabric of learning, a collective sense of identity and duty. Matthew Arnold was to suggest something similar in the mid-nineteenth century and the 1945 Labour Government attempted to implement a socialist version, but Milton preempted both. The pamphlet is influenced by Milton's experiences in St. Paul's, Cambridge and Italy. He suggests that all citizens (aged between 12 and 21) should be instructed not only in the classics but in contemporary literature and thought (no doubt recalling Gill at St. Paul's) and that a network of institutions should be set up throughout the nation which would combine the perceived roles of school and university. Instruction and freethinking would productively interact. Again he is projecting this thesis into the idyll of the nation beyond the war, united and at peace with itself.

Milton's most debated and celebrated pamphlet is the *Areopagitica* (1644). It was prompted partly by an ordinance passed by the Commons in June of the same year by which the immense output of the London presses would thereafter be monitored and regulated by Parliament. By this time the Commons was dominated by an inbuilt majority of hardcore Presbyterians who were becoming unsettled by opinions, publicly voiced, and radical factions which had spun out of what was effectively a prototype republic. The Independents were arguing for the establishment of a Constitution which would licence freedom of expression and religious commitment. They were themselves Protestants but they envisaged a post-war state in which no specific school of belief would dominate the secular organs of government. The Parliamentary ordinance was a reaction by the Presbyterians against the growing popularity of the Independents, whose spokesmen were making use of pamphlets to promote their ideas. It was as though the repressive dictatorship of Charles had been inherited by the Presbyterians who similarly feared anything that might threaten their autocratic preeminence.

Milton, while remaining committed to the Cromwellian cause, was unsettled by the image of a post-war nation that was an authoritarian, Presbyterian, version of its High Church predecessor, and *Areopagitica* is an argument for religious freedom and free speech. He addresses the Parliament of England as if it were the democratic assembly of ancient Athenians assembled on the Areopagus, the hills of Ares near Athens (hence the title). *Areopagitica* promotes a condition of liberty and freedom of choice that would not properly feature in the socio-political mainstream of British life until the nineteenth century. It would, long after Milton's time, be plundered by those who wished to underpin their own libertarian ideas with quotations from what is often regarded as the first systematic defence of free speech. Consider, for example, the following assault upon the practice of censorship.

As good kill a man as kill a good book; who kills a man kills a
reasonable creature, God's image; but he who destroys a good book,
kills reason itself, kills the image of God, as it were, in the eye.

(*WJM*, IV: 297–8)

Milton's presentation of himself in *The Reason of Church Government*
as a poet with the wisdom and authority of a philosopher is here fully
justified. The passage deploys figurative devices not as decoration but
as constituents of a powerful, logically argued thesis, and it typifies
the manner and technique of the rest of the pamphlet.

Milton was aware that *Areopagitica* was a provocative and, for him,
potentially dangerous piece of work; arrest and imprisonment seemed
distinct possibilities. In fact, Parliament responded in an unexpected
and quite effective manner; they ignored it. They did not even discuss
the repeal of the printing ordinance. Six months after it was published
William Prynne, a supporter of Presbyterianism, published a Parliament-
sponsored pamphlet called *Fresh Discovery* in which he assailed critics
of the licensing laws. Milton was not mentioned, and one wonders if
it had become an official government policy to pretend that he did not
exist; if so, this might perhaps be taken as a perverse compliment to
his abilities.

Did Milton regard his treatment by the authorities as a personal
slight? Perhaps, because little more than a year afterwards he produced
a short poem which reads like *Areopagitica* versified and written by an
angrier man. 'On the New Forcers of Conscience Under the Long
Parliament' is a direct attack upon the Presbyterians, whom he presents
as an assembly of tyrants, compares Parliament with the notorious
Catholic Council of Trent and closes with the statement that, 'New
Presbyter is but old *Priest* writ large'. [84–5]

(i) MARRIAGE, SEPARATION AND THE DIVORCE TRACTS

Milton had married Mary Powell in July 1642. He was thirty-three,
she was seventeen. Their brief courtship and subsequent relationship
have become the stuff of legend and imaginative speculation, the most
sardonic example of the latter being Robert Graves's novel *Wife to Mr.
Milton* (1942). Some facts are known. Milton visited Oxford in June
1642 partly to examine documents in the Bodleian Library and partly,
at the request of his father, to deal with some family business: a loan
of £300 that Milton senior had some years before made to one Richard

Powell of Forest Hill near Oxford and repayments of which had recently become infrequent. There is no record of how the financial difficulties were settled but, as guest of the Powells, Milton met their eldest daughter Mary and within a month they were married. The sequence of events has an air of romance about it as, during the summer of 1642, Oxford was already being talked of as a base for the King and his military advisors, although Charles's presence there was not at the time permanent. Units of the Royalist and Parliamentarian armies were encamped at various points in the counties between Oxfordshire and London and within three months of Milton's visit one of the first major battles of the war would take place at Edgehill, twenty miles from Oxford, with more than 5000 killed. The Powells, moreover, were ardent Royalists and what they thought of their unexpected visitor, already known to be the author of radical pro-Parliamentarian pamphlets, can only be imagined. However, Richard Powell agreed to the marriage and to a £1000 dowry, money he did not really have. Mary returned with her husband to Aldersgate Street in late July and if love-at-first-sight had prompted their sudden union, the sensation would appear to have worn off with almost equal rapidity. It soon became evident to Milton that his bride, while beautiful and delicate in appearance, was in disposition and temperament his complete opposite. She had no interest in literature or contemporary ideas; her religion, High Church, was more an inheritance and habit than a fabric of beliefs.

After less than a month in Aldersgate Street Mary received a request from her father to return home to Oxford, which she did. No one knows why this request was made or what prompted the newly married woman to leave. At the time Royalists were leaving London in droves and perhaps her family feared for her safety. Edward Phillips, Milton's nephew, pupil and co-resident of Aldersgate Street, would have witnessed some of these events and in his biography of his uncle (1694) he tells of how Milton assumed that her absence was temporary and was expecting her back for Michaelmas, 29 September. They would not meet again until 1646, after the defeat of the King.

The connection between Mary's departure and the publication less than a year later by Milton of a pamphlet called *The Doctrine and Discipline of Divorce* (1643) seems so obvious as to be hardly worth comment, but the relationship between the event and the nature of the text is by no means straightforward. Critics have scoured the pamphlet for evidence of autobiographical inspiration and anger; there is little, if any. Mary's disappearance might have prompted the writing of it but the breadth and balanced complexity of the argument indicates clearly that Milton had been pondering and researching the topic long before he met his wife. The *Divorce* pamphlet was well planned and intended as another element of his programme of political and religious ideas. Divorce had been legalised for entirely selfish reasons by Henry VIII – it was indeed a contributory factor in his break with Rome – but over the subsequent century it had rarely been made use of by anyone else. It involved complex, potentially humiliating, and enormously expensive legal procedures. Milton's pamphlet was, as he made clear, designed as a cure for unhappiness, a proposal that couples who found themselves to be incompatible should be given an easier opportunity to end their state of mutual distress. Existing canon law permitted divorce only in extreme circumstances, such as non-consummation or if either party is found to be planning the murder of the other, but Milton argued that the distress caused by the enforced continuation of a relationship between 'two incoherent and uncombining dispositions' should, legally, be alleviated.

Parker states that 'It took almost fanatical courage that comes with overwhelming conviction in the face of accepted opinion, that kind of courage that will stand alone if it can stand on solid truth' (1968: 242). He means that while Milton's reputation as a prose writer on politics and religion rivals that of Milton the poet, it should be remembered that in 1643 he was writing as an independent, without the official protection or prompting of any of the parties and factions of a divided nation. He lived in a Cromwellian city and favoured the anti-Royalist cause but he was attacking enshrined canon law, and its advocates, the prelates, the bishops and hierarchy of the Anglican Church, still held power within both camps. What exactly did he propose? His most controversial proposition was that marriage involved a meeting of minds, that the mutual sense of intellectual and temperamental compatibility was of far greater significance than such fundamental and provable issues as procreation or sexual betrayal. In his view a marriage which is comprised of 'two incoherent and uncombining dispositions' (*WJM*, III: 417) calls for its own dissolution. If this is denied the discontented party will find themselves 'bound fast to an uncomplying discord of nature', 'an image of earth and phlegm' (*WJM*, III: 344–400), so much so that the result will be the worst imaginable: since marital love is a token of God's love for man, its failure and absence will cause the believer even to sink from 'despair to thoughts of atheism' (*WJM*, III: 405–6).

However, before citing parallels between Milton's ideas and the liberal divorce legislation of the later twentieth century one should note that in all instances Milton presents the man as the suffering party. He does not deny that the woman also might suffer, but consistently she is portrayed as the potential cause of the state in which 'instead of being one flesh, they will be rather two carcasses chained unnaturally together' (WJM, III: 478). She is presented as such not because Milton regards women as more prone than men to such specifics as infidelity, but because more often than not it is the woman who has to prove her potential for social and intellectual compatibility. He gives an example: 'who knows that the bashful muteness of a virgin may oft times hide all the unliveliness and natural sloth which is really unfit for conversation? ... nor is it therefore that for a modest error a man should forfeit so great a happiness – and no charitable means to release him' (WJM, III: 394). This might seem to us a somewhat patronising, almost misogynistic, representation of womanhood – the temptingly mute virgin might well prove to be genuinely stupid – but at the time it was radical, in that it is founded upon the assumption that a woman is at least capable of being the intellectual equal of a man.

Two points should be made about the significance of the divorce tract. First, its substance reinforces the contention that it was not a perverse, personal diatribe. Mary evidently was not the model for the hypothetical wife who failed the test of intellectual compatibility: why else would he want her back and not sue for divorce? Second, the models for gender distinction and marriage presented in the tract prompt comparison with his treatment of the same issues in his poetry, particularly his presentation of the Lady in Comus and, of course, the original couple, Adam and Eve in Paradise Lost. In the former the woman is the intellectual equal of her potential seducer, the obverse of the 'bashful muteness of a virgin'; for her, virginity (pre-marital) is part of an ethical fabric and not a tempting façade. She is, one must assume, the kind of woman who would be an active participant in Milton's idealised marriage of minds, while Comus the demon is the worst kind of man, unable to recognise the mental capacities of a woman [72–4]. Adam and Eve are a more complex pairing. Divorce in the modern (i.e. post Old-Testament) sense is not an issue in Paradise Lost but in Book IX Adam faces a choice which is at least comparable with that of the injured party in a marriage. She has eaten the forbidden fruit. If he does likewise he will stay with his beloved, indeed his intellectual equal; if he does not he will obey God's law, but lose her. He eats [114–15]. In the light of this moment in Paradise Lost consider Parker's summary of the divorce pamphlet.

> He [Milton] makes it quite clear that, in his opinion, divorce should not be permitted for malice, or for any 'accidental, temporary, or reconcilable offence' – not even for 'stubborn disobedience against

the husband'. It should be permitted only for genuine and certain incompatibility, amply demonstrated.

(1968: 243)

The parallels between the divorce tract and the Book IX passage in *Paradise Lost* are striking, and unsettling. Eve's act does indeed involve 'stubborn disobedience against the husband', but does Adam's choice to follow her mean that he sees this as an 'accidental, temporary, or reconcilable offence'? It involves the breaking of God's law (the eating of the fruit), but so do 'malice' or for that matter adultery, both 'reconcilable', according to Milton.

Paradise Lost and its complex questionings of the human condition were 25 years away but what is known is that the divorce tract caused a massive public disputation. In December 1644 Milton was summoned before the House of Lords for examination. According to Phillips (1694: 24) the case against him was 'soon dismissed'. What exactly this case was remains open to speculation. In September 1644 William Prynne in *Twelve Considerable Serious Questions* had called for the suppression of Milton's pamphlet, accusing it of irreligious liberality, but the legalistic-theological specifics of the case against Milton are lost. In his *Tetrachordon* and *Colasterion* (4 March 1645) Milton vindicates himself not by particularising the case of his accusers but by reinforcing the proposals of his first divorce pamphlet. At the centre of all this are the tensions caused by the religious differences of the period. Milton's accusers were not exclusively Anglo-Catholics (for whom divorce was forbidden and sacrilegious): Prynne for example was a Presbyterian. Essentially, Milton seemed to be averring toward a radical, Arminianist position of free will, in the sense that he interpreted scripture in a way which suggested that intellectual competence was as important as the acceptance of foregoing, conventional interpretations, irrespective of their allegiance. A subjective and revealing account of Milton's perception of all this is available in his Sonnet XII, discussed below **[83–4]**.

The battle of Naseby in 1645 was the turning point in the Civil War. Over the previous three years Oliver Cromwell had orchestrated what was the first modern military campaign. He treated his troops as professional soldiers, equipped them well with the most sophisticated armour and weaponry and planned encounters with cold circumspection. His colleague Lord Fairfax became commander-in-chief of this so-called New Model Army. After Naseby the Royalist forces were reduced to irreparable disarray and Oxford, the King's headquarters, surrendered to the Parliamentarians, commanded by Fairfax, in 1646. Charles fled but was captured a few months later and remained prisoner until his execution in 1649. The final, decisive battle was the siege of Colchester of 1648, at which the remaining, monarchless Royalists were routed by Fairfax's forces.

The years between 1645 and 1649 seem for most biographers of Milton to represent if not quite a hiatus then at least a period of reflection in his career as a writer. Between the two dates he produced no pamphlets. He wrote no more than two brief poems per year, all of which addressed themselves to ongoing civil, political and religious issues [79–90]. He worked on his *History of Britain* and a related document called *The Character of the Long Parliament*, which would be published respectively in 1670 and 1681. Both reflect and are consistent with the religious and political ideas of the pamphlets but lack their energy. Perhaps he was more concerned with the new, or rather renewed, experience of married life. Some time, probably during the spring, in 1645 Milton was summoned mysteriously to the house of his friends the Blackboroughs where waiting for him, alone in a backroom, he found Mary. Edward Phillips (Phillips 1694: 66–7) claims that Mary was penitent and submissive, 'begging Pardon on her knees before him'. They were reconciled and she joined him in his new house in the Barbican. Less than a year later their first child, Anne, was born. They would have three more: a son, John (March 1651) and two other daughters Mary (October 1648) and Deborah (May 1652). Mary Senior died two days after the birth of Deborah on May 5th. Childbirth in the seventeenth century was the most frequent cause of death for younger women. Mary was 28.

After his reconciliation with Mary – their marriage, despite their differences in temperament and disposition, was thereafter by all accounts a happy one – Milton made peace with her family: indeed he effectively rescued her father Richard from bankruptcy. His own father died in March 1647, leaving Milton his various properties and investments: the management of these would involve a further distraction from his writerly activities. Phillips in his biography offers little more than a paragraph on his uncle's intellectual life during the 1645–49 period. He moved from the Barbican to a smaller house in High Holborn: 'Here he liv'd a private and quiet life, still prosecuting his studies and curious search into knowledge, the grand affair perpetually of his life ...' (1694: 68).

It was a puzzling time. *Samson Agonistes*, a lengthy pseudo-epic poem on the story of Samson and Delilah, would not be published until 1671, but some, Parker (1968) particularly, argue that he was preparing it in the late 1640s. There are biographical parallels. Consider Delilah's speech when she returns to her husband.

> With doubtful feet and wavering resolution
> I came, still dreading thy displeasure, Samson,
> Which to have merited, without excuse,
> I cannot but acknowledge; yet if tears
> May expiate (though the fact more evil draw
> In the perverse event than I foresaw)
> My penance hath but slackened, though my pardon
> No way assured. But conjugal affection
> Prevailing over fear, and timorous doubt
> Hath led me on desirous to behold
> Once more thy face, and know of thy estate. (732–42)

Was he here recollecting his meeting with Mary in the Blackborough's house?

More significantly, Samson was blind, and in the late 1640s Milton was becoming increasingly aware of severe problems with his own eyesight. By 1652 he would become, like Samson, completely blind. Blindness features as a somewhat ghostly yet insistent theme in Milton's life and writing. In 'L'Allegro' and 'Il Penseroso' there is a curious tension between the enjoyment of the perceived world, what could be fully experienced and *seen*, and the contemplative mode, the life of the mind. His meeting with Galileo, who had seen and reported a new universe but was by then unable to see anything at all, intrigued him, and he would contemplate the strange, almost ironic, relationship between matters perceived and things known without sight in his 1650s 'blindness' sonnets **[88–9]**and in Book III of *Paradise Lost* **[101–2]**.

(j) THE EXECUTION OF THE KING AND MILTON IN THE POLITICAL CENTREGROUND

The trial and the execution of Charles I drew Milton back into the maelstrom of English political and religious debate. Two weeks after Charles was beheaded Milton published, in February 1649, a pamphlet called *The Tenure of Kings and Magistrates*, which was and has remained a controversial document. It was written during the trial of the king, the progress and details of which Milton is thought to have been aware;

and, with only indirect reference to these events, he investigates their premises and contexts. His thesis is that monarchy holds power by virtue of a tacit contract with the people. If the former fails in this stewardship – and Milton suggests rather than explicitly claims that Charles had done so – it should be called to account by its subjects. Milton's thesis was not in itself revolutionary or unprecedented. James I, Charles's predecessor, had, thirty years before, produced a document called *Basilikon Doron* in which he acknowledged that monarchy should involve an awareness of and a sympathetic response to the complexities, opinions and uncertainties of the kingdom (Shakespeare's *Measure for Measure* was a dramatic enactment of James's abstractions). However, no nation before this had tried its monarch for his failures, found him guilty and killed him.

It has sometimes been suspected that when writing *The Tenure of Kings and Magistrates* Milton was in contact with members of the republican government-in-waiting, many of whom attended Charles's trial and were signatories to his death warrant. Nothing evidential is known, but the pamphlet involves such a depth of detail regarding ongoing political developments that his acquaintance with some of the individuals involved seems more than likely. As well as a justification for regicide the document involves a lengthy attack upon the Presbyterian party of the Commons, whom he treats as hypocrites. They who had campaigned energetically against the Royalist party at the beginning of the war now actively denounced those who had decided to prosecute the king. Milton's argument carries a magisterial logic. Men, created in God's image, were 'born free ... born to command and not to obey'. Adam's transgression had caused confusion and disarray and it is only now that fallen man can claim to be returning to a state which at least corresponds with his prelapsarian condition. None among mankind can claim authority by right; governance shall be determined by a collective sense of justice and reason (8–11). In short, Milton is citing the Old Testament as justification for the overthrow, indeed the execution, of a monarch who stood against man's attempt to make the best of his postlapsarian condition. The validity of his thesis is a matter for historians and theologians, but what is particularly striking about it is its relationship to his later, ever-puzzling interpretation of the Old Testament in *Paradise Lost*. He seems in *The Tenure of Kings and Magistrates* to be suggesting that in England, in 1649, fallen man was at last becoming aware of how a diminished but honourable equivalent of his prelapsarian state might be implemented in terms of a new political consensus. The Cromwellian, republican commonwealth, the shadowy precursor to modern democracy, was imminent. By the time *Paradise Lost* went to press in 1667 this project had failed horribly and at the end of the poem the foreseen prospects for Adam's lineage are informed with far less optimism than can be found in *The Tenure*.

Milton was soon drawn into a practical involvement with contemporary politics. In March 1649, a month after *The Tenure* was published, he was appointed Secretary of Foreign Tongues to the newly organised Council of State, the republican cabinet. He had no executive function in the Council but he would operate as its intermediary with other nations. In practical terms his talents and range as a linguist qualified him for this, but it was known also that Milton's skill as a rhetorician, along with his sympathetic affiliations, would be of enormous benefit in the Council's early dealings with the rest of Europe: even intrinsically rebellious and unorthodox states such as Holland were variously horrified and confounded by the news of Charles's execution, while others, such as Spain, regarded the act as Satanic.

A few weeks after Milton's *Tenure* appeared, a bestseller hit the streets of London. *Eikon Basilike* (literally the 'King's Image', but popularly known as the 'King's Book') was a compilation of prayers, reflections and pietistic meditations allegedly authored by Charles during his imprisonment and trial. No absolute proof of its origin, such as manuscript copies, has ever been produced but at the time its readers did not doubt its authenticity, and there were many readers. The book aroused a popular feeling of abhorrence among the literate public at the apparent murder of a sensitive, Christian leader committed by the Council and in the people's name. Parliament attempted to suppress it, but failed; its popularity guaranteed its continued production by discrete, unacknowledged presses inside and outside London. It fell to Milton to defend the government, which he did in a book called *Eikonoklastes* ('The Image Breaker'), published in October 1649. *Eikonoklastes* returns to the argument of *Tenure* but with far less restraint. Milton presents the king as a criminal; hedonist, thief, hypocrite, and in his Papal allegiances, traitor. He pitches the argument at a level that he knows will register with the ordinary reader, claiming that much of the *Eikon* is a fabric of plagiarism, with stealings from the work of Sidney and Shakespeare: modified passages from *Richard III* are, Milton states, ironically appropriate, given the parallels between the two monarchs (*CPW*: 84).

An important feature of *Eikonoklastes* is its style, which invites contrast with earlier documents. In *The Reason of Church Government* the prose reflects Milton's optimistic, some might argue naively optimistic, imaginings of the outcome of the Civil War; it is shamelessly ebullient and energised. *Areopagitica* is more studied and calculating in its manner: by 1644, Milton knew that his idealism was somewhat premature, that he was obliged to address factions and political-religious constituencies that bespoke various levels of extremism, authoritarianism and ambition. Anger and frustration inform *Eikonoklastes*. It reads in one sense as an obligation, a task undertaken by Milton reluctantly, and while we have no reason to doubt the sincerity of his arguments they sometimes remind one of the savage editorials of modern tabloid newspapers, shot through with a blend of political contingency and forced rhetoric. Consider the following passage on the state of the new republic.

It were a nation miserable indeed, not worth the name of a nation, but a race of idiots, whose happiness and welfare depended on one man [the King]. The happiness of a nation consists in true religion, piety, justice, prudence, temperance, fortitude and the contempt of avarice and ambition. They in whomsoever these virtues dwell eminently, need not kings to make them happy, but are the architects of their own happiness, and whether to themselves or others are not less kings.

(WJM: 254)

Now compare this with the passage from the *Reason of Church Government,* quoted above **[27–8]**. In the latter the syntax virtually cascades with its author's imaginings, while *Eikonoklastes* reads more like a document prepared by a man who feels obliged to instruct and specify.

In November 1649 a document called *Defensio Regia Pro Carolo I* ('A Defence of King Charles I') by the celebrated classical scholar Claudius Salmasius appeared in Europe. It was not translated into English, probably because it was aimed at the educated classes: a meticulous point-by-point trawl through biblical, theological and classical sources which sought to prove beyond doubt that the execution of Charles involved the overturning of all divine and natural laws. (Salmasius's method mirrors that of Milton in the *Tenure,* published earlier the same year, and while this rhetorical technique was not uncommon at the time, one suspects that Salmasius deployed it partly as an act of personal provocation.) Again Milton was appointed as respondent, his *Defensio pro populo Anglicano* ('A Defence of the English People') came out in early 1651 and its title reflects its thesis. The people of England had punished the king because he stood between them and their realisation of the best that could be hoped for in man's attempts to create some counterpart to the world lost after the Fall. Milton matches Salmasius in his citation of sources, indeed ridicules his unscholarly misuse of them, and supplements this with a blend of nationalism and ideological commitment that we usually associate with twentieth-century political discourse; in Milton's presentation the Cromwellian regime is licensed by scripture, it involves collective responsibility and not the adoration of a debauched figurehead, and the wise, courageous people of England will monitor its implementation.

Milton was becoming, in the public consciousness and professionally, the official spokesman for the fledgling Cromwellian State. Our perception of his own opinions and ideals regarding politics and religion can be assembled from our slight knowledge of what he privately said – Phillips is our principal, though by no means verifiable or trustworthy, source for this – and what we intuit from his contemporaneous writing. His primary allegiance was to the Independents. But to capitalise the Independents and by implication treat them as a unit or sect is in itself a contradiction in terms. Independency involved the belief in Christ as the only true head of the Church, and the Bible, variously interpretable, as its only rule for faith. Milton, without using the term, defined Independency as coming 'from the true freedom of Christian doctrine and church-discipline subject to no superior judge but God only' (Hunter 1978, IV: 101). Independents treated the individual believer as the sage and determinant of his own theological centre-ground and religious practice. Often they would attach themselves to specific institutions, chiefly the Church of England, but would treat institutionalised religion more as a pragmatic necessity than an organising principle for faith and thought. It could be argued that Independency was the driving force for the early Parliamentarian cause but during the years involving the close of the Civil War and the establishment of a republic it inevitably involved a paradox: many Independents were now faced with the practicalities of government, were becoming instruments of institutionalisation. Milton addressed the specifics of this more in his, albeit slight, poetic output of the late 1640s to early 1650s than in his prose writings. In many ways the chronology of these poems reflects his growing sense of unease regarding the development of the new state. For example Sonnet XII (1646) **[83–4]** rails against the objections in Parliament inspired by the Presbyterians to his divorce pamphlets, and 'On the New Forcers of Conscience…' (1646) **[84–5]** names senior Presbyterian clerics and theologians as the Protestant counterparts to Catholic authoritarianism. Both reflect anger while being lit by a confident, inspired sense of Independency, particularly his own, as able to resist the power of religious factionalism. However, two years later his sonnet in praise of Fairfax (August 1648) **[86]** carries more a sense of anxiety. Fairfax, one of Cromwell's senior generals, was an Independent and Milton implores him to save the fledgling state from threats both internal and external, and not only from remaining Royalists. In 1652 **[86–7]** he produced a similar sonnet, this time addressed to Cromwell (who was not so much the official leader of the Independents as their most powerful advocate). He asks Cromwell to stand against Members of Parliament, mainly Presbyterians, who were campaigning for the reorganisation of an established Church which would exclude dissidents in much the same way as the Pro-Catholic High Church of Charles had done, albeit according to an antithetical core doctrine. Later that same year he addressed a sonnet to Sir Henry Vane as his ally against established religion **[87]**. These poems were not published at the time but they circulated in manuscript form among Milton's friends, colleagues and seniors, some of whom were their direct addressees. As such they offer an intriguing insight into his personal opinions on the state of government. He was and would remain an Independent, an advocate of the fundamental rights of free speech and manner of worship. However, he was himself being drawn more into the practicalities of government in which idealism and circumstantial necessity were rarely the same thing.

In 1649 the government gave him accommodation near Westminster and a small army of scribes was employed to set on paper the immense output of this near-blind political and religious theorist. He was appointed as author of the so-called *Observations*, a year-by-year explanation and justification of government policy, in which Milton employed his rhetorical skills to deal with such issues as Cromwell's Irish campaign and the imprisonment of the more active members of such republican splinter groups as the Diggers and Levellers. These, particularly the Diggers, advocated a political system that was close to modern democracy. Gerrard Winstanley, the leader of the Diggers, virtually preempted socialism in his call for the common ownership of land.

In 1651 Milton's duties were supplemented by his appointment as Chief Censor, a magnificently ironic choice on the part of the government given that central to practically all of Milton's pro-republican writings was his belief in and defence of free speech. He was, to say the least, a libertarian censor; only those publications which directly incited the overthrow of the government were suppressed. Indeed, he permitted the publication of *The Moderate*, the argumentative news-sheet of the Levellers, which continually called for the empowerment of the common people. He co-edited the official government newspaper

41

called *Mercurius Politicus*, the mid-seventeenth-century equivalent of the Thatcherite *Sun* and *Times* of the 1980s. It could be argued that the office of Censor in the Cromwellian commonwealth was perceived, not least by its occupant, more in its original classical specification as a person who comments upon and engages with the opinions and conduct of others than in its modern sense of a figure who licenses or bans publications. London teemed with newspapers and pamphleteering was reaching crescendo proportions. John Lilburne, the most vocal, fanatical spokesman for the Levellers published pieces advocating that Parliament should reform itself and provide representation for the seventeenth-century forerunners of the working classes, the artisans, yeomen and craftsmen who existed in a political vacuum. The Presbyterians, outside Parliament, counted among their number some of the best pamphleteers in the country. Milton lasted little more than a year as Chief Censor. In late 1652 he had licensed the publication of a notorious, heretical tract called the *Racovian Catechism*, which amongst other things denied the doctrine of the Trinity. The Council was unsettled and summoned Milton to justify his act. He stated to them that he was enacting his own principles of free speech, stated in *Areopagitica* and elsewhere, and in effect resigned. He would continue as Latin Secretary, officially, until 1655 when his blindness and other commitments caused these duties to become impractical. He did not completely give up his activities as the Council's international representative and a compromise was agreed. His salary of £288 was reduced to a life pension of £150 and in return for this he would be available to the Council if his skills were required. He would remain so until the Restoration of the monarchy in 1660.

By 1656 the Foreign Tongues Secretariatship had effectively been taken over by Andrew Marvell, while Milton, in deference to his classical learning, still held prominence regarding important communications in Latin (Marvell would replace Milton as the Latinist in 1657). Marvell had become Milton's assistant three years earlier, and their subsequent relationship is enshrined in the folklore of literary biography. Marvell's most debated, if not most famous, poem is his 'Horation Ode Upon Cromwell's Return from Ireland' (1650). It is an ambiguous piece, an implementation of ambiguity more as a tactically propitious device than as an intellectual-poetic exercise. It celebrates Cromwell, with whom Marvell was personally acquainted, but it also in a shadowy manner acknowledges the disturbing resonances of the act of King killing. Few facts are known about the friendship between Milton and Marvell, but, as the cliche has it, opposites attract, and Marvell's 'Ode' indicates a great deal. Marvell was a pragmatist, a man whose beliefs and opinions were at once genuine and adaptable to circumstances. He knew that the concept of monarchy was not something that could be suddenly transformed into collective republicanism. In Marvell's poem the stanza most frequently cited involves the much-reported demeanour of Charles at his execution.

> He nothing common did or mean
> Upon that memorable scene.

Had Milton read these lines when he wrote the *Defensio Anglicano* , his justification for regicide and republicanism published a year later? In the final page of it there is a sentence which almost cites Marvell's poem, and, if it does, shifts the focus from the soon to be executed King to the people of England.

> After so glorious a deed, you ought to think, you ought to do nothing that is mean and petty, nothing but what is great and sublime.

Milton's 'you ought' is addressed to the collective consciousness of the nation; he believed that his readers could accept his own perception of the execution as a 'glorious' and 'sublime' step towards the implementation of religious and political freedom. He was an idealist. Marvell was a Machiavellian pragmatist; he remained on good terms with the quietened but still powerful Royalist factions, and after the Restoration profited from this. After 1660, when the monarchy was restored, he would use his political contacts – he would then be Member of Parliament for Hull – to rescue his old friend Milton from the vengeful punishments visited upon many of the regicides.

No one is certain of when Milton began the poem that will forever guarantee his status as one of the great English poets, *Paradise Lost*; but it is possible to connect incidents from his life with this work's at once puzzling and universalised message.

Some time in the mid-1650s, when his work for the government was becoming less burdensome, Milton began to assemble a document known as *De Doctrina Christiana*. It would not be published in his lifetime and indeed no-one was certain of its existence until it was discovered in manuscript form in the Public Record Office in 1823. Even after it went into print in 1825 some doubted its authenticity; it was difficult, even during the relatively enlightened ethos of the early nineteenth century, to accept that Milton had contemplated such heretical, wayward, deviant thoughts. The parallels between *De*

Doctrina Christiana and *Paradise Lost* would have been evident to anyone familiar with both, but the implications of accepting that the former was a rehearsal for the latter were too unsettling to be addressed publicly until the twentieth century (see Kelley 1941).

Paradise Lost has endured as a controversial book because it involves a cautiously, respectful transcription of the book of Genesis alongside very radical questionings of what it meant to John Milton. *De Doctrina Christiana* discloses the origins of these questionings. It deals with familiar doctrinal and theological issues, but in a manner that would not become licensed until the end of the eighteenth century: rationalism, empiricism and individuality threaten the sovereignty of immutable absolutes. In it, God is treated by Milton almost as a person; His motives, objectives and inclinations become unnervingly actual and contingent: there are parallels with Arminianism, but it goes much further. For example, early in *De Doctrina* (*WJM*, XIV: 24–6) Milton asks why God created man, not in the characteristically Socratic-theological manner of someone who has foreknowledge of the answer, but as someone who is engaging in an ongoing exchange with God. Did God know that Adam and Eve would fall of their own free will? If so, should we question His love for us, given that He knew in advance of our Fate? Yes and no, answers Milton, because while God could foresee the future of man He could not determine it: this is up to us 'in the exercise of [our] uncontrolled liberty' (82). Milton's encounters in his youth with Calvinist notions of predestination and their antitheses are in the background, but he has moved beyond stark dichotomies towards a more complex yet flexible engagement with belief. He deals with contradictions, inconsistencies – Adam's 'fall was ... certain, but not necessary; it proceeded from his own free will, which is incompatible with necessity' (82–6) – but he does not attempt to resolve them; they are, he implies, part of our inheritance, our condition, a state that we should contemplate and further investigate.

Throughout the document Milton engages with scripture as though he is conversing with God and offers his own perceptions of what God has been and is doing, and how we should accommodate these notions. Milton declares his anti-Trinitarianism; God is one person, irrespective of the faulty conception of Him as Father, Son and Holy Spirit. We, as the inheritors of the Fall, can only properly understand Good because we have become aware of Evil; our understanding of Redemption is consequent upon this. Monogamy is the ideal condition, but compatibility is a fact; divorce is acceptable in that it enables individuals to locate a more secure enactment of marital harmony. He even implies that, since there is no record of God forbidding polygamy, it should

44

perhaps be permitted. (This was the feature of *De Doctrina* which most disturbed the early Victorian skeptics – surely our most eminent Christian poet could not be suggesting that God would approve of promiscuity?)

The question which attends our knowledge of *De Doctrina*, its genesis in the late 1650s and its relationship with *Paradise Lost*, is of how Milton's life and experiences influenced his ongoing conceptions of God and the human condition. He had witnessed, been part of, events in Christian Europe that were unprecedented, almost apocalyptic. Monarchs were and had always been perceived as the secular agencies of God, but England had shifted the focus.

The Cromwellian republic was founded upon the principle that the nation, not the king, would organise itself, with the assistance of its wisest servants, according to its own conception of God's will. Sadly, and evidently to Milton, this ideal was falling apart. The Cromwellian regime, by the late 1650s, was riven with uncertainty, contradiction and factionalism. Cromwell himself, who had begun his political and military career as the representative of a collective endeavour, was becoming a dictator. Gone was the plain black suit and hat, to be replaced by thick purple robes and the ornaments of magisterial high office: while he kept to title of Lord Protector of the Commonwealth, his wife became Her Highness the Lady Elizabeth.

Most of Milton's official duties had been taken over by Marvell and others (in 1658 a young scholar called John Dryden would become one of Marvell's assistants), but he was still called upon as scripteur and translator of government documents. He remained in contact with the centre of power and by 1658, after the death of Cromwell, he would have been aware that even among Parliamentarians, particularly the Presbyterians, the restoration of the monarchy was being openly talked of.

In 1658 he wrote what would be his last sonnet, no. XIX, in which he tells of being visited by the spirit of his late wife – though of which one, Mary Powell or the recently departed Katherine Woodcock (m. 1656, d. 1658), we cannot be certain. It involves a moment of pathos, remembered optimism and a confirmation of life beyond the grave, but it is a dream **[90]**.

> I waked, she fled, and day brought back my night.
>
> (*TP*: 14)

He might be referring to his blindness, but it is just as likely that the night referred to in this closing line involves a more general feeling of pessimism and disappointment. The dream had involved a particular person, but for Milton another dream had died.

The fact that *De Doctrina Christiana* would remain as a collection of incomplete drafts reflects its status as an internalised, personalised expression of Milton's ideas and reflections. It is informed by a sense of isolation, of a man whose perceptions of God and how God's will could be practically implemented by man had been overtaken by events that would destroy them. An epic, involving a literary representation of the book of Genesis and addressing the question of why we are as we are, had always been a possibility – evidenced by the abandoned *Adam Unparadised*. During the 1650s Milton had virtually exchanged his identity as a poet for that of political theorist and theologian, but the fragmentary, animated nature of *De Doctrina* indicates that he was thinking again about how verse could be his medium, his focus. He had begun *Paradise Lost*.

(k) THE RESTORATION AND *PARADISE LOST*

Frequently, regimes instilled by revolution die a natural death. The radical fervour that brought about the transformation of France at the end of the eighteenth century and Russia at the beginning of the twentieth was replaced by combinations of stagnation and corruption followed by decay. The Cromwellian commonwealth established the precedent for this, and by the closing years of the 1650s even ardent republicans had become resigned to the fact that an experiment had failed, although what exactly would replace it was still a matter for speculation. Richard Cromwell had briefly replaced his father, but by 1659–60 it was apparent to everyone that the fate of the nation would be determined by General George Monck who commanded the army. In April 1660 Monck, who had for five years been governor of Scotland, brought his forces south, took control of a directionless bureaucracy of government (Richard Cromwell had already been forced to resign by Monck's London-based military colleagues) and a month later Charles II, after twelve years of exile, rode into London as the new King. There was public rejoicing, but no violence: it seemed to all who witnessed the event, pro- and anti-monarchists, inevitable.

The regime of Charles II would be different from that of his predecessors. The centre of power had shifted irrevocably toward Parliament, but, nevertheless, the ardent monarchists took revenge for what they regarded as a decade of injustice. Several members of the Cromwellian

Council were tried by Parliament and executed and Milton, as the most prominent apologist for regicide and republicanism, had to go into hiding. In June 1660 Parliament took steps to have him arrested and declared that his *Defensio pro populo Anglicano* and *Eikonklastes* should be publicly burned. In August Parliament licensed the burning, by the official hangman, of all of his available works in print. In late August Parliament passed an Act of Indemnity, which listed those associated with the execution of Charles I and the subsequent Cromwellian regime who were condemned to death; some were in custody, some still at large. Milton was not on the list but while he no longer had to fear for his life his exclusion did not exempt him from punishment. In late October he was arrested and imprisoned.

His release on 15 December was brought about through the influence of a number of individuals. His own brother Christopher had sided with the Royalists during the war and his affiliations were not altered by a decade of republicanism. He had by 1660 become a successful barrister and his promotion to the Judiciary on 25 November is surely not coincidentally related to John's release from prison little more than a fortnight later. Andrew Marvell was now Member of Parliament for Hull and, despite his previous associations with the Commonwealth, a Pro-Restorationist. Marvell publicly addressed a case for the pardoning of Milton that was for some self-evident. He pointed out that Milton had become blind shortly after the execution of the King, that this was God's retributionary strike against a good man who had been led astray by politicians and that he should be left to endure and reflect upon this righteous punishment.

Marvell's presentation of his friend's condition to Milton's accusers was both accurate and calculatedly selective. Milton had indeed endured circumstances that might be regarded as punitive: a blind man dependent continually upon his friends and family being led, probably in disguise, from one hiding place to another. However, Marvell's characterisation of him as repentant and submissive was, to say the least, sympathetically biased. In March 1660, when the Restoration was inevitable, Milton had published a pamphlet called the *Ready and Easy Way to Establish a Free Commonwealth*, a document which forcefully reiterated the arguments of ten years before, for a republic, and made clear that its author regarded the imminent reinstitution of a monarch as disastrous for the state of the nation. The pamphlet was heroic and potentially suicidal in that Milton was aware that it would have no effect upon what was about to happen. Marvell's plea for tolerance, to those who would have been aware of Milton's pamphlet, was obviously a masterpiece of persuasive rhetoric.

47

The last fourteen years of Milton's life, after his release in 1660, are treated economically by most of his biographers, because little happened. He was no longer part of the political life of his country. His career as a pamphleteer was over. In 1673, a year before his death, he returned briefly to the practice with *Of True Religion, Heresy, Schism, Toleration, and what best means may be used against the growth of Popery*, which Wilson refers to as a 'dull little work' (1983: 257).

In 1663 he married again; Elizabeth Minshull (thereafter known as 'Betty'), a woman of decent, moneyed, middle-class stock, took control of the new household 'in the Artillery Walk, leading to Bunhill fields' (Phillips 1694: 75). His daughters from his first marriage had, during the previous decade, been looked after by their maternal grandmother but had now returned to their father's house: Anne (17), Mary (15) and Deborah (10). The relationship between Milton and his daughters would become the stuff of gossip and scurrilous legend, little if any of it founded upon attributable comments by the women themselves. Frequently cited is the alleged statement by the family maidservant Elizabeth Fisher that Mary, on being informed that her father was to remarry, professed indifference and added that 'if she could heare of his death that was something' (French, IV 1949–58: 374–5). Stories circulated, after Milton's death, that he had obliged Mary and Deborah to read to him in at least eight languages which they did not understand and, when others were not available, to transcribe what were then his own almost equally obscure compositions (French, V 1949–58: 109). Parker, among many, questions the authenticity of this account, noting that it is entirely incongruous with Milton's perfectionism as a linguist and stylist.

The only major events of his remaining years would be the plague of the summer of 1665 and the Great Fire of September 1666: Thomas Ellwood, a Quaker, a neighbour and regular acquaintance of Milton arranged for the family to take a property in Chalfont St. Giles to avoid the former. The Fire did not affect the Bunhill House, situated as it was beyond the city, but it destroyed the original family home in Bread Street. The loss of Bread Street might seem of no enormous consequence in the life of the poet, but for two reasons it was. Despite the fact through the 1650s and early 1660s Milton had produced very few poems his reputation in England and Europe, partly from his early literary works and subsequently his career as a political-religious theoretician, was immense. During the Cromwellian regime and the early years of Charles II European visitors to London would ask to be shown the Bread Street house, where the legend had begun. It became the iconic centrepiece for speculation: what, if anything, was Milton doing, writing, now? For Milton himself the loss of Bread Street was a financial catastrophe. His income from government work had, with the Restoration, ceased; Bread Street was his last piece of real estate and in 1666 fire insurance, as we understand it, did not exist.

What happened next answered the above question, but, with an irony that Milton would probably not have enjoyed, left the monetary situation unbettered. *Paradise Lost* was published in August 1667 by Samuel Simmons (Parker, cited on the 1667 title page, was his representative). Within two years it had sold almost 4000 copies; it was one of the bestsellers of the century. Royalties, in the modern understanding of a writer's percentage of sales, were not a feature of seventeenth-century publishing. The printer-publisher made the object and sold it. The writer was paid mainly in advance for its contents. By 1669 Milton had received £20, roughly one-tenth of his annual salary as a Cromwellian civil servant.

He had written what even its earliest respondents, pro and anti, perceived to be the most important poem in English. He would spend his remaining years in a state of relative poverty while being celebrated as a poet almost beyond compare. At the beginning of the poem, when he seeks the aid of the 'heavenly muse' in his great task, one wonders if he is already aware of the paradoxical relationship between what he was about to do and what he had already done, been and experienced. He had been at the centre of events that would significantly affect the history of Europe, its political and religious destiny, and his presence had been forthright, vocal, tangible. Now he was going to explain to everyone why we are as we are; the verse would speak for him and he, partly by choice, partly by circumstance, would retire into the background.

No one is certain of exactly when he began *Paradise Lost*. The manuscript is by various hands, but so was everything else Milton produced after the early 1650s; he was blind. Clearly it was related to some of the thinking behind *De Doctrina*, but he would continue to contribute to this peculiar work almost until his death and it would be wrong to claim that the prose work was a plan for the poem or that the latter grew directly out of the former. The draft manuscript of *Adam Unparadised* (held in the library of Trinity College, Cambridge) shows that at least as early as 1639–40 the fundamentals of the project were in his mind, but this was conceived as a drama and there are no verbatim borrowings from it in the 1667 poem. It is assumed by most scholars that he started planning and making early drafts for *Paradise Lost* in the mid-1650s, but that he gave his time almost exclusively to its completion in the five years between 1661 and 1666. This of course raises the questions of whether or how the events of these years, the 1650s and 1660s, as perceived and experienced by Milton, affected his treatment of the poem's central themes: the rebellion of Satan and his compatriots against God; their defeat; the creation of man; the Fall of man, instigated by Satan; and its immediate consequences – effectively the contents of the first book of the Old Testament, Genesis. These questions will be looked at in detail when the specifics of the poem are dealt with below in Part II [94–121], but some potential parallels between his life and work ask for preliminary consideration.

Milton had witnessed, been part of, a series of events that were without precedent in the history of Christian Europe. Wars between noble households over their respective claims to a title or piece of land were an ongoing feature of the medieval world and, more recently, religious difference had fuelled conflicts throughout northern Europe, but the English Civil War was different. It began as a rebellion against an undisputed head of state that was founded upon, in modern parlance, ideology; a combination of economic, political, philosophical and religious discourses. It resulted in the execution of a monarch who was regarded by himself and his supporters as God's secular representative, and the foundation, for the first time ever, of a Christian republic. The events of the Civil War were shocking enough but a more fundamental state of uncertainty was caused by the fact that they had no established theoretical or practical precedents; and Milton during the 1650s was one among many who attempted, with reference to religious doctrine and classical learning, to make sense of what was happening.

In the seventeenth-century literary works were not, in our sense of the word, reviewed. Studied responses in print to *Paradise Lost* would have to wait until the 1680s, but we can make some confident assumptions regarding the nature of the early discussions which Milton knew he would prompt. First there would be a question. The original story, the book of Genesis, was known to everyone, so why was Milton rewriting it; moreover why was he causing it to share a genre, the epic, with Homer's and Virgil's pre-Christian pieces? Milton did not change any of the detail of the Old Testament narrative – if he had this would have been spotted by his successor, the government Censor, and the poem banned; it was not – but what he did was to make the participants of this narrative, and himself as its coordinator, speak in a way that was different from the language of the English Bible. All of the imaginative, stylistic and rhetorical resources of English Renaissance verse were channeled into *Paradise Lost*, and more: Milton individualised and universalised them. Milton did not alter Genesis but he modernised it, so that its figures would become as actual and immediate as the very real presences who had been part of the events of the previous thirty years.

He invited, virtually obliged, his first readers to consider parallels, allegorical relationships between his poeticisation of the original story of mankind and a more recent one, but the rest was up to them. Was Milton's Satan Cromwell? Was God Charles I? Perhaps Cromwell was God's proper representative and the collapse of his project, followed by the Restoration, was evidence of how Satanic forces still informed the condition of fallen men? These questions, even now, are still unresolved. Romantic poets, Blake particularly [137–8], thought that Milton empathised with Satan and more recent interpreters, notably Empson in this century, found that Milton's Satan was an anticipation of modern rationalism [152–3]. Christopher Hill, a Marxist, regarded God as a version of outdated, feudalist authoritarianism and Satan as representative of the newly empowered mercantile classes [176–8]. Such detailed interpretations would not be publicised for at least a century after the poems appeared in print but their essence would have been anticipated, experienced by contemporary readers. The only evidence of this comes from one Theodore Haak, who in the 1680s translated *Paradise Lost* into his native German and told a friend of how, fifteen years before, London had been alive with speculation about what the poem really meant. (Hill 1977: 391–2). Was it only about God and Satan, Adam and Eve, or was it also using them figuratively, as a means of examining a more recent Fall and its consquences?

What we do know is that, alongside the tragic, violent polemicism of the Civil War, Milton's early life would have played a part in his writing of the poem. The conflict between fundamentalist Calvinism and Arminianism – is our fate predetermined or is it a matter of choice? – is central to *Paradise Lost*. Did God, omniscient as He is, know that Satan would rebel and was He aware that Adam and Eve, when He created them, would eat the fruit? Or, having given all of them the gift of free will, how did He respond to the unanticipated consequences of their acts? English politics of the mid-seventeenth century resonate through the poem but also, carried into it, we encounter the fundamental disputes of all Europe during the sixteenth and seventeenth centuries. Milton's tutor, Thomas Young, his father's Protestantism and its family history, St. Paul's school, Cambridge: all of these formative experiences fed the uncertainties and questionings that characterise the poem.

For the remaining, seven, years of his life Milton continued to write, but what he had wanted to do was done. The rest was reflective, retrospective. Betty, his new wife, looked after the practicalities and

51

when Milton wasn't writing he entertained visitors and friends, Marvell regularly. He was encouraged by publishers, aware of the popularity of *Paradise Lost*, to do more, and studious pieces, previously written, went into print: *The History of Britain* (1670), *Accedence Commenc't Grammar* (1669) and the *Art of Logic* (1672).

He wrote *Paradise Regained* (1671), a pseudo epic about Jesus's temptation by and rejection of Satan. The subject in itself should, we might assume, have caused even more dispute than *Paradise Lost*, but the poem has been either ignored by Milton's critics or treated as a slight, peripheral footnote to his more important work. Understandably perhaps. It was about the conflict between God, or at least His Son, and Satan; not about the relationship between God and us. And it is a subdued, unprovocative poem. It reflects the state of mind of an old man who is aware, if not content with, what he knows and has experienced. Little more can be said or done **[121–6]**.

Milton died quietly and without evident distress sometime between the 8th and 10th of November 1674. He was buried in the Churchyard of St. Giles, Cripplegate. There was no great ceremony. Little is known of who attended the funeral; Marvell perhaps, but no one is sure. His mortal life concluded without much notice but he has lived on, perhaps more insistently than any other English literary writer, through the most turbulent periods of three subsequent centuries. He still speaks to us. He still asks us questions about the existence of God, and, consequently, about how and why we treat each other as we do.

FURTHER READING

Biographical accounts of Milton began to appear soon after his death, principally: Aubrey (1681), Skinner (1687), Wood (1691), Phillips (1694) and Toland (1698). Generally, these relied on three sources: interviews and word of mouth anecdotes; passages from Milton's own pamphlets in which he digresses into autobiography, particularly *The Reason of Church Government* (1642) and *Defensio Secunda* (1654); known but disputable accounts of seventeenth-century politics and the Civil War. Phillips had a special advantage in that he was Milton's nephew and from the 1640s onwards his pupil and close acquaintance. His is the most cited of the early biographies, and, despite Phillips's occasionally careless deployment of dates and chronology, remained the principal source for most surveys before Masson (1859–94). Apart from Skinner, all of the above are reprinted in Darbishire (1932).

In the eighteenth century practically all biographical accounts were prefaces to collections of Milton's work, the best known being Richardson's (1734, reprinted in Darbishire), Birch's (1738) and Newton's (1749). These contained further material gleaned from interviews with surviving relatives and acquaintances (some questionable; see French) and began, with the benefit of retrospective distance, to consider causal relations between the life and the work. The most controversial and influential example of the latter appeared in the later eighteenth century: Johnson's 'Life of Milton' (1779). Johnson was an anti-Miltonist, partly because his verse did not attend to the ongoing conventions of Augustan writing, partly because of his radical, regicidal republicanism **[135–6]**.

The Romantics' enthusiasm for Milton **[137–42]** was mirrored in several sympathetic biographies, principally Hayley (1794) and De Quincey (1838) **[140–1]**, and this tendency for the author's affiliation to contemporaneous moods and trends to influence biography continued through the nineteenth century (see Ivimay 1853) **[144–5]**. The exception is David Masson's magisterial account (1859–94) **[146]**. Masson effectively initiated the second period of Milton biography, in that while the early studies from Aubrey onwards were based on random, selective and often very partial accounts, Masson collected and reassembled chronologically all available information on seventeenth-century history, literature and Milton's involvement with both.

Masson's twentieth-century counterpart is W.R. Parker (1968). Parker builds on and adds to Masson's fund of indisputable facts, but tends to give less attention to the broader historical and literary contexts – Parker incorporates all known and relevant written material but he generally leaves it to the reader to decide on whether or how the life affected or became part of the work.

Most earlier twentieth-century biographies made no serious attempts to add to or challenge what was previously accepted; rather they offered fairly objective surveys for the contemporaneous reading public: Raleigh (1900), Belloc (1935), Hanford (1949), Bush (1964).

Since Parker, the two most interesting biographies have been Wilson's (1983) and Levi's (1996). The former reflects its author's conservative disposition in that he treats Milton as a kind of counterbalance for the late twentieth-century state of dissolute, irreligious philistinism, while Levi's is the first comprehensive modern attempt to treat Milton's writings as a coded autobiography. Brown (1995) is more a survey of the literary, cultural and socio-political contexts of the life and work than a conventional biography. The shortest, most accessible and pleasantly illustrated modern biography is Wedgwood (1969).

Fletcher's *The Intellectual Development of John Milton* (1956) is, as its title suggests, a comprehensive survey of the philosophical, cultural and religious dimensions of Milton's life. French's *Life Records* (1949–58) provides access to the basic printed material upon which Milton biographies from Aubrey onwards have depended. *The Milton Encyclopedia* (Hunter 1978) is an excellent reference guide for biographical issues.

PART II
WORK

(a) INTRODUCTION

The volume of Milton's poems to which, unless noted, I will refer is the one edited by Carey and Fowler (1968). I shall treat the poems according to the chronology followed by Carey and Fowler and I refer the reader to their footnotes for details of the scholarly debates attending the precise date of a poem's composition. Problems can arise regarding, in particular, the Sonnets, many of which are numbered but lack specific titles: it is sometimes the case that Carey and Fowler's numberings differ from those in some critical or biographical works. I will follow Carey and Fowler's numeration.

What is certain is that during Milton's life there were six significant publications. *A Maske Presented at Ludlow Castle* (generally known as *Comus*) (1637) was the first. The second was *Poems of Mr. John Milton* (1645) containing most but not all of his early shorter verse. *Paradise Lost* was first published in 1667, followed by a 1674 second edition in which the poem was largely unchanged in substance but redrafted as 12 rather than the original 10 books. *Paradise Regain'd. A Poem in IV Books. To which is added Samson Agonistes* appeared in 1671 and the 1673 *Poems etc. Upon Several Occasions* contains many, although not all, of his previously unpublished shorter works. Some poems, mainly the more contentious political pieces of the 1640s and 1650s, did not appear until after Milton's death; publication dates for these will be given.

Milton wrote a number of poems in Latin and Italian. Some of these are referred to above in Part I, but they will not be dealt with here: this is a study of Milton's English poetry (translations of the non-English pieces can be found in Carey and Fowler). One might be caused to wonder why below there is an apparent intermission between Sonnet I [60] and Sonnet VII [69]: the intervening sonnets were not in English.

(b) EARLY POEMS

The Psalms

Milton's paraphrases of Psalms 114 and 136 are his first poems in English, in that they are the only ones of the mid-1620s that survived to go into print. They are referred to in the headnote of his *Poems* (1645) as follows: 'This and the following Psalm were done by the Author at fifteen years old'. The original psalms were in Hebrew, a language of which in 1624 Milton was ignorant, and his source would have been the Latin versions.

He does not in any significant way alter their content: 114 is an account of the flight of the tribe of Abraham to Canaan; 136 is a straightforward celebration of the God of the Old Testament. They are relevant to his later poetry only in that they are the first recorded instance of his use of English metrical structures, which he does correctly and with confidence. (The pentameter couplet is deployed in 114, and 136 involves four-line stanzas, with four stresses per line.)

On the Death of a Fair Infant Dying of a Cough

This was thought to have been written about a year after the psalms, in 1625–26 and after Milton had gone up to Cambridge (it first appeared in print in Milton's *Poems* of 1673). It belongs to the genre of the funerary elegy. Milton would have written Latin versions of this, memorialising the deaths of eminent figures and entirely as student exercises. It is, in effect, his first original poem in English and two initial points should be made about it.

First, the funerary elegy, particularly on the death of a child, was popular with young poets because it obliged them to test their rhetorical skills on a tragic subject. (Note that John Dryden's first published piece was his 'Elegy on the Death of Lord Hastings', 1649.) This should be borne in mind in relation to debates on who exactly Milton's 'Fair Infant' might have been. Phillips (1694: 62) claimed that it was his sister's child, Anne, while Parker (1968: 802) pointed out that Anne, aged two, died in 1629, two years after the poem was written. It is likely that Milton did not have a specific infant in mind (he mentions no names and the plague of 1625 would have offered him many examples of infant mortality); rather, he was trying his hand at addressing a standard, tragic theme: part of the poem (stanzas 2–4) alludes to well known classical accounts of child-death from Ovid.

Second, it uses the 'royal rhyme' stanza (seven iambic pentameters followed by an alexandrine and rhyming ab abb cc). This he would later employ in the more famous 'On the Morning of Christ's Nativity' and it is likely that he was testing himself against the complexities of the kind of difficult, baroque stanza favoured by the likes of John Donne **[15–16]**.

In much of the poem (11 stanzas in total) Milton addresses questions to the soul of the dead child, gender unspecified, and discourses on the meaning of death, mortality and the afterlife. It is largely an exercise, an attempt to interweave familiar theological precepts and human experiences with his ongoing ambitions as a poet. Its success might be judged by a couplet from the final stanza, addressed to the grieving mother of the child.

> Think what a present thou to God hast sent,
> And render him with patience what he lent;

The mother's 'patience', her faith and the knowledge that she will eventually be reunited with her child, sits at the centre of a beautifully compressed exercise in emotive rhetoric and versification.

At a Vacation Exercise in the College, part Latin, part English

---

As the title suggests this was a light-hearted version of student exercises. The latter are acknowledged in the first section, in Latin, which is full of obscenities and personal references – the poem was first performed before an audience of fellow students just before the university closed for the summer vacation in 1628. Farcical, mildly irreverent exercises such as this were a standard feature of the closing of the academic year and tolerated by dons: the shift into English in sections 2 and 3 symbolises the change from classically based, academic discourse to the non-university pragmatics of everyday language.

Section 2 begins with a mock heroic treatment of English ('Hail native language...', line 1) as a rough, demotic pretender; just as celebrated as its classical precursors but part of an Englishman's life. But half way through this Milton allows the mask of deference to slip and refers to his own thoughts about English, or rather English poetry.

> Yet I had rather, if I were to choose,
> Thy service in some graver subject use,
> Such as to make thee search thy coffers round,
> Before thou clothe my fancy in fit sound:
> Such where the deep transported mind may soar
> Above the wheeling poles, and at heaven's door
> Look in ...
>
> (TP: 29–35)

The message is unambiguous. He wants to write in English an epic poem which will rival its classical precedents and which will centre upon the essential difference between classical and contemporary writing: the Christian God. Aged 19, Milton was thinking about what would eventually become *Paradise Lost*. He finishes the section as follows:

> Then quick about my purposed business come,
> That to the next I might resign my room.
> *(TP: 57–8)*

This is calculatedly ambiguous. He wishes as soon as possible to set about his 'purposed business' as a poet. He will of course 'resign' his room in college to the 'next' resident, but at the same time he will also 'resign' the spacious room of his intellect and talent to the 'next' business; writing poetry.

The third section (lines 59–100) is an address to mythical and classical antecedents and of no great significance. What should be noted is his use in the poem of the pentameter couplet; this is far more controlled and elegantly precise than in Psalm 114. His confidence as a poet was increasing.

Sonnet I

The significance of this poem, thought to have been written in 1626, is more symbolic than intrinsic: it is Milton's first recorded attempt at the sonnet form. In total he would produce 23 (six in Italian) and the most important ones in English were written in the late 1640s to early 1650s and engaged with contemporaneous, political, issues **[79–90]**.

Milton's versification in his sonnets follows the Italian (Petrarchan) metrical scheme of two quatrains and two tercets, as opposed to the more widely used Shakespearean format of ab ab cd cd ef ef gg. Each, stylistically, is equally demanding but one can assume that Milton's choice implied that he wished to ally himself with the works of the European Renaissance – the fact that he also wrote in Italian supports this thesis.

This one is a stylistic rehearsal for his later sonnets and in itself is no more than a celebratory evocation of the nightingale as a bird with poetic associations (Keats's similar gesture almost two centuries later is well known). Milton would later refer to the bird in 'Il Penseroso' (55–64), *Comus* (233–4, 556) and *Paradise Lost* (III, 37–40) and continue to invoke the two associations first treated in this sonnet: the bird's connections with chastity and female purity (Philomela); and with singularity of voice and nocturnal song, the natural counterpart to the song of the poet.

Song. On May Morning

Its placing in Milton's 1673 volume, shortly before 'On Shakespeare', causes most editors to assume that this poem was written in 1629–30. Like most of the early pieces produced at Cambridge it carries an air of self-conscious apprenticeship, as if Milton is choosing random, relatively insignificant topics on which to practice his skills. It comprises five couplets of varying lengths and is a conventional celebration of spring becoming summer. No mythical presences usher in the new season but his evocations of nature's abundance are very similar to the imagery of 'L'Allegro', there used as background to the introduction of Euphrosyne, the spirit of Mirth: again Milton appears to be rehearsing for larger projects.

On the Morning of Christ's Nativity

Chronologically, this was Milton's fifth poem in English; qualitatively it was the first of his major poems, at least those to be credited as such by later critics. He told Diodati that he began the poem before dawn on Christmas Day 1629. It first appeared in print in the 1645 *Poems* and seems to be a relatively straightforward account of the events surrounding the birth of Christ – as dictated by convention, the event itself is not specifically referred to. There were many precedents for poetic accounts of the Nativity and the one which is thought to have influenced Milton most was in Italian, Tasso's *Nel giorno della Natività* (1621).

Milton does not alter the detail of the Biblical account, but the feature of the poem which has maintained its accredited significance is its tendency to cause the reader to think closely about the very notion of God's incarnation, the intersection of the timeless and ineffable with the transient and fragile state of mortality.

Structurally the poem is in three sections, of roughly equal length. Stanzas 1 to 8 describe the setting of the Nativity, which is characterised by a reduction of light and sound to a bare minimum – the natural world seems respectfully to have suspended its activities. Stanzas 9 to 17 are principally concerned with the angelic choir whose celestial music symbolises the harmony and order which briefly descends upon the world with the birth of Christ. The third section, stanzas 18 to 26, is about the effect of the birth upon the false deities of the pre-Christian world.

In stanza 14, in the middle section, Milton evokes the effect of the angelic choir.

For if such holy song
Enwrap our fancy long,
Time will run back and fetch the age of gold,
And speckled vanity
Will sicken soon and die,
And lep'rous sin will melt from earthly mould,
And hell itself will pass away,
And leave her dolorous mansions to the peering day.

(*TP*: 133–40)

This and the stanza following it are ambiguously optimistic. The birth of Christ seems to offer a relatively painless and generous form of redemption. Sin, hell, mortality ('the dolorous mansions' and 'the peering day') are briefly removed; humanity seems to have been returned to 'the age of gold'. But as we should be aware, this age, our prelapsarian state, is irretrievable, and in stanza 16 Milton reminds us of the fact.

But wisest fate says no
This must not yet be so.

(*TP*: 149–50)

The child in the manger must be crucified:

The babe lies yet in smiling infancy,
That on the bitter cross
Must redeem our loss.

(*TP*: 151–3)

This concertinaing of Christ's life, most specifically the image of a crucified infant, is deliberately shocking. The effect of the image underpins Milton's message – before we can return to the golden, prelapsarian state there is much suffering to be done, by Christ and us.

Throughout the poem Milton interweaves his presentation of the events attending the birth of Christ with intimations of theological truths that underpin it. In the first two stanzas he notes that

Nature in awe to him
Had doffed her gaudy trim

(*TP*: 32–3)

Nature has chosen to 'hide her guilty front with innocent snow', has thrown 'the saintly veil of maiden white' upon her 'foul deformities'. Later in stanza 7 he returns to this theme and tells of how the sun

> Hid his head for shame
> As his inferior flame
> The new enlightened world no more should need.
>
> (*TP*: 80–2)

The natural world was presented frequently in Renaissance verse as an approximation of its timeless counterpart, its beauty a part of God's design, but Milton turns this strategy around and reminds the reader that nature, incorporating man, is an element of our post-lapsarian state. Its attractions are but 'foul deformities' compared with what we have lost and appropriately it hides itself from the coming of Christ.

In stanza 19 Milton turns his attention to the pagan, pre-Christian cosmos. The 'oracles' who advised Apollo are literally struck 'dumb' by the birth of Christ; their prophesies can no longer run 'through the arched roof in words deceiving'. And at a stroke Milton reduces classical mythology to the same state as nature; it too is part of our fallen condition and is unworthy of the presence of the true God incarnate.

The music and light which accompany the birth are described in terms of their absence and inaccessibility. They are those things which 'Before was never made'; the music 'was never by mortal finger struck' (stanza 9). The pure light of God and the music of heaven are indescribable because they are part of the state from which man, when he fell, cut himself off; language, our means of description incorporates our fallen condition.

The poem is striking in that it continually projects its ostensible topic into a broader, all-inclusive contemplation of man's relationship with God, focusing particularly upon the reason for the coming of Christ – man's original act of disobedience and its consequences. Again, we should note that while this was an ever-present feature of Renaissance, post-Reformation consciousness, its emphatic resurfacings in Milton's early verse suggests that as a poet he had an agenda, a scale of priorities. And he would eventually address himself directly to its apex; *Paradise Lost*, the fall of man.

The Passion

The opening stanza acknowledges Milton's previous poem on the 'joyous news of heavenly infant's birth' and declares its own subject:

> ... now to sorrow must I tune my song
> And set my harp to notes of saddest woe
>
> (*TP*: 1–2)

It would deal with the crucifixion and resurrection of Christ and it was, appropriately, written during Easter 1630. It is comprised of only eight stanzas, less than a quarter the length of its predecessor, and Milton appended a prose note to its 1645 printing. 'This subject the author finding to be above the years he had when he wrote it, and nothing satisfied with what was begun, left it unfinished.' Milton's claim that he was too young to deal properly with its subject seems rather modest, given the breadth and quality of his other work at the time. What we have makes no direct reference at all to the crucifixion and subsequent events and is a discursive, unfocused series of digressions on the nature of suffering, pain and their significance. Parker 1968: 73) claimed that '*He was writing a poem about himself writing a poem*'. Martz (1980: 167–8) suggests that his failure was due to ideological-doctrinal forces, that he found himself involved in contemplative, meditative processes which some saw as more favoured more by Catholics than Puritans.

On Shakespeare

This is a brief, 11-line epigram in heroic couplets, a tribute to the memory and reputation of Shakespeare which first appeared, anonymously, among the prefatory metrical to Shakespeare's Second Folio of 1632. The fact that Milton had been asked to contribute it testifies to his own growing reputation in literary London.

It involves an extended conceit in which Shakespeare's writings are praised as a far more fitting and enduring tribute to his greatness than a traditional monument 'in piled stones'. This device is something of a literary commonplace, dating back to Horace's '*Exegi monumentum aere perennius*' ('I have built a monument more lasting than bronze').

While never questioning Shakespeare's eminence, Milton at one point suggests that his artistry was more inspired and natural than the consequence of intellectual endeavour.

... to the shame of slow-endeavouring art,
Thy easy numbers flow ...

(*TP*: 9–10)

Patronizing perhaps? Milton considers, tentatively, the effect of Shakespeare's work upon subsequent writers and offers two lines which are somewhat ambiguous.

Then thou our fancy of itself bereaving
Dost make us marble with too much conceiving;

(*TP*: 13–14)

The syntax is deliberately confusing. Is Milton suggesting that 'too much conceiving' (i.e. an excess of figurative language) on Shakespeare's part, or by those who follow his example, can indeed make us 'marble'?: to 'marble', used as a verb rather than a noun, refers to the reproduction of the variegated and unstructured texture of that stone.

On the University Carrier

There are two versions of this poem, both written in 1631, in memory of Thomas Hobson (d. 1 January 1631), a well-known Cambridge figure who hired out carriages and horses to members of the University.

Both versions involve heroic couplets and a style and mood that might seem irreverent but which, at the time, were thought fitting tributes to persons of Hobson's class and intellect. For example,

Merely to drive the time away he sickened,
Fainted, and died, nor would with ale be quickened,
Nay, quoth he, on his swooning bed outstretched,
If I may not carry, sure I'll ne'er be fetched,

(second version *TP*: 15–18)

These are the only examples of mock-heroic, comic verse in Milton's work and, although the puns and rough-hewn couplets are competently dispatched, they also carry a sense of their author engaged in a task that does not quite suit his temperament.

An Epigraph on the Marchioness of Winchester

Jane Paulet, the Marchioness of the title, died on 15 April 1631 of an infection after being delivered of a dead baby boy. Milton did not know her but she was connected by family to Earl Holland, Chancellor of the University, and Milton was not the only member of the institution to produce a tribute, probably in expectation of a published miscellany; none appeared.

The poem itself is of no great significance. It is done in octosyllabic couplets with occasional variations and generally its style defers to the baroque, hyperbolic tendencies of poets such as Richard Lovelace, John Suckling and Thomas Carew. These men earned the collective title of Cavalier Poets because their combination of precise, idiomatic diction and self-concsciously urbane and graceful wit carried overtones of the courtly gallantry practised by aristocratic supporters of Charles I. Milton's poem is affected and deferential to its subject's aristocratic lineage, with frequent references to her 'noble birth', 'high birth' and 'noble house' interspersed with classical and biblical antecedents for distinguished women who had died in childbirth. In short, Milton was disposing his talents in the hope of patronage from a wealthy family; none came.

L'Allegro and Il Penseroso

These two pieces are poeticised versions of the academic or classical debating exercise, the synkriseis, in which one person displays his skills as an orator and rhetorician by arguing the relative values of two opposing ideas or propositions. Milton himself is thought to have done this at Cambridge in spring 1631, before an academic audience; E.M.W. Tillyard (1938: 1–28) contends that his subject was 'Whether Day or Night is more Excellent' and argues that the two poems, addressing respectively the same contentions, grew out of it. No-one is certain of when exactly they were written; they first appeared in print in the 1645 *Poems*.

They have, along with the 'Nativity Ode', been ranked by Milton's critics as two of his most important early poems and for a number of reasons. Principally, it is thought that while Milton was attempting to balance equally two contending views of life his temperament intervened and he disclosed to us, involuntarily, aspects of his intrinsic disposition.

John Florio's *Dictionary* (1598) defines the word 'Allegro' as 'joyfull, merie, jocund, sportfull, pleasant, frolike' and Milton's 'L'Allegro' attempts to do justice to this state of easy, uncorrupt hedonism. It is a celebration of daytime pleasures, mostly undertaken in a rural setting. The speaker of the poem wakes with sunrise and 'On the light fantastic toe' (34) begins to savour the joys of the English countryside during what appears to be early summer. The poem is effectively a list, a catalogue of people, creatures and activities, which seem to reflect a state of pastoral ease and contentment. Critics have remarked that 'L'Allegro' often gives the impression that Milton is performing a duty, listing and documenting the pleasures of the day in a manner that is effective yet perfunctory. During the 1930s, for example, an exchange took place between Milton scholars on who or what exactly is referred to in lines 45–6.

> Then to come in spite of sorrow
> And at my window bid good morrow
> (*TP*: 45–6)

None of the scholars seemed certain of who would come to the window: was it the mountain nymph (referred to in line 36), the singing lark (line 41) or Milton himself? The debate, documented by Stanley Fish (1980: 112–35), raises the question of whether Milton, when composing this section, was so personally uninspired by this listing of easy pleasures that he did not give proper attention to exactly which subject would be connected with the verb 'to come'.

The title of 'Il Penseroso' indicates its predominant theme. It addresses the state of pensiveness, a thoughtful and not necessarily pleasurable condition of introspection. The sunny daytime of 'L'Allegro' is exchanged for night, the tactile, visual sensations of light for the more contemplative mood of darkness. Milton does his best to balance and equalise the states of mind promoted in each poem, even to the extent of repeating similar frames of reference. In 'L'Allegro' he is

> Sometime walking not unseen
> By hedgerow elms, on hillocks green,
> Right against the eastern gate,
> Where the great sun begins his state
> (*TP*: 57–60)

while in 'Il Penseroso'

> I walk unseen
> On the dry smooth-shaven green,
> To behold the wandering moon
> (*TP*: 65–7)

But, try as he might, Milton cannot quite prevent himself from allowing his personal predisposition to interfere with this state of balance. For example, in 'Il Penseroso' he rejoices in being hidden from 'day's garish eye' (141) while 'L'Allegro' contains no equivalent rejection of night. At the conclusion of 'Il Penseroso' he asks night-time to

> Dissolve me into ecstasies
> And bring all heaven before mine eyes
> (TP: 165–6)

inferring that only the inner eye, the contemplative state, can enable human beings to properly understand what lies beyond the given world. In 'L'Allegro' he celebrates the pleasure of daytime as

> Such sights as youthful poet's dream
> On summer eves by haunted stream
> (TP: 129–30)

and one should note that these sights inspire 'youthful' poets, implying that their more mature counterparts have moved beyond such distractions, to thought.

The closing couplets of both poems are intriguing. The one from 'L'Allegro' is conditional.

> These delights, if those can'st give,
> Mirth with thee, I mean to live.
> (TP: 151–2)

This suggests, subtly, that he could live with Mirth, if only ... Compare this with the certainty of 'Il Penseroso'.

> These pleasures Melancholy give,
> And I with thee will choose to live.
> (TP: 175–6)

These poems are important because they cause us to look beyond them to more emphatic disclosures of Milton's state of mind in later work. They readdress a theme raised in the 'Nativity Ode', where the diversions and attractions of the known world are temporarily suspended for the birth of Christ. Milton would eventually go blind and his sonnet on this condition [88–9] recaptures the mood of 'Il Penseroso'; the contemplative, unseeing state is now an obligation, not a choice, and it seems to suit his temperament. More significantly, in the so-called 'Address to Light' at the beginning of Book III of *Paradise Lost* Milton revisits 'Il Penseroso'. He is about to create God in a poem and the lines on how darkness might 'bring all heaven before mine eyes' written thirty years before must surely have registered for the now blind poet **[101–2]**.

Sonnet VII

This is an unexceptional exercise in reflective sonneteering, its subject being the passage of time as experienced by Milton himself in, as he puts it, '[his] three and twentieth year!' (2) He concludes that while his youth has been 'Stol'n', his future, 'however mean or high', will be of more significance.

> If I have grace to use it so
> As ever in my great task-master's eye.
> (*TP*: 13–14)

The only line which has held the attention of critics is,

> But my late spring no bud or blossom sheweth.
> (*TP*: 4)

which refers presumably to his own perception of his poetic reputation. He had written a fair amount of poetry, but little of it had as yet (1631) appeared in print.

Arcades

This piece resembles the form of the masque, the combination of song, music, costume drama, dance and verse generally performed before an aristocratic sponsor. Its brevity (109 lines in total) suggests that it was written and performed as the prelude to a more extensive series of events. The prose preface (it first appeared in print in 1645) calls it *'Part of an entertainment presented to the Countess Dowager of Derby at Harefield...'*. Alice, the Countess Dowager, was about 72 in 1633, when the piece was written and performed, and was nominal head of the family who would be Milton's principal patrons during the early 1630s. The more significant, full-length masque, *Comus*, would be performed before Alice's son-in-law, Thomas, Earl of Bridgewater, a year later.

The substance of 'Arcades' is an address of about sixty lines, done in heroic couplets, by the so-called 'Genius of the Wood', a version of whom would reappear in *Comus* as the 'Attendant Spirit'. This is topped and tailed by a short sequence of 'Songs' performed by younger members of the Countess's family. The address is little more than a celebration of the presence and grand status of the Countess:

> To the great mistress of yon princely shrine
> Whom with low reverence I adore as mine
> *(TP: 36–7)*

The phrase 'yon princely shrine' typifies the way in which 'Arcades', and the masque form in general, continually crosses the border between actuality and a part-classical, part-Christian spirit world. With 'yon' the Genius and audience are aware of the material presence of Harefield House (the masque would have been performed in the grounds), while 'shrine' elevates the house's 'mistress', the noble Dowager, to a higher, mythical status – her young relatives, the singers, are referred to as 'nymphs'.

Milton, characteristically, embeds this elegant diversion in a core of religious-philosophical reference. He introduces the 'celestial sirens' (63), figures borrowed from Plato's *Republic* whose voices harmonise the concentric whorls of the universe, and blends this image with his by now familiar notion of

> ... the heavenly tune, which none can hear
> Of human mould with gross unpurged ear
> *(TP: 72–3)*

This, like the music which accompanies the birth of Christ in the 'Nativity Ode', is an expression of God's presence from which the Fall has detached human beings.

The most intriguing section of 'Arcades' is the conclusion of the Genius's address (74–84), in which Milton finds himself having to reconcile the notion of music which is beyond human comprehension with the newly elevated, almost otherworldly, status of the Dowager. To have caused her to hear it would have been both sacrilegious and sycophantic, and Milton provides a deftly evasive compromise: '[S]uch music' would be worthy of 'her immortal praise' if only 'my [Milton's] inferior hand or voice could hit/Inimitable sounds' (75–8). The 'heavenly tone' would indeed be a fitting tribute to her status, but she is attended by lowly human beings who cannot produce it.

'At A Solemn Music', 'On Time', 'Upon the Circumcision'

These three poems have no common theme or subject but I place them together because each involves a stylistic exercise. They were written at around the same time in early 1633 (all published 1645) and it appears that in each Milton was experimenting with flexible and unorthodox verse forms, testing and exercising his individuality.

Their topics are variously familiar and circumstantial. As its title suggests, 'At A Solemn Music' returns us to the contrast between mortal and celestial music and looks forward to the moment of redemption when the two might be united. 'On Time' reworks the central theme of Sonnet VII, the passage of time, evidenced by death and decay, compared with our immortal, timeless destiny. 'Upon the Circumcision' could be a versified footnote to the 'Nativity Ode'; it is a brief celebration of the feast of Christ's circumcision, January 1.

The formal model for 'At A Solemn Music' was Petrarch's 'canzone' form (see Prince 1954: 62). Most of the brief, 28 line poem involves iambic couplets, which vary between eight and 12 syllables, counterpointed against much shorter lines, such as 'Singing everlastingly' (16), which rhyme apparently at random with much earlier closing syllables (in this case 'jubilee', line 9). 'On Time' is even more flexible, with couplets and quatrains of different line lengths contrasting with compressed patterns such as:

> So little is our loss,
> So little is thy gain.

> (*TP*: 7–8)

'Upon The Circumcision' returns to the Italian 'canzone' form, this time modelled upon poems by Milton's favourite, Tasso.

The common feature of all three is their tendency to deploy flexible, unpredictable elements of metrical and sound pattern in a manner that appears to replicate the improvised, sometimes hesitant manner of ordinary speech. As poems in their own right they are of no great significance, but they could be regarded as stylistic rehearsals for what would be recognised as his most important early work, 'Lycidas', written four years later. This too involves unpredictable line lengths and variable rhyme schemes, indicating that the mood of the speaker and the complexity of his topic are constantly battling against the abstract structure of the verse form. All of this looks forward to the radical use of blank verse in *Paradise Lost*.

Comus [18-19]

This masque was first performed at Ludlow on 29 September 1634 as part of the ceremonies to mark the investiture of the Earl of Bridgewater as Lord Lieutenant and President of the Council of Wales. Bridgewater was the senior member of the aristocratic family which sponsored much of Milton's work in the early 1630s. Henry Lawes, Milton's friend, was music tutor to Bridgewater's children, who played the parts of 'The Lady' and the two 'Brothers' in the masque; Lawes wrote the music for the piece and took part in it as the 'Attendant Spirit'.

The plot is relatively simple in that the Lady, lost in a 'wild wood', is virtually kidnapped by Comus, a spirit of not-quite demonic but less than creditable status, who transports her to a partly imagined 'palace'. She resists his lecherous designs and, with the assistance of her brothers, escapes. The Attendant Spirit functions rather like the narrator in fiction, setting the scene for the audience and withdrawing to allow the principal characters and their exchanges centre stage.

The theme of *Comus* is transparent and uncomplicated: God-given virtue can resist evil and corruption. It has attained significance as one of Milton's major, formative works because it subtly engages with issues that are central both to his status as poet and to more recent critical controversies; principally the Fall, freedom of choice and the influence of gender upon both.

The most important section of *Comus* is lines 558-812, in which The Lady is 'set in' and apparently unable to remove herself from 'an enchanted chair'. The section is a dialogue between The Lady and Comus, who appears to have entrapped her in a fantastic, enchanted realm. Comus is attempting to seduce her and the following are examples of his rhetorical technique:

> If all the world
> Should in a pet of temperance feed on pulse,
> Drink the clear stream, and nothing wear but frieze,
> The All-giver would be unthanked, would be unpraised,
> Not half his riches known, and yet despised.
> (719-23)

> Beauty is nature's coin, must not be hoarded,
> But must be current, and the good thereof
> Consists in mutual and partaken bliss,
> Unsavoury in the enjoyment of itself.
> It you let slip time, like a neglected rose

It withers on the stalk with languished head.
(738–43)

The passages are significant because they transcend their immediate context and involve Milton in an engagement with contemporary poetic and social conventions. They invite comparison with the amatory mode of Metaphysical poetry in which the male addresser makes use of his considerable stylistic and referential abilities to persuade the female addressee of something; frequently that sex with him is entirely consistent with God's design for the universe and the status of human beings within it. Comus argues that nakedness is God's gift and that He would be 'unthanked' if it were not fully appreciated and indeed made use of 'in mutual and partaken bliss'. Beauty is transient and will 'like a neglected rose' wither if not enjoyed. These strategies are almost cliches and are abundant in Donne's 'The Flea' and 'The Ecstasy' and in Marvell's 'To His Coy Mistress'. But while Donne's and Marvell's addressees remain silent and, one assumes, enchanted, Milton allows The Lady to reply, and she does.

I had not thought to have unlocked my lips
In this unhallowed air, but that this juggler
Would think to charm my judgement, as mine eyes,
Obtruding false rules pranked in reason's garb.
(755–8)

The closing line of this extract is remarkable: 'false rules pranked in reason's garb' is a succinct and unambiguous rejection of the tendency in the verse of the Metaphysicals for the use of figurative language as a means of undermining the customary perceptions of the listener [15–16]. Indeed it anticipates Samuel Johnson's famous dismissal of this technique: 'their learning instructs and their subtlety surprises; but the reader commonly thinks his improvement dearly bought ...' (Johnson 1779–81). The Lady continues,

Thou hast not the ear nor soul to apprehend
The subtle notion, and high mystery
That must be uttered to unfold the sage
And serious doctrine of Virginity ...
Enjoy your dear wit and gay rhetoric
That hath so well been taught her dazzling fence
Thou art not fit to hear thyself convinced.
(783–91)

There are very few women in Renaissance literature who use language with such confidence and authority as Milton's Lady. Portia in *The Merchant of Venice* (1596–97) and Isabella in *Measure for Measure* (1603–04) are clever and effective advocates for their respective causes, but their status is undermined by the fact that the former is only listened to when disguised as a man and the latter, irrespective of her intellectual capacities, is a pawn in male-dominated game.

The Brothers eventually arrive 'with swords drawn' and transport their sister from Comus's realm of debased enchantment, but The Lady has already effectively disempowered Comus by dismantling his rhetoric. As he puts it, 'I feel that I do fear/Her words set off by some superior power' (799–800).

Printed editions did not carry the title *Comus* until 1738; previously it had been known just as *A Masque Presented at Ludlow Castle, 1637*. The question why the demon of the piece acquired titular status a century after it was written can be answered by noting that in 1738 its late author was known principally as the creator of the biblical epic *Paradise Lost*, one of whose central characters was Satan. The exchange between Comus and The Lady anticipates the one that would take place in Book IX of *Paradise Lost*, between Satan and Eve, with one obvious difference: Eve is persuaded and precipitates the Fall of mankind.

Lycidas

Edward King, a Fellow of Christ's College, Cambridge, died on 10 August 1637. He was drowned in the Irish Sea when his ship, destined for Dublin, sank in a storm shortly after leaving Anglesey. Later that year a volume of memorial verses was commissioned by King's Cambridge acquaintances, and 'Lycidas' was Milton's contribution. King and Milton were almost the same age (Milton four years King's senior) and would have known each other in Cambridge, but there is no hard evidence to suggest that they were close friends. The legend that 'a particular friendship and intimacy' existed between them was begun by Edward Phillips (1694: 54), principally to add biographical poignancy to the status of the poem. The title and name of Lycidas carry a number of literary resonances; he is a piper in the world of Theocritus, and a shepherd in Virgil's *Eclogues*. These roles are customarily associated with those of poet and priest and Milton presents Lycidas-King as both: King was indeed an ordained minister in the Anglican Church and had published a number of poems.

'Lycidas' is brief, 193 lines in total, and, given the amount of intense critical scrutiny and scholarly decoding that has attended it, could claim to be the most complex and enigmatic short poem in English. It should also be regarded as exemplary in its respectful misuse of the sub-genre to which it belongs, the elegy, as while its ostensible subject is King, his brief life and tragic death, it deploys this as a framework for Milton's own ruminations on poetry in general, religious belief and other aspects of the contemporary world (Percy Bysshe Shelley's 'Adonais', Matthew Arnold's 'Thyrsis' and W.H. Auden's 'In Memory of W.B.Yeats' follow a similar line).

The opening is at once conventional and slightly puzzling.

> Yet once more, O ye laurels, and once more,
> Ye myrtles brown, with ivy never sere,
> I come to pluck your berries harsh and crude,
> And with forced fingers rude,
> Shatter your leaves before the mellowing year.
>
> (*TP*: 1–5)

The references invoke tradition: laurels were sacred to Apollo and formed the crown of poetic achievement; myrtle formed Venus's crown and ivy Bacchus's. The entire poem is embedded in such classical-poetic allusions and references (best decoded in Carey's edition); there is nothing unusual about this routine Renaissance strategy but what causes us to suspect that something else is about to occur is the phrasing of 'with forced fingers rude/Shatter your leaves...'. 'Rude' in the seventeenth century was used to signify an act that was unskilled, shocking and vigorously sincere; its general association with matters ribald or unsophisticated is a modern habit. Milton is announcing his intention to rudely 'Shatter' a number of complacent expectations.

Next, Lycidas is celebrated as shepherd and poet and the passage which has been looked at as both biographical and controversial is the verse paragraph of lines 25–6, in which Milton presents himself and Lycidas-King together as shepherd-poets in what is assumed by editors to be the gardens and meadows surrounding Cambridge colleges. It is, allegedly, controversial because the 'Rough Satyrs', and 'Fauns with cloven heel' (34) who danced to their music are assumed to be their fellow undergraduates who were evidently their intellectual inferiors (see Pyle 1948).

Milton appears to be as much promoting his own extraordinary talents as he is memorializing King's, and a little later (37–8) he reminds us that 'now thou art gone/Now thou art gone, and never must return!'

He follows this (50–63) with a strange passage which deals specifically with King's death, referring to 'Mona' (Angelsey) and 'Deva' (the nearby river Dee) – strange because he also infers that King's poetic and intellectual promise were of no practical benefit at his untimely death.

> Where were ye nymphs when the remorseless deep
> Closed o'er the head of your loved Lycidas?
> (*TP*: 50–1)

The twenty-line passage following the reflection on King's departure (64–84) is a disquisition on the function, practice and status of poetry. 'Fame' (70) would be the 'spur' to poetic eminence; and those who do not wish to 'meditate the thankless Muse' (66), that is, write serious poetry, can 'sport with Amaryllis' (68). Amaryllis was the young woman praised by Virgil's poet-swain Tityrus and for contemporary readers the reference would have evoked the ongoing Metaphysical tradition of amatory verse which, Milton implies, is a diversion. Counterpointed with 'Fame' is 'blind Fury' (75), the most violent and nastiest of the Muses: her wrath is a key element of the human condition; she embodies the stark reality of life which poetry and poets, if they are to deserve respect, should address.

Lines 85–102 constitute a section that is both cohesive and transitional. In the former respect it centralises and emphasises a theme which features throughout the poem, water. Here the water in which Lycidas drowned, the sea, is contrasted with the constantly mobile, purer liquid of rivers, specifically the Sicilian fountain-stream of 'Arethuse' (85) and the 'Mincius' (86), Virgil's native river. This shift towards the somewhat detached pastoral mode is brief and is partly a means by which Milton can alter the perspective again, because at line 103 a third river brings us much closer to home and the present day.

It is the 'Camus', the latinate name for the Cam which flows past the ancient colleges of Cambridge, and it opens the passage (103–31) which is the most debated and problematical of the entire poem. Cambridge has already been introduced as the intellectual home of King and Milton and it is generally accepted that Milton takes the reader there a second time in order to address a particular religious-political agenda. Suddenly we are introduced to 'the pilot of the Galilean lake' (109) who bears 'Two massy keys ... of metal twain'. The pilot is assumed to be St. Peter, to whom Christ gave the symbolic keys of the true Church (hence the term 'pilot'). It should also be noted that the Papacy is regarded by Roman Catholics as the legacy of St. Peter, its authority similarly licensed by Christ, while Protestants regarded the

Pope as the corrupt usurper of the word of Christ and status of St. Peter. This allusion to the central, divisive issue of the Reformation is significant because, as noted in Part 1 **[12–15]**, Cambridge at this time was well populated by powerful supporters of the official, Anglican Church of Archbishop Laud, effectively Anglo-Catholics who in alliance with Charles I sought to marginalise and suppress the more radical Puritan constituency. The former are introduced as 'Blind mouths!' (119). This image is much debated, and the most enduring and widely accepted interpretation comes from John Ruskin (*Sesame and Lilies*, I: 22). Ruskin commented that 'A "Bishop" means "a person who sees". A "Pastor" means "a person who feeds"' and went on to decode Milton's 'Blind mouths' as referring to the higher clergy of the Laudian church, who deserved neither the title of bishop, since they had blinded themselves to Christian truth, nor the generic term pastor since they were greedy and corrupt.

The next 12 lines (119–31) avoid specific reference either to religion or to individual practitioners of it – Christopher Hill, a Marxist critic, points out that 'Critics who complain of Milton's obscurity here forget the censorship' (1977: 51). All interpreters of the poem agree that the section is a savage indictment of the Laudian, Anglican Church as a debasement of scripture. Its senior members

> Scarce themselves know how to hold
> A sheep-hook, or have learned aught else the least
> That to the faithful herdsman's art belongs
> (*TP*: 119–20)

They are not the shepherd-pastors who would care for their flock, but corrupt hedonists more concerned with the 'lean and flashy songs' of high ceremony. 'The hungry sheep' (125) have already become prey to 'the grim wolf with privy paw' (125) who 'Daily devours apace, and nothing said' (129) – the Roman Catholic Church. However, Milton warns that the

> ... two handed-engine at the door,
> Stands ready to smite once, and smite no more.
> (*TP*: 130–1)

The 'two handed engine' is the most debated image of the poem (see Carey and Fowler: 238–9). The general consensus is that it signifies a two handed broadsword, or possible axe, and anticipates the Protestant reaction to the Anglo-Catholic hierarchy, a shrewd diagnosis of the religious and political tensions that in less than a decade would lead to the Civil War.

The remainder of the poem returns us to pastoral figures and images, the most notable being that of Lycidas, 'Sunk though he be beneath the watery floor,' (16) transmuted to another realm of existence, 'mounted high', and united with 'the dear might of him (Christ) that walked the waves' (173). This enables Milton to integrate the contrasting images of sea and freshwater which inform the poem. Lycidas is now with 'other groves and other streams' (174) which 'With nectar pure his oozy locks he laves' (174). The 'other' streams are the brooks of Eden which, according to the book of Revelations, run with nectar. Lycidas can in these wash from his hair the oozy, salty memory of his drowning at sea. Milton finishes his celebration-remembrance of King with Lycidas as 'the genius of the shore' (187), 'genius' here meaning a beneficent protective spirit.

The closing verse paragraph (186–93) is curious because Milton switches from the 'I', with which he introduced himself at the opening of the poem, to the third person mode: 'Thus sang the uncouth swain...' (186). The key to this is his choice of the word 'uncouth'. In the seventeenth century it was used in our understanding of it as meaning awkward or amateurish, but it also just as frequently indicated someone as yet unknown. In the first instance Milton is modestly understating his talents and in the second his yet to be realised potential. Significantly, via the switch to the third person, he is saying goodbye to both. The couplet which concludes the poem looks to the future, his own.

> At last he rose, and twitched his mantle blue:
> Tomorrow to fresh woods, and pastures new.
> (*TP*: 192–3)

Milton would set out on his European tour a few months after he completed 'Lycidas' and, while the 'fresh woods and pastures new' might have been a private allusion to this, the phrases also incorporate the sense of personal destiny as a poet which features in his early verse. 'Lycidas' itself, while occasioned by a tragic accident, is informed by a sense of something already planned. The metrical experiments of four years earlier, in 'At A Solemn Music', 'On Time' and 'Upon the Circumcision' anticipate the more complex structure of 'Lycidas', with their varying line lengths, stress patterns and rhyme schemes. It was as though Milton was preparing himself stylistically for a major poem that would receive wider public scrutiny, and King's death offered him just this opportunity. Oras (1953) shows that 'Lycidas' involves an arrangement in which the verse paragraphs operate almost as poems in miniature; generally each paragraph begins and ends with relatively conventional schemes such as the couplet and quatrain and reserve the more complex, unpredictable patterns for the central part. This was not simply a display of stylistic dexterity and flamboyance. It should be remembered that Milton uses each paragraph as a means of subtly shifting the perspective, sometimes toward King in particular and just as frequently toward a more universal agenda involving religious truth and the ultimate purpose of poetry. Oras has noted that the formal structure of the poem was, like those of its minor predecessors, influenced by Milton's knowledge of Italian poetry, Tasso's in particular. But, more significantly, its curious balance between regularity and unpredictability was unprecedented in English verse; it was deliberately, self-consciously radical in form. Milton seemed to be demonstrating his command of poetic design, his ability to reformulate its conventional demands so as to guarantee the uniqueness of the poem's speaking presence, a voice that would make us pause, and listen.

(c) POLITICAL POEMS

During the 1640s and 1650s, Milton's activities as a propagandist for the Cromwellian side during the Civil War and his subsequent role as civil servant to the Cromwell government occupied most of his time. He produced vast amounts of prose; pamphlets and discourses on theology, law and politics. It was long assumed that *Samson Agonistes* was written after *Paradise Lost* in the late 1660s but W.R. Parker (1949) has cited evidence, albeit circumstantial, that Milton produced it during the years of 1647–53. It remained unknown and in manuscript form until its publication in 1671. Indeed, all but three of the other, mostly brief, poems verifiably produced during the 1640s and 1650s would not go into print until the 1673 edition of *Poems*. In effect Milton's career as a poet was suspended.

These shorter poems are his least scrutinised and celebrated. The majority are sonnets occasioned by specific events and experiences. They often engage with controversial aspects of contemporary politics, but as poems in their own right they are uncontroversial; they reflect their author's talents as a versifier but, compared with their predecessors up to and including 'Lycidas', they are largely unambiguous, transparent and, for their interpreters, undemanding. The best scholarly guide to the style and versification of the sonnets and their often contemporary frame of reference is still John Smart's edition, *The Sonnets of John Milton* (1921). Honigman (1966) extends Smart's commentary to include more recent critical and scholarly issues.

Sonnet VIII

This, in print, was subtitled as 'When the assault was intended to the City'. It was written in 1642, the City was London and the assault was that of the Royalist forces, made after the battle of Edgehill had left the road to the capital largely undefended. Milton was living in Aldersgate Street.

It is addressed to

> Captain or colonel, or knight in arms,
> Whose chance on these defenceless doors may seize,
> *(TP: 1–2)*

and is largely a plea for mercy by 'him within'; Milton. It cites the sacking of Thebes by Alexander the Great (referred to as the 'Emathian conqueror') after which the house and descendants of Pindar were spared, and paraphrases a passage from Plutarch which describes how, after the Spartans had taken Athens, a song from Euripides's *Electra* had prevented them from razing a city that had produced so great a poet.

It is a peculiar piece because, superficially, it seems to involve on Milton's part abject surrender and a rather selfish request for compassion. The lines 5–6, paraphrased, state that 'I John Milton, poet, will repay your mercy with words of praise'.

> He can requite thee, for he knows the charms
> That call fame on such gentle acts as these
> *(TP: 5–6)*

However, it is generally assumed that the sonnet's candid evocation of fear and desperation on the poet's part is an act of solidarity with his fellow citizens of London, a realistic and personal register of the feeling of terror and panic that gripped the city at the prospect of its largely Parliament-affiliated inhabitants being massacred by their vengeful Royalist captors.

Sonnet X: To The Lady Margaret Ley

Margaret Ley was a neighbour of Milton's in Aldersgate Street and Phillips (1694: 64) suggests that he sought her company as compensation for his departed wife. Ley's husband Hobson was away, a captain in Cromwell's army, but there is no evidence that the poem celebrated anything more than mutual respect. In fact, most of it refers to her father, Earl of Marlborough, who had resigned as President of the Council under Charles I in 1628. A year later Charles directed that Parliament should be adjourned and Milton (lines 5–6) infers that Marlborough's death soon afterwards was in some way related to this: 'the sad breaking of that Parliament/Broke him' (5–6). So although Margaret Ley is its ostensible subject the poem is as much concerned with events that had led to the Civil War.

Sonnet IX

The 'Lady' (1) of this sonnet has not been identified as an actual person. She is rather an embodiment of virtue, someone who maintains the biblical tradition of 'Mary' and 'Ruth' (5); the former sat at Jesus' feet and both thereafter restrained their baser inclinations.

As a celebration of virtuous womanhood this seems to be a brief reengagement with 'The Lady' of *Comus*. Equally it could be regarded as an endorsement of Puritan and Cromwellian morality. One should note that the celebration of women as figures who would be enjoyed and enjoy sensual acts was a persistent theme in the verse of the Metaphysicals and their successors, the so-called Cavalier poets, and that both were associated with the corrupt, hedonistic culture of Royalism [15–16].

Its closing lines, at least for many modern readers, are nauseating. Milton advises the Lady to

> Therefore be sure
> Thou, when the bridegroom with his feastful friends
> Passes to bliss at the mid-hour of night,
> Hast gained thy entrance, virgin wise and pure.
> (*TP*: 11–14)

In short, while your husband has pleasured himself with drink, food, boisterous male company and the eventual deflowering of you, you should be proud that he is the first. It is not beyond the bounds of credibility to interpret Christ as the Bridegroom of the Church, 'bliss' as death and the consummation as a spiritual one, but Milton invests the poem with such a degree of sensual/celestial ambiguity as to reinforce the impression of essentially male control, physical and intellectual. As we shall see **[166–74]** feminist critics of Milton concentrate predominantly upon *Paradise Lost* and pay hardly any attention to his early lyric poems. One might assume from this that his early presentations of gender were ranked as consistent with those of his peers, while the mythical, originary presences of Adam and Eve were thought to deserve special scrutiny.

Sonnet XIII: To Mr. H. Lawes, on his Airs

Henry Lawes, addressed as Harry in the first line, was a close friend of Milton's: they had co-written *Comus*. He had been a member of the King's Music, Charles I's assembly of composers and musicians, was a Royalist, and it is thought that Milton composed the poem shortly after Lawes's brother William was killed fighting for the King at Chester (1645): it was first printed in Henry Lawes's *Choice Psalms* (1648) (the 'Airs' of the title).

Mostly the poem is a catalogue of praise for Lawes's musical and poetic talents but the closing three lines alter this private register.

> Dante shall give fame leave to set thee higher
> Than his Casella, whom he wooed to sing
> Met in the milder shades of Purgatory.
>
> (*TP*: 12–14)

Dante in *Purgatorio* meets the ghostly presence of his old friend Casella, a musician. Everything is implied but Milton's frame of reference suggests an intriguing parallel between Dante's encounter and Milton's and Lawes's circumstances. They are still friends, still sharers of a respect for the aesthetics of music and verse, but their lives have been altered by their respective affiliations – a kind of purgatory, albeit the milder shades. Even those poems of the 1640s which do not address directly the state of England at that time often carry a subtle resonance of lives changed.

Sonnet XII: On the Detraction which followed upon my writing of Certain Treatises

---

The 'Treatises' referred to in the title are Milton's divorce pamphlets **[30–6]**. The sonnet was not published until 1673 but it was circulated in manuscript form when it was written in 1646. It begins:

> I did but prompt the age to quit their clogs
> By the known rules of ancient liberty
> When straight a barbarous noise environs me
> Of owls and cuckoos, asses, apes and dogs.
>
> (*TP*: 1–4)

The Renaissance English sonnet was associated predominantly with a one-to-one relationship between an addresser and addressee, usually involving a particular amatory theme (Shakespeare being the exemplar) or some other intensely personal issue (Donne's so-called 'Holy Sonnets' for example). Milton in his 1640s sequence of sonnets altered this agenda significantly: while retaining an autobiographical scenario these poems usually become vehicles for political dialectic, and this is one of the most acerbic of all.

The animal imagery of the fourth line sums up Milton's opinion on the New Parliamentarians, evoking classical, mainly Ovidian, associations: owl = ignorance; cuckoo = ingratitude and vanity; ass = stupidity and obstinacy; ape = empty mockery; dog = obtuse quarrelsomeness. These verbal cartoons reflect Milton's mood of anger, but they are underpinned by a more considered treatment of the men who had summoned him to answer for his ideas, focusing on the notion of 'liberty' (line 20). He presents his detractors, mainly the Presbyterian element of Parliament, as those who

> Bawl for freedom in their senseless mood,
> And still revolt when truth would set them free.
> Licence they mean when they cry liberty;
> For who loves that, must first be wise and good;
> But from that mark how far they rove we see
> For all this waste of wealth, and loss of blood.
>
> (*TP*: 9–14)

By 'licence' Milton means dictatorial authoritarianism, as opposed to the ideal of 'liberty'. The latter had been the 'cry', the unifying principle, of the Parliamentarian cause in the War, and in Milton's view requires its advocates to be both 'wise and good'. The 'revolt', in Milton's view, has gone backward; a terrible 'loss of blood' will have been for nothing if the new government cannot accept and institute genuine liberty – in short, to allow the likes of Milton to offer radical ideas in print.

On the new Forcers of Conscience in the Long Parliament

This, stylistically, is an adaptation of the Italian 'Sonetto Caudato', a sonnet with a coda; here an extra six lines. There can be no other reason for this extension than to allow Milton ample space for a further attack upon the Presbyterians in Parliament. It was, like its predecessor, written in 1646 (published 1673) and was thought to have been occasioned by a series of Parliamentary ordinances which, in Milton's view, were gradually replacing the ideals of religious liberty with a new orthodoxy; beginning with the replacement of the Book of Common Prayer with the more regulated Directory for Public Worship as the basis for religious services (January 1645).

In the poem he actually names some of the, in his view, most authoritarian and illiberal Presbyterians, such as Dr. Adam Stewart, Samuel Rutherford (8), Thomas Edwards and the 'Scotch What-d'ye-call', thought to be Robert Baillie (12), all senior academics and theologians in Scotland and Continental Europe. He presents them as the new generation of theological dictators and most significantly he compares them with the Roman Catholic hierarchy. Their influence upon Parliament is compared with the Council of Trent (14–15) in which the Catholic Church had reformulated its doctrines after the Reformation. He closes: 'New *Presbyter* is but old *Priest* writ large' (20). He does not suggest theological parallels between Catholicism and Presbyterianism; rather that both usurp civil and religious liberty and enforce doctrinaire belief as law. He contrasts the Presbyterians with

> Men whose life, learning, faith and pure intent
> Would have been held in high esteem with Paul,
> (*TP*: 8–9)

the Independents, with whom he sympathised; those who advocated civil liberty as the basis for a fabric of theological difference but who are 'now ... named and printed heretics' (11). This line is thought to refer to the five authors of the tract called *Apologetical Narration* (1646), sharply opposing the regulations of the Presbyterians and demanding toleration and freedom of conscience (see Smart 1921: 129), and who, like Milton, would be made to answer to Parliament.

Sonnet XIV

This poem, unlike most of its peers, makes no claim to political or theological significance. It is personal; a memorial to his recently deceased friend, Mrs. Catherine Thomason. In it, Milton exercises his practised and considerable skills as a versifier, mainly in adding an extra stylistic quality to the cliché that the deceased has preceded us, through her goodness, to a better world, where she will 'drink [her] fill of pure immortal streams' (14). The poem's significance is more circumstantial than inherent, in that if Milton had not achieved, via *Paradise Lost*, nation-wide eminence it would probably never have appeared in print, as it did in 1673.

Sonnet XI

Thought by Carey (Carey and Fowler: 305) to have been written later than Sonnet XII, this one, despite its accepted numbering, returns us to the controversy of the divorce pamphlets **[30–6]**, particularly *Tetrachordon,* which is mentioned in the opening line. It gives the impression that this pamphlet was the mid-seventeenth-century equivalent of a bestseller ('it walked the town awhile' ... (3)). More significantly, this is the poem in which Milton comes closest to bombastic satire. The 'stall reader' (5) is confused by the classical roots of *Tetrachordon* ('Bless us! What a word on/A title page is this!' 5–6) and for Milton their reaction is symptomatic of the Presbyterians' refusal to accept open debate; theological absolutism is ranked with philistinism. Milton himself lowers his register, suggesting that the Scottish names 'Gordon, Colkitto, or Macdonnel, or Galasp' are just as obscure but more 'rugged' than his own pamphlet title and implies that their non-Anglo-Saxon roots testify to a new level of barbarism, names 'that would have made Quintilian stare and gasp.' (11) (The surnames themselves echo those of known Scots Presbyterians (Carey and Fowler: 305)). He invokes the presence of 'Sir John Cheke' (12), the first Professor of Greek at Cambridge and one of the most famous English classicists and humanists, implying that the new age of reason and learning ushered in by the likes of Cheke, the Renaissance, is being dismantled by the Presbyterian fundamentalists.

Psalms LXXX – LXXXVIII

These are translations from the Hebrew, scrupulously executed by Milton and of little importance beyond the fact that at the time (1648) the Lords and the Commons were quarrelling regularly over which translation (there were already two in print) best transferred the style of the originals to an English that would be appreciated by worshippers in the new Protestant republic. It is not known if Milton was commissioned by his allies in Parliament to do the translations or if he contributed them independently. Either way, the fact that they did not appear in print until 1673 indicates their slight relevance at the time.

On the Lord General Fairfax at the Siege of Colchester

Colchester, one of the last towns to be held by the Royalists, fell on 27 August 1648 and this poem was written shortly afterwards. It celebrates the military career of Fairfax, who took Colchester, was commander in chief of the New Model Army and was arguably the most skilled and effective general on the Parliamentarian side.

The Civil War was effectively over but Milton refers to 'new rebellions' which 'raise/their hydra heads' (6–7). The Homeric beast with nine heads embodies the sense of there still being numerous threats to the Parliamentarian ascendancy: principally the Royalist uprisings in Kent and Wales and the Scots invasion from the North. Fairfax, implies Milton, would play the role of Hercules and slay the beast.

The sestet (closing six lines) of the sonnet is important because it states that 'yet a nobler task awaits thy hand' (9). Milton suggests that Fairfax should, in effect, take command of peacetime England. Milton admired him as a man of balanced conviction, a figure who would at once temper the extremism of the Presbyertians and impose a version of military discipline upon the variously corrupt and anarchistic elements among the disunited victors. In fact after the war Fairfax retired from public life (he disapproved of the execution of the King), which might explain Milton's decision to leave the poem out of his 1673 volume: it eventually appeared in print after Milton's death in 1694.

To the Lord General Cromwell

This is virtually a rerun of its predecessor. When it was written, in 1652, Cromwell had replaced Fairfax as the most eminent military tactician on the Parliamentarian side (he would not become Lord Protector until 1653) and like the Fairfax sonnet the octave (first eight lines) celebrates its subject's brilliance as a general. Cromwell had commanded the armies which defeated the Scots, first at Preston in 1648 – 'While Darwen stream with blood of Scots imbrued' (7) – then at Worcester in 1651 (9). Again the sestet shifts the emphasis to the subject's peacetime role; 'yet much remains to conquer still ... new foes arise/Threatening to bind our souls with secular chains' (9–12). The 'new foes' are generally taken to be those who argued in Parliament for a reformulated established church with limited tolerance of dissenters. The 'Committee for Propagation of the Gospel' had been set up to oversee these matters and Cromwell was a member. Milton had argued in *Areopagitica* for unrestricted liberty of speech and worship and in the 1650s campaigned for the practical implementation of these ideals within the new republic. That fact that Milton's views proved to be more radical than those of the eventual Cromwellian regime is probably the reason why this sonnet, like its predecessor, remained out of print until 1694.

To Sir Henry Vane the Younger

After Fairfax and Cromwell comes Vane, the third figure in whom Milton invests his hopes for the future of England. In 1652, when this sonnet was written, the first naval skirmishes in the eventual war between England and Holland took place (even Holland, one of the most solidly Protestant European states, had taken issue at the execution of Charles I). Vane had become, in effect, foreign minister in the Council of State and the octave urges him to 'unfold/the drift of hollow states' (5–6), 'hollow' being part-pun on Holland, part-reference to its physical 'state' below sea level, part-condemnation of its moral hollowness or inconsistency. As usual, the sestet shifts the frame of reference to the condition of England and Vane is presented as a figure competent 'to know/Both spiritual power and civil, what each means./ What savers each. Thou hast learned, which few have done' (9–11). Once more emphasis is given to Milton's hoped-for republic, in this case where 'civil' and 'spiritual' (religious) power will remain separate, and to the sonnet's subject as one of its leaders. Vane was allied with the Independents, and, like Milton, he was utterly opposed to an established Church. Although he did not support the King's execution he was excluded from the Act of Indemnity and executed in January 1662. Milton, bravely, allowed this sonnet to be printed in Sikes's *Life and Death of Sir Henry Vane* later that same year.

Sonnet XVI *and* To Mr Cyriack Skinner Upon His Blindness

I treat these two poems, both sonnets, together because each deals with Milton's blindness. The first, Sonnet XVI, was thought to have been written in 1652 shortly after Milton became completely blind. The opening lines have puzzled scholars.

> When I consider how my light is spent
> Ere half my days, in this dark world and wide,

The question is what Milton means by 'half my days'. He would have been 42–3 when the poem was written, so does he assume that, given that his father died aged 84, he also will reach that age and spend the second 'half of his days' in 'this dark world'? The rest of the sonnet contains ruminations on his condition and state of mind that are, to say the least, oblique. He appears to be uncertain about how his blindness will affect his life as a writer: 'Doth God exact day-labour, light denied,/I fondly ask' (7–8). The closing line, much quoted and debated, seems to be his maxim.

> They also serve who only stand and wait.

Interpreted simply, this would appear to suggest that Milton now regards himself as physically disqualified from his previous role as apologist for the Parliamentarian cause. But hardly any critic espouses such a reading. Instead legions of them have investigated the deeper meaning of 'stand', variously decoding it as standing like angels who await the orders of God or, in a military context, taking up position against enemies (such as the Scots and Presbyterians). Carey (329–30), offers a brief survey of the scholarly debates surrounding the poem.

Sonnet XVI is a curious, endlessly ambiguous sequence of reflections and as such contrasts sharply with the one addressed to Skinner, written, it is assumed, three years later. This is far more direct and unhesitant. He has been 'Bereft of light' (3) for 'three years' (1) and no longer does he 'argue.../Against heaven's hand or will' (6–7). 'What supports' (9) him through this is 'conscience', the knowledge that he has 'lost them' (sight in both eyes),

> overplied
> In liberty's defence, my noble task,
> Of which all Europe talks from side to side.
> *(TP: 10–12)*

He seems to regard his blindness as a kind of war wound suffered, presumably because he has read and written so much, in the defence of political and religious liberty.

Both sonnets should be read alongside the opening of Book III of *Paradise Lost* **[101–2]**. All three disclose slightly different reflections by Milton upon the significance of his blindness.

Sonnet XVII

It is likely that the 'Lawrence' to whom the sonnet is addressed sometime in the early 1650s was Henry Lawrence, an Independent and a member of the Cromwellian Council of State. Beyond that the poem is of no great significance. Lawrence and Milton were obviously on good terms and the sonnet is a celebration of their co-enjoyment of the 'fire' on a 'sullen day' (3–4), and wine, particularly when the weather allows them to talk in the garden. They share, apparently, an 'Attic taste' (10) for simple and refined elegance.

Sonnet XV: On the Late Massacre in Piedmont

This comes very close to the appropriation of an act of genocide as shamelessly political rhetoric. The Vaudois people existed as a semi-independent religious community on the borders of France and Italy. They had been collectively excommunicated in 1215 and since the sixteenth century been regarded by many as the original Protestants, a status which caused the Catholic Duke of Savoy to send in an army originally to expel them; instead almost 2000 were massacred. This occurred in 1655 and Cromwell took up their cause as martyrs to religious freedom. Milton joins in, offering an account of how a mother, child in arms, had been hurled from a cliff (7–9). He goes on to imagine that 'their martyred blood' (10) will in 'Italian fields' fertilise greater rebellion against the 'Babylonian woe' – English Protestants frequently identified Rome with the Babylon of *Revelation*.

Sonnet XVIII

Along with the 'Piedmont' sonnet this one marks the end of Milton's career as a 'political' poet, in the sense that he used verse to engage with immediate and identifiable issues – *Paradise Lost* would echo with less transparent political resonances. It is addressed to the Cyriack Skinner of his second blindness sonnet (both written in 1655). Skinner is thought to have been one of Milton's early pupils, but beyond that little is known of him: Parker (*TLS*, 13 September 1957) speculates from purely circumstantial evidence that Skinner might have been the real author of the early biography of Milton which practically everyone else ascribes to Phillips. In any event the 'Cyriack' of the sonnet becomes a springboard for Milton's ruminations on European politics, particularly the wars between Sweden and Poland, France and Spain, both shot through with the Protestant-versus-Catholic divisions of a fragmented continent. The mood of the piece is stoical, imagining a time (11) when God will ordain a more 'cheerful hour'.

Sonnet XIX

Many regard this as the last poem to have been completed by Milton before *Paradise Lost* (Carey's chronology of texts reflects this). If it was written in 1658, as is generally assumed, its context is as significant as its content: the Restoration had become more than a possibility.

The 'late espoused saint' brought to Milton 'like Alcestis from the grave' (1–2) might refer either to Katherine Woodcock, his second wife, who had died in February 1658, or to his first, Mary Powell (d. 1652), or both. Euripides's Alcestis had given her life for her husband Admetus and was rescued from the grave by Hercules but, decent women as both had been, neither of Milton's wives quite merits this hyperbolic treatment. Alternatively, the Alcestis of the poem might be regarded as a symbolic presence, an imagined collection of all the love and generosity offered to him by his late partners. He has 'Full sight of her in heaven without restraint' (8), a line loaded with self-focused irony – he now had 'full sight' only of memories. Just before he can 'embrace' this ghostly figure, reality intervenes.

> I waked, she fled, and day brought back my night.
>
> (*TP*: 14)

The resonant density of this line might move even the most cynical reader of Milton. He seems to exist in a world comprised only of personal, recalled images: everything else is pure darkness. He is remembering, perhaps, not only his late beloveds but an all-encompassing, almost visionary enterprise. Cromwell had recently died and the broader vision he once embodied seemed also to be departing.

(c) TRAGIC AND EPIC POETRY

The incorporation of *Samson Agonistes*, along with *Paradise Lost* and *Paradise Regained*, in this section is more a reflection of its generic status than an implied dating of it between the political verse and *Paradise Lost*. The question of when exactly it was written remains unresolved [92–3].

Samson Agonistes

The myth, the story, of Samson is located principally in the Old Testament, specifically Judges XII–XVI. Milton's dramatic poem generally follows the biblical account, with a number of changes. In the Bible Delilah is Samson's mistress. Milton makes her his wife, presumably to emphasise the intensity of their relationship. Also, the biblical Samson is presented as a folklorish giant with no special claim to intellect while Milton's figure continually reflects upon and scrutinises his past, his condition and his future. Along with the biblical legend, Aeschylus's *Prometheus Bound* and Sophocles's *Oedipus at Colonus* both have tragic-heroic figures respectively imprisoned and blinded.

Milton's work is relatively short (1758 lines) and while he subtitled it as 'A Dramatic Poem' most critics suggest that its brevity and the presence of a predominant character and speaker, Samson, indicated that he did not intend it for public performance. The plot is straightforward.

The opening 330 lines are an exchange between Samson and the 'Chorus of Danites' which informs us of his past and current state. He is, or rather was, a military hero of the Jewish people (the Chorus is comprised of lamenting Jews). He was betrayed by his wife Delilah, who belonged to the tribe with whom the Jews were at war, the Philistines. They, as a result, captured him and cut off the hair upon which his God-given strength depended; next he was blinded and cast into imprisonment and slavery.

The exchange between Samson and the Chorus is interrupted by the arrival of his father, Manoa (332). Manoa proposes that a ransom be paid to secure his release (483) (this is Milton's invention and not part of the Biblical account). Samson responds that, while the suggestion is tempting, he is aware that his punishment is just. He betrayed the secret of his strength to his wife, not because of love but because he responded vainly to her flattery and was willingly entrapped by her physical charms (521–40). He feels that he deserves his humiliating plight.

His next visitor is Delilah herself (724), who supports his father's proposal, and seeks his forgiveness in return for the alleviation of his sufferings (733–818). Samson replies that, while he cannot pardon himself, her crime is still more unpardonable (819–42, 871–902, 928–50).

The third visitor is Harapha (1076), the Philistine giant, who comes to mock and taunt him. Strengthened by his exchanges with his father and Delilah, Samson resists Harapha's verbal assaults with discourses that emphasise his own sense of tragic certainty, and Harapha departs 'somewhat crestfallen' (1244).

Finally, an Officer from the Philistine court arrives (1308) and summons Samson to perform feats of strength before them. He departs with the Officer (1426) and the poem ends with the Chorus and Manoa being informed by a Messenger from the court of what has happened (1596–1660): Samson has rooted up the two pillars which supported the building in which he was supposed to perform, bringing down the roof and killing himself and the assembled dignitaries.

It is useful to keep in mind a basic synoptic account of the text because, more than any other of Milton's works, our opinions on its complexities of meaning are affected as much by its assumed provenance and context as they are by our close readings of it: we need to have before us the stark unchangeable features of the story in order to properly appreciate how a change in our perspective can variously complicate them.

The problem, still unresolved, is of when *Samson Agonistes* was written. Carey's introduction gives a thorough account of the debate. Most pre-twentieth-century commentators assume that it was written in the mid-to-late 1660s, after *Paradise Lost* and alongside *Paradise Regained*; it was published along with the latter in 1671. Parker (1949 and 1968) offers the most detailed and convincing argument that it was produced during the period 1647–53, based mainly upon evidence that the amanuenses who prepared the Trinity MS were probably those of the early 1650s (Milton was totally blind by 1652). All manner of textual-autobiographical parallels have been cited to support arguments for the poem's earlier or later provenance and, in the absence of any irrefutable evidence for either case, the final decision rests with the reader, who must balance what they understand of Milton's life against their interpretation of the text.

First of all there are parallels between the Samson–Delilah relationship and Adam and Eve in *Paradise Lost*. Samson was betrayed and, to an extent, so was Adam: Eve fell, ate the forbidden fruit, before him, and Milton presents his eating of it as at least partly inspired by his

fear of losing her. One might argue that this supports the later provenance argument; that Milton was further exploring a principal theme
of books IX and X of *Paradise Lost*. Alternatively, one could argue that
Milton in the early 1650s saw parallels between himself and Samson;
his wife had left, if not exactly betrayed him; and she had done so
because of her familial attachment to a cause, the Royalist Party,
opposed to his. Moreover Samson, like Milton, had very recently been
struck blind (by the late 1660s blindness had become a long endured
element of Milton's life) and, although Milton was aware that there
was no connection between his visual impairment and his martial
problems, the myth of Samson might have sounded an obliquely
relevant chord.

One could argue against this that in the late 1660s Milton felt himself
to be in a situation not unlike Samson's. He had not like his hero been
a military presence, but there are parallels between the presentation of
Samson as the massive, apparently undefeatable symbol of Israelite
rebellion and Milton's role as the brave defender against all theological
and political assaults upon the Cromwellian cause. At the beginning
of the poem Samson reflects upon his state.

> Promise was that I
> Should Israel from Philistian yoke deliver;
> Ask for this great deliverer now, and find him
> Eyeless in Gaza at the mill with slaves,
> Himself in bonds under Philistine yoke;
> (*TP*: 38–42)

Substitute Cromwellian for 'Israel' and 'Royalist' for 'Philistine' and
picture Milton reflecting upon the fact that he too had, albeit briefly,
been imprisoned after his cause was defeated. Also, throughout
Samson's exchanges with his father he frequently emphasises that his
punishment is deserved not because his cause was unjust; but quite
the contrary, that it is his destiny.

This passage is important because it brings to a head a constant
feature of the poem, the insistent issue of choice. Although Milton
made relatively few changes from the Biblical legend the element of
the text that brings it closer both to the mood of the pre-Christian
stories of Prometheus and Oedipus and to Renaissance poetry and
drama is the impression of a character beset by uncertainty and
contingency: Hamlet's tortured contemplation of 'that is the question'
is brought to mind. Samson's father offers him one solution to his

problem, and, more significantly, the woman who has caused his imprisonment complicates this with the supplementary argument that if he accepts it they could be reunited as man and wife.

All of this invites comparisons with *Paradise Lost*. Satan in Book II similarly involves himself in a complex series of speculations and hypotheses on what he as leader of the defeated angels should do next. In *Samson Agonistes* Delilah is frequently compared with a snake (763) or a viper (997–1000), which is the disguise used by Satan during his tempting of Eve: Delilah is the tempter of Samson and the parallels are intriguing. Throughout *Samson Agonistes* bird, reptile and animal imagery constantly attends each character's image of themselves and each other: Samson, for example, is before his imprisonment a 'lion' (28, 139) and later becomes subject to 'the labour of a beast' (37). In *Paradise Lost* the scale of being from animal through to angelic-spiritual states is a persistent theme, deployed to frame the action within God's overall construction of the natural world, with human beings at its centre. These similarities between the two texts return us to the question of when *Samson Agonistes* was written, and generally favour the 1650s argument, given that many aspects of *Samson Agonistes* seem more like preliminary explorations of, even rehearsals for, the precise orchestrations of *Paradise Lost* than further engagements with them.

The metre of *Samson Agonistes* is another feature of the poem that raises questions about position in the chronology of Milton's writings. Parts of it involve a pattern then unprecedented in English and which Milton in his prose introduction compares with the Greek 'apolelymenon' (freed from any particular stanza scheme) and 'alloestropha' (irregular strophes). In fact it resembles modern free verse, with lines sometimes having irregular rhyme, sometimes unrhymed, and varying in length between 12 and 6 syllables. Milton was experimenting with the relation between the abstract structure of verse and the less predictable form of improvised speech (see for example lines 95–110 of Samson's opening monologue on his state and condition). He had tried something similar but much less radical in *Comus* and 'Lycidas', which could favour the argument that *Samson Angonistes* belongs to an experimental tendency in his writing of the 1640s and 1650s. My placing of it prior to *Paradise Lost* reflects the strength of this case.

Paradise Lost

Paradise Lost is a poetic rewriting of the book of Genesis. It tells the story of the fall of Satan and his compatriots, the creation of man, and, most significantly, of man's act of disobedience and its consequences: paradise was lost for us. It is a literary text that goes beyond the traditional limitations of literary story telling, because for the Christian reader and for the predominant ethos of Western thinking and culture it involved the original story, the exploration of everything that man would subsequently be and do. Two questions arise from this and these have attended interpretations of the poem since its publication in 1667. First, to what extent did Milton diverge from orthodox perceptions of Genesis? Second, how did his own experiences, feelings, allegiances, prejudices and disappointments, play some part in the writing of the poem and, in respect of this, in what ways does it reflect the theological and political tensions of the seventeenth century?

Paradise Lost was probably written between 1660–65, although there is evidence that Milton had had long term plans for a biblical epic: there are rough outlines for such a poem, thought to have been produced in the 1640s, in the Trinity MS, and Edward Phillips (1694: 13) claims that Milton had during the same period shown him passages similar to parts of Book IV of the published work. The first edition (1667) was comprised of 10 books and its restructuring to 12 book occurred in the 1674 edition.

Prefatory material

There are two significant pieces of prefatory material; a 54-line poem by his friend Andrew Marvell (added in 1674) and Milton's own prose note on 'The Verse' (added to the sixth issue of the 1667 first edition).

Marvell's poem is largely a fulsome tribute to Milton's achievement but this is interposed with cautiously framed questions which are thought to reflect the mood of awe and perplexity which surrounded *Paradise Lost* during the seven years between its publication and the addition of Marvell's piece (lines 5–8, 11–12, 15–16).

Milton's own note on 'The Verse' is a defence of his use of blank verse. Before the publication of *Paradise Lost* blank verse was regarded as occupying a middle ground between poetic and non-poetic language and suitable only for plays; with non-dramatic verse there had to be rhyme. Milton claims that his use of blank verse will overturn all of these presuppositions, that he has for the first time ever in English created the equivalent of the unrhymed forms of Homer's and Virgil's classical epics. He does not state exactly how he has achieved this and subsequent commentators (see particularly Prince 1954 and Emma 1964) have noted that while his use of the unrhymed iambic pentameter is largely orthodox he frames within it syntactic constructions that throughout the poem constitute a particular Miltonic style. In fact 'The Verse' is a relatively modest citation of what would be a change in the history of English poetry comparable with the invention of free verse at the beginning of the twentieth century. Effectively, *Paradise Lost* licensed blank verse as a non-dramatic form and without it James Thomson's *The Seasons* (1730), William Cowper's *The Task* (1785) and William Wordsworth's *Tintern Abbey* (1798) and *The Prelude* (1850) would not be the poems that they are.

Book I

The first twenty-six lines of Book I introduce the theme of the poem; 'man's first disobedience, and the fruit/Of that forbidden tree, whose mortal taste/Brought death into the world...' (1–3) – and contain a number of intriguing statements. Milton claims to be pursuing 'things unattempted yet in prose or rhyme' (16) which can be taken to mean an enterprise unprecedented in non-literary or literary writing. While theologians had debated the book of Genesis and poets and dramatists engaged with it, no-one had, as yet, rewritten it. This raises the complex question of Milton's objectives in doing so. He calls upon 'the heavenly muse' to help him 'assert eternal providence,/And justify the ways of God to men' (25–6). Both of these statements carry immense implications, suggesting that he will offer a new perspective upon the indisputable truths of Christianity. The significance of this intensifies as we engage with the developing narrative of the poem.

In lines 27–83 Milton introduces the reader to Satan and his 'horrid crew', cast down into a recently constructed hell after their failed rebellion against God. For the rest of the book Milton shares his third person description with the voices of Satan, Beelzebub and other members of the defeated assembly.

The most important sections of the book are Satan's speeches (82–124, 241–264 particularly). In the first he attempts to raise the mood of Beelzebub, his second in command, and displays a degree of heroic stoicism in defeat: 'What though the field be lost?/All is not lost' (105–6). His use of military images has caused critics, William Empson particularly, to compare him with a defeated general reviewing his options while refusing to disclose any notion of final submission or despair to his troops. By the second speech stubborn tenacity has evolved into composure and authority.

> The mind is its own place, and in itself
> Can make a heaven of hell, a hell of heaven

What matter where, if I be still the same,
And what I should be, all but less than he
Whom thunder hath made greater? Here at least
We shall be free; the almighty hath not built
Here for his envy, will not drive us hence:
Here we may reign secure, and in my choice
To reign is worth ambition though in hell:
Better to reign in hell, than serve in heaven.

(I: 254–63)

While not altering the substance of Genesis, Milton's style would remind contemporary readers of more recent texts. Henry V addressing his troops, Mark Antony stirring the passions of the crowd, even Richard III giving expression to his personal image of the political future, all exert the same command of the relation between circumstance, rhetoric and emotive effect. Milton's Satan is a literary presence in his own right, an embodiment of linguistic energy. In his first speech he is inspired yet speculative but by the second the language is precise, relentless, certain: 'The mind *is* its own place ... We *shall* be free... We may reign *secure*'. The arrogant symmetry of line 263 has turned it into an idiom, a cliché of stubborn resistance: 'Better to reign in hell, than serve in heaven'. The question raised here is why Milton chose to begin his Christian epic with a heroic presentation of Satan.

The most striking and perplexing element of Book I is the fissure opened between Milton's presence as guide and co-ordinator in the narrative and our perception of the characters as self-determined figures. Consider, for example, his third-person interjection between Satan's first speech and Beelzebub's reply:

So spake the apostate angel, though in pain,
Vaunting aloud, but racked with deep despair.

(I: 125–6)

Milton is not telling anyone familiar with the biblical account anything they do not already know, but he seems to find it necessary to restrain them, to draw them back slightly from the mood of admiration that Satan's speeches create. When he gives an itemised account of the devils, he begins with Moloch.

First Moloch, horrid king besmeared with blood
Of human sacrifice, and parents tears.

(I: 392–3)

This version of Moloch is accurate enough but Milton is being a little imaginative with chronology, given that at this point in the history of the cosmos children, parents and the blood of human sacrifice did not yet exist. Indeed, his whole account of the sordid tastes and activities of the devils is updated to give emphasis to their effects upon humanity. Again, we have cause to suspect that Milton is attempting to match the reader's impulse to sympathise with the heroic (in Satan's case almost charismatic) condition of the devils with a more orthodox presentation of them as a threat to human kind, moral, physical and spiritual. Later (777–92) he employs a mock heroic style and presents them as pygmies, shrunk to a physical status that mirrors their spiritual decadence. Here it could be argued that he is attempting to forestall the reader's admiration of the efforts and skill in the building of Pandemonium (710–92) by ridiculing the builders.

In Book I Milton initiates a tension, a dynamic that will attend the entire poem, between the reader's purely literary response and our knowledge that the characters and their actions are ultimates, a foundation for all Christian perceptions of the human condition. The principal figures of Homer's and Virgil's poems are our original heroes. The classical hero will face apparently insurmountable tasks and challenges and his struggles against the complex balance of fate and circumstance will cause us to admire, to identify with him. Milton in Book I invoked the heroic, cast Satan and his followers as tragic, defeated soldiers, and at the same time reminded the Christian reader that it is dangerous to sympathise with these particular figures. Throughout the book we encounter an uncertainty that is unmatched in English literature: has the author unleashed feelings, inclinations within himself that he can only partially control, or is he in full control and cautiously manipulating the reader's state of perplexity?

Book II

Book II is divided into two sections. The first (1–628) is the most important and consists of a debate in which members of the Satanic Host – principally Satan, Moloch, Belial, Mammon and Beelzebub – discuss the alternatives available to them. There are four major speeches. Moloch (50–105) argues for a continuation of the war with God. Belial (118–228) and Mammon (237–83) encourage a form of stoical resignation – they should make the best of that to which they have been condemned. It is Beelzebub (309–416) who raises the possibility of an assault upon Earth, Eden, God's newest creation. Satan, significantly, stays in the background. He favours Beelzebub's proposal, which eventually wins the consensual proxy, but he allows his compatriots freedom of debate, and it is this feature of the book – its evocation of open exchange – that makes it important in our perception of *Paradise Lost* as in part an allegory on contemporary politics. Milton's attachment to the Parliamentarians during the Civil War, along with his role as senior civil servant to the Cromwellian cabinet, would have well attuned him to the fractious rhetoric of political discourse. Indeed, in the vast number of pamphlets he was commissioned to write in defence of the Parliamentarian and Republican causes, he was a participant, and we can find parallels between the speeches of the devils and Milton's own emboldened, inspirational prose.

For example, one of Milton's most famous tracts *Eikonoklastes* **[38–9]**, in which he seeks to justify the execution of Charles I, is often echoed in Moloch's argument that they should resume direct conflict with God. Milton invokes the courageous soldiers who gave their lives in the Civil War 'making glorious war against tyrants for the common liberty' and condemns those who would protest against the killing of Charles 'who hath offered at more cunning fetches to undermine our liberties, and put tyranny into an art, than any British king before him'. For Milton the Republicans embody 'the old English fortitude and love of freedom' (*CPW*, III: 343–4). Similarly Moloch refers to those who bravely fought against God and now 'stand in arms, and longing wait/The signal to ascend' (55–6). Charles, the author of 'tyranny' in Milton's pamphlet, shares this status with Moloch's God; 'the prison of his tyranny who reigns/By our delay …' (59–60). Both Milton and Moloch continually raise the image of the defence of freedom against an autocratic tyrant.

Later in the book when Beelzebub is successfully arguing for an assault upon Earth he considers who would best serve their interests in this enterprise:

> … Who shall tempt with wandering feet
> The dark unbottomed infinite abyss
> And through the palpable obscure find out
> His uncouth way, or spread his airy flight
> Up borne with indefatigable wings
> Over the vast abrupt, ere he arrive
> The happy isle; what strength, what art can then
> Suffice, or what evasion bear him safe
> Through the strict sentries and stations thick
> Of angels watching round? …

for on whom we send
The weight of all our last hope relies.
(II: 404–16)

The heroic presence to whom Beelzebub refers is of course Satan,
their leader. In Milton's pamphlet *A Second Defence of the English People*
(1654) he presents England as almost alone in Europe as the bastion of
liberty and he elevates Cromwell to the position of heroic leader.

> You alone remain. On you has fallen the whole burden of our affairs.
> On you alone they depend. In unison we acknowledge your
> unexcelled virtue ... Such have been your achievements as the
> greatest and most illustrious citizen ... Your deeds surpass all
> degrees, not only of admiration but surely of titles too, and like
> the tops of pyramids bury themselves in the sky, towering above
> the popular favour of titles.
>
> (*CPW*, IV: 671–2)

The parallels between Beelzebub's hyperbolic presentation of Satan
and Milton's of Cromwell are apparent enough. Even Milton's subtle
argument that Cromwell deserves a better status than that conferred
by hereditary title echoes the devil's desire to find their own replacement for the heavenly order, with Satan at its head. It is likely that
many early readers of *Paradise Lost* would spot the similarities between
the devils' discourse and Milton's, produced barely fifteen years before
– which raises the question of what Milton was trying to do.

To properly address this we should compare the two halves of Book
II. The first engages the seventeenth-century reader in a process of
recognition and immediacy; the devils conduct themselves in a way
that is remarkably similar to the political hierarchy of England in the
1650s. In the second, which describes Satan's journey to Earth, the
reader is shifted away from an identification with the devils to an
abstract, metaphysical plane in which the protagonists become more
symbolic than real. Satan is no longer human. At the Gates of Hell he
meets Sin, born out of his head when the rebellion was planned, and
Death, the offspring of their bizarre and inhuman coition (II: 666–
967). Then he encounters Chaos, a presence and a condition conducive
to his ultimate goal (II: 968–1009).

Book II is beautifully engineered. First, we are encouraged to identify
with the fallen angels; their state and their heroic demeanour are very
human. Then their leader, Satan, is projected beyond this and equated
with ultimates, perversely embodied abstracts; Sin, Death and Chaos.

One set of characters have to deal with uncertainties, unpredictable circumstances, conflicting states of mind. The others are irreducible absolutes.

Milton is establishing the predominant, in effect the necessary, mood of the poem. For much of it, up to the end of Book IX when the Fall occurs, the Christian reader is being projected into a realm that he/she cannot understand. This reader has inherited the consequences of the Fall, a detachment from any immediate identification with God's innate character, motives and objectives. On the one hand our only point of comparison for the likes of Satan (and eventually God and his Son) is ourselves; hence Milton's humanisation of the fallen angels. On the other, we should accept that such parallels are innately flawed; hence Milton's transference of Satan into the sphere of ultimates, absolutes, metaphysical abstracts.

Critics have developed a variety of approaches to this conundrum. Among the modern commentators, C.S. Lewis read the poem as a kind of instructive guide to the self-evident complexities of Christian belief. Waldock (1947) and Empson (1961) conducted humanist readings in which Satan emerges as a more engaging character than God. Blake (followed by Coleridge and Shelley) was the first humanist interpreter, claiming that Milton was of the 'Devil's Party' without being able to fully acknowledge his allegiance **[137–8]**. Christopher Hill (1977), a Marxist, is probably the most radical of the humanist critics and he argues that Milton uses the Satanic rebellion as a means of investigating his own 'deeply divided personality'.

> Satan, the battleground for Milton's quarrel with himself, saw God as arbitrary power and nothing else. Against this he revolted: the Christian, Milton knew, must accept it. Yet how could a free and rational individual accept what God had done to his servants in England? On this reading, Milton expressed through Satan (of whom he disapproved) the dissatisfaction which he felt with the Father (whom intellectually he accepted).
>
> (366–7)

Book III

It begins with the most candid, personal passage of the entire poem, generally referred to as the 'Address to Light' (1–55). In this Milton reflects upon his own blindness. He had already done so in Sonnet XVI. Before that, and before his visual impairment, he had in 'L'Allegro' and 'Il Penseroso' considered the spiritual and perceptual consequences of, respectively, light and darkness. Here all of the previous themes seem to find an apotheosis. He appears to treat his blindness as a beneficent, fatalistic occurrence which will enable him to achieve what few if any poets had previously attempted, a characterisation of God.

> So much the rather thou celestial light
> Shine inward, and the mind through all her powers
> Irradiate, there plant eyes, all mist from thence
> Purge and disperse, that I may see and tell
> Of things invisible to mortal sight.
>
> (III: 51–55)

Milton is not so much celebrating his blindness as treating it as a fitting correlative to a verbal enactment of 'things invisible to mortal sight', and by invisible he also means inconceivable.

God's address (56–134) is to his Son, who will of course be assigned the role of man's redeemer, and it involves principally God's foreknowledge of man's Fall. The following is its core passage.

> So will fall
> He and his faithless Progeny: whose fault?
> Whose but his own? Ingrate, he had of me
> All he could have; I made him just and right,
> Sufficient to have stood, though free to fall.
> Such I created all the etherial powers
> And spirits, both them who stood and them who failed;
> Freely they stood who stood, and fell who fell.
> Not free, what proof could they have given sincere
> Of true allegiance, constant faith or love,
> Where only what they needs must do, appeared,
> Not what they would? What praise could they receive?
> What pleasure I from such obedience paid,
> When will and reason (reason also is choice)
> Useless and vain, of freedom both despoiled,
> Made passive both, had served necessity,
> Not me.
>
> (III: 95–111)

The address tells us nothing that we do not already know, but its style has drawn the attention of critics. In the passage quoted, and throughout the rest of it, figurative, expansive language is rigorously avoided; there is no metaphor. This is appropriate, given that rhetoric during the Renaissance was at once celebrated and tolerated as a reflection of the human condition; we invent figures and devices as substitutes for the forbidden realm of absolute, God-given truth. And God's abjuration of figures will remind us of our guilty admiration for their use by the devils.

At the same time, however, the language used by an individual, however sparse and pure, will create an image of its user. God, it seems, is unsettled: 'whose fault?/Whose but his own?' He is aware that the Fall will occur, so why does he trouble himself with questions? And why, moreover, does God feel the need to explain himself, to apparently render himself excusable and blameless regarding events yet to occur: 'Not me'.

If Milton was attempting in his presentation of the devils to catch the reader between their faith and their empirical response, he appears to be doing so again with God. Critics have dealt with this problem in different ways. C.S. Lewis reminds the reader that this is a poem about religion but that it should not be allowed to disturb the convictions and certainties of Christian faith.

> The cosmic story – the ultimate *plot* in which all other stories are episodes – is set before us. We are invited, for the time being, to look at it from the outside. And that is not, in itself, a religious experience ... In the religious life man faces God and God faces man. But in the epic it is feigned for the moment, that we, as readers, can step aside and see the faces of God and man in profile.
> (1942: 132)

Lewis's reader, the collective 'we', is an ahistorical entity, but a more recent critic, Stanley Fish (1967) has looked more closely at how Milton's contemporaries would have interpreted the passage. They, he argued, by virtue of the power of seventeenth-century religious belief, would not be troubled even by the possibility that Milton's God might seem a little too much like us. William Empson (1961) contends that the characterisations of God and Satan were, if not a deliberate anticipation of agnostic doubt, then a genuine reflection of Milton's troubled state of mind; 'the poem is not good in spite of but especially because of its moral confusions' (p.13).

Such critical controversies as this will be dealt with in detail in Part 3, but they should be borne in mind here as an indication of *Paradise Lost*'s ability to cause even the most learned and sophisticated of readers to interpret it differently. Lewis argues that Milton would not have wanted his Christian readers to doubt their faith (though he acknowledges that they might, implying that Milton intended the poem as a test), while Fish contends that querulous, fugitive interpretations are a consequence of modern, post-eighteenth-century, states of mind (a strategy generally known of Reader-Response Criticism). Empson, who treats the poem as symptomatic of Milton's own uncertainties, is regarded by Fish as an example of the modern reader.

The first half of the Book (1–415) comprises God's exchange with the Son and includes their discussion of what will happen after the Fall, anticipating the New Testament and Christ's heroic role as the redeemer. The rest (416–743) returns us to Satan's journey to Earth, during which he meets Oriel, the Sun Spirit, disguises himself and asks directions to God's newest creation which, he claims, he wishes to witness and admire. By the end of the Book he has reached Earth.

Book IV

Here the reader is engaged in two perspectives. We are shown Adam and Eve conversing, praying and (elliptically described) making love, and this vision of Edenic bliss is juxtaposed with the arrival and the thoughts of Satan. Adam's opening speech (411–39) and Eve's reply (440–91) establish the roles and characteristics that for both of them will be maintained throughout the poem. Adam, created first, is the relatively experienced, wise figure of authority who explains their status in Paradise and the single rule of obedience and loyalty. Eve, in her account of her first moments of existence, discloses a less certain, perhaps impulsive, command of events and impressions.

> That day I oft remember, when from sleep
> I first awaked, and found myself reposed
> Under a shade of flowers, much wondering where
> And what I was, whence thither brought, and how.
> Not distant far from thence a murmuring sound
> Of waters issued from a cave and spread
> Into a liquid plain, then stood unmoved
> Pure as the expanse of heaven; I thither went
> With unexperienced thought, and laid me down
> On the green bank, to look into the clear
> Smooth lake, that to me seemed another sky.
> As I bent down to look just opposite
> A shape within the watery gleam appeared
> Bending to look on me; I started back,
> It started back, but pleased I soon returned,

Pleased it returned as soon with answering looks
Of sympathy and love; there I had fixed
Mine eyes till now, and pined with vain desire,
Had not a voice thus warned me, What thou seest,
What there thou seest fair creature is thyself,
With thee it came and goes: but follow me,
And I will bring thee where no shadow stays
They coming, and thy soft embraces, he
Whose image thou art, him thou shall enjoy
Inseparably thine, to him shalt bear
Multitudes like thyself, and then be called
Mother of human race: what could I do,
But follow straight, invisibly thus led?
Till I espied thee.

(IV: 449–77)

This passage is frequently cited in feminist surveys of Milton [166–74]. It introduces his most important female figure, indeed the original woman, and it does so by enabling her to disclose her innate temperamental and intellectual characteristics through her use of language.

We do not require textual notes or critical commentaries to tell us that Eve's attraction to her own image in the water (460–5) is a straightforward, indeed candid, disclosure of narcissism. Her first memory is of vain self-obsession. However, before we cite this as evidence of Milton's portrayal of Eve, who will eat the forbidden fruit first, as by virtue of her gender the prototypical cause of the Fall, we should look more closely at the stylistic complexities of her speech.

For example, when she tells of how she looked 'into the clear/Smooth lake' (458–9) she is performing a subtle balancing act between hesitation and a more confident command of her account. 'Clear' in seventeenth-century usage could be both a substantive reference to clarity of vision ('*the* clear') and be used in its more conventional adjectival sense ('clear smooth lake'). Similarly with 'no shadow stays/Thy coming' (470–1), the implied pause after 'stays' could suggest it first as meaning 'prevents' and then in its less familiar sense of 'awaits'. The impression we get is confusing. Is she tentatively feeling her way through the traps and complexities of grammar, as would befit her ingenuous, unsophisticated state as someone recently introduced to language and perception? Or is Milton urging us to perceive her as, from her earliest moments, a rather cunning actress and natural rhetorician, someone who can use language as a means of presenting herself as touchingly naïve and blameless in her instincts? In short, is her language a transparent reflection of her character or a means by which she creates a persona for herself?

This question has inevitably featured in feminist readings of the poem [168–9], because it involves the broader issue of whether or not Milton was creating in Adam and Eve the ultimate and fundamental gender stereotypes – their acts were after all responsible for the postlapsarian condition of humankind.

To return to the poem itself we should note that it is not only the reader who is forming perceptions of Adam and Eve. Satan, in reptilian disguise, is watching and listening too. Beginning at line 505, Milton has him disclose his thoughts.

> all is not theirs it seems:
> One fatal tree there stands of knowledge called,
> Forbidden them to taste: knowledge forbidden?
> Suspicious, reasonless. Why should their Lord
> Envy them that? Can it be sin to know,
> Can it be death? And do they only stand
> By ignorance, is that their happy state,
> The proof of their obedience and their faith?
> O fair foundation laid whereon to build
> Their ruin! Hence I will excite their minds
> With more desire to know ...
>
> (IV: 513–24)

Without actually causing us to question the accepted facts regarding Satan's malicious, destructive intent Milton again prompts the reader to empathise with his thoughts – and speculations. Satan touches upon issues that would strike deeply into the mindset of the sophisticated Renaissance reader. Can there, should there, be limits to human knowledge? By asking questions about God's will and His design of the universe do we overreach ourselves? More significantly, was the original act of overreaching and its consequences – the eating of the fruit from the tree of knowledge as an aspiration to knowledge – intended by God as a warning?

The rest of the book returns us to the less contentious, if no less thrilling, details of the narrative, with Uriel warning the angel Gabriel of Satan's apparent plot, Gabriel assigning two protecting angels to Adam and Eve, without their knowledge, and Gabriel himself confronting Satan and telling him that he is contesting powers greater than himself.

Before moving further into the poem let us consider whether the various issues raised so far in the narrative correspond with what we know of Milton the thinker and not simply our projected notion of the thoughts which underlie his writing of the poem. Most significantly, all of the principal figures – Satan, God, Adam and Eve – have been caused to affect us in ways that we would associate as much with literary characterisation as with their functions within religious belief; they have been variously humanised. In one of Milton's later prose tracts, *De Doctrina Christiana,* begun, it is assumed, only a few years before he started *Paradise Lost,* we encounter what could be regarded as the theological counterparts to the complex questions addressed in the poem. In a passage on predestination, one of the most contentious topics of the post-reformation debate, Milton is, to say the least, challenging:

> Everyone agrees that man could have avoided falling. But if, because of God's decree, man could not help but fall (and the two contradictory opinions are sometimes voiced by the same people), then God's restoration of fallen man was a matter of justice not grace. For once it is granted that man fell, though not unwillingly, yet by necessity, it will always seem that necessity either prevailed upon his will by some secret influence, or else guided his will in some way. But if God foresaw that man would fall of his own accord, then there was no need for him to make a decree about the fall, but only about what would become of man who was going to fall. Since, then, God's supreme wisdom foreknew that first man's falling away, but did not decree it, it follows that, before the fall of man, predestination was not absolutely decreed either. Predestination, even after the fall, should always be considered and defined not so much the result of an actual decree but as arising from the immutable condition of a decree.
>
> (*CPW,* VI: 174)

If after reading this you feel rather more perplexed and uncertain about our understanding of God and the Fall than you did before, you are not alone. It is like being led blindfold through a maze. You start with a feeling of relative certainty about where you are and what surrounds you, and you end the journey with a sense of having returned to this state, but you are slightly troubled about where you've been in the meantime. Can we wrest an argument or a straightforward message from this passage? It would seem that predestination (a long running theological crux of Protestantism) is, just like every other component of our conceptual universe, a result of the Fall. Thus, although God knew that man would fall, He did not cause (predetermine) the act of disobedience. As such, this is fairly orthodox theology, but in making his point Milton allows himself and his readers to stray into areas of paradox and doubt that seem to run against the overarching sense of certainty. For instance, he concedes that 'it will always seem that necessity either prevailed upon his (man's) will by some secret influence, or else guided his will in some way'. Milton admits here that man will never be able to prevent himself ('it will always seem') from wondering what actually caused Adam and Eve to eat the fruit. Was it fate, the influence of Satan, Adam's or Eve's own temperamental defects?

The passage certainly does not resolve the uncertainties encountered in the first four books, but it does present itself as a curious mirror-image of the poem. Just as in the poem the immutable doctrine of scripture sits uneasily with the disorientating complexities of literary writing, so our trust in theology will always be compromised by our urge to ask troubling questions. Considering these similarities it is possible to wonder if Milton decided to dramatise Genesis in order to throw into the foreground the very human tendencies of scepticism and self-doubt that exist only in the margins of conventional religious and philosophic thought. If so, why? As a form of personal catharsis, as an encoded manifesto for potential anti-Christianity, or as a means of revealing to readers the true depths of their uncertainties? All of these possibilities have been put forward by commentators on the poem, but as the following pages will show, the decision is finally yours.

Books V–VIII

These four books, the middle third of the poem, will be treated as a single unit because they are held together by a predominant theme; the presence of Raphael, sent by God to Paradise at the beginning of book V as Adam and Eve's instructor and advisor. The books show us the growth of Adam and Eve, the development of their emotional and intellectual engagement with their appointed role prior to the most important moment in the poem's narrative, their Fall in book IX.

At the beginning of book V God again becomes a speaking presence, stating that he despatches Raphael to 'render man inexcusable ... Lest wilfully transgressing he pretend/Surprisal, unadmonished, unfore-warned' (244–5). Line 244 offers a beautiful example of tactical ambiguity. Does 'Lest' refer to man's act of 'transgressing'? If so, we are caused again to consider the uneasy relation between free will, predestination and God's state of omniscience: surely God knows that man will transgress. Or does 'Lest' relate, less problematically, to man's potential reaction to the consequences of his act? Once more the reader is faced with the difficult choice between an acceptance of his limited knowledge of God's state and the presentation to us here of God as a humanised literary character.

The arrival of Raphael (V: 308–576) brings with it a number of intriguing, often puzzling, issues. Food plays a significant part. Eve is busy preparing a meal for their first guest.

> She turns, on hospitable thoughts intent
> What choice to choose for delicacy best,
> What order so contrived as not to mix
> Tastes, not well-joined, inelegant, but bring
> Taste after taste upheld with kindliest change.
>
> (V: 332–6)

This passage might seem to be an innocuous digression on the domestic bliss of the newlyweds – with Eve presented as a Restoration prototype for Mrs. Beaton or Delia Smith – but there are serious resonances. For one thing her hesitant, anxious state of mind appears to confirm the conventional, male, social and psychological model of 'female' behaviour – should we then be surprised that she will be the first to transgress, given her limitations? Also, the passage is a fitting preamble for Raphael's first informal act of instruction. Milton sets the scene with, 'A while discourse they hold;/No fear lest dinner cool' (395–6), reminding us that fire would be part of the punishment for the Fall; before that neither food nor anything else needed to be heated. The 'discourse' itself, on Raphael's part, treats food as a useful starting point for a mapping out of the chain of being. Raphael, as he demonstrates by his presence and his ability to eat, can shift between transubstantial states; being an angel he spends most of his time as pure spirit. At lines 493–9 he states that

> Time may come when men
> With angels may participate, and find
> No inconvenient diet, nor too light fare;
> And from these corporal nutriments perhaps
> Your bodies may at last turn to spirit,
> Improved by tract of time, and winged ascend
> Ethereal

Raphael will expand upon this crucial point throughout the four central books: it is God's intention that man, presently part spirit, part substance, will gradually move up the chain of being and replace Satan's fallen crew as the equivalent of the new band of angels. How exactly this will occur is not specified but Raphael here implies, without really explaining, that there is some mysterious causal relationship between such physical experiences as eating and the gradual transformation to an angelic, spiritual condition: his figurative language is puzzling. It would, however, strike a familiar chord for Eve, who at the beginning of the book had described to Adam her strange dream about the forbidden fruit and an unidentified tempter who tells her to 'Taste this, and be henceforth among the gods/Thyself a goddess, not to earth confined' (V: 77–8). Later in Book IX, just before she eats the fruit, Satan plays upon this same curious equation between eating and spirituality, 'And what are gods that man may not become/As they, participating godlike food?' (IX: 716–17).

Milton appears to be sewing into the poem a fabric of clues for the attentive reader, clues that suggest some sort of causal, psychological explanation for the Fall. In this instance it might appear that Raphael's well meant, but perhaps misleading, discourse creates for Eve just the right amount of intriguing possibilities to make her decision to eat the fruit almost inevitable. In consequence, God's statement that Raphael's role is to 'render man inexcusable' sounds a little optimistic.

Books VI–VIII are concerned almost exclusively with Raphael's instructive exchanges with Adam; Eve, not always present, is kept informed of this by Adam during their own conversations. Book VI principally involves Raphael's description of Satan's revolt, the subsequent battles and God's victory. Book VII deals mainly with the history of Creation and in Book VIII Raphael explains to Adam the state and dimensions of the Cosmos. The detail of all this is of relatively slight significance for an understanding of the poem itself. Much of it involves an orthodox account of the Old Testament story of Creation and the only notable feature is Milton's decision in Book VIII to follow, via Raphael, the ancient theory of Ptolemy that the earth is the centre of the universe. Copernicus, the sixteenth-century astronomer, had countered this with the then controversial model of the earth revolving around the sun, which Raphael alludes to (without of course naming Copernicus) but largely discounts. Milton had met Galileo and certainly knew of his confirmation of the Copernican model. His choice to retain the Ptolemaic system for *Paradise Lost* was not alluded to in his *ex cathedra* writing and was probably made for dramatic purposes; in terms of man's fate the earth was indeed at the centre of things.

More significant than the empirical details of Raphael's disclosures is Adam's level of understanding. Constantly, Raphael interrupts his account and speaks with Adam about God's gift of reason, the power of the intellect, which is the principal distinction between human beings and other earthbound, sentient creatures. At the end of Book VI Raphael relates reason (563–76) to free will (520–35). Adam is told (and the advice will be oft repeated) that their future will depend not upon some prearranged 'destiny' but upon their own decisions and actions, but that they should maintain a degree of caution regarding how much they are able, as yet, to fully comprehend of God's design and intent. In short, their future will be of their own making while their understanding of the broader framework within which they must make decisions is limited and partial. At the end of Book VI, for example, after Raphael has provided a lengthy account of the war in heaven he informs Adam that he should not take this too literally. It has been an allegory, an extended metaphor, a 'measuring [of] things in Heaven by things on Earth'. (893)

In Book VIII, before his description of the Cosmos, Raphael again reminds Adam that he is not capable of fully appreciating its vast complexity.

> The great architect
> Did wisely to conceal, and not divulge,
> His secrets to be scanned by them who ought
> Rather admire; or if they list to try
> Conjecture, he his fabric of the heavens
> Hath left to their disputes, perhaps to move
> His laughter at their quaint opinions wide
>
> (VIII: 72–8)

This is frequently treated as an allusion to the ongoing debate on the validity of the Ptolemaic or the Copernican models of earth and the planets, but it also has a rhetorical function in sustaining a degree of tension between man's gift of reason and the at once tantalising yet dangerous possibilities that might accompany its use. All of this carries significant, but by no means transparent, relevance from a number of theological issues with which Milton was involved; principally the Calvinist notion of predestination versus the Arminianist concept as free will as a determinant of fate **[9–11]**.

Later in Book VIII (357–451) Adam tells Raphael of his first conversation with God just prior to the creation of Eve, which resembles a Socratic dialogue. Socrates, the Greek philosopher, engaged in a technique when instructing a pupil of not imposing a belief but sewing his discourse with enough speculations and possibilities to engage the pupil's faculties of enquiry and reason. Through this exchange of questions and propositions they would move together toward a final, logically valid conclusion. God's exchange with Adam follows this pattern. The following is a summary of it.

Adam laments his solitude. God says, well you're not alone, you have other creatures, the angels and me. Yes, says Adam, but I want an equal partner. God replies: Consider my state. I don't need a consort. Adam returns, most impressively, with the argument that God is a perfect self-sufficiency, but man must be complemented in order to multiply. Quite so, says God. This was my intention all along. And He creates Eve.

The relevance of this to Adam's ongoing exchange with Raphael is unsettling. Stanley Fish suggests that it is meant to offer a further, tacit reminder to the reader of the rules and preconditions that attend man's pre-fallen state. 'If the light of reason coincides with the word of God, well and good; if not reason must retire, and not fall into the presumption of denying or questioning what it cannot explain' (1967: 242). It reminded William Empson (1961) of the educational phenomenon of the Rule of Inverse Probability, where the student is less concerned with the attainment of absolute truth than with satisfying the expectations of the teacher: in short, Adam has used his gift of reason without really understanding what it is and to what it might lead. Is Adam being carefully and adequately prepared for the future (Fish) or is Raphael's instruction presented to us as some kind of psychological explanation for the Fall (Empson)?

This interpretative difference underpins our reading of Books V–XII, and, to complicate matters further, indeed to heighten the dramatic tension of the narrative, Milton places Adam's account of his exchange with God not too long before a similar conversation takes place between Eve and Satan, in Book IX just prior to her decision to eat the fruit.

Book IX

Eve's conversation with Satan (532–779) is the most important in the poem; it initiates the Fall of mankind. Satan's speeches, particularly the second (678–733), display an impressive and logical deployment of fact and hypothesis. Eve does not understand the meaning of death, the threatened punishment for the eating of the fruit, and Satan explains:

> ye shall not die:
> How should ye? By the fruit? It gives you life
> To knowledge. By the threatener? Look on me,
> Me who have touched and tasted, yet both live,

And life more perfect have attained than fate
Meant me, by venturing higher than my lot.
Shall that be shut to man, which to the beast
Is open?

(IX: 685–93)

Having raised the possibility that death is but a form of transformation beyond the merely physical, he delivers a very cunning follow-up.

So ye shall die perhaps, by putting off
Human, to put on gods, death to be wished,
Though threatened, which no worse than this can bring.
And what are gods that man may not become
As they, participating godlike food?

(IX: 713–17)

In short, he suggests that the fruit, forbidden but for reasons yet obscure, might be the key to that which is promised.

Eve's reply to Satan's extensive, even-handed listing of the ethical and practical considerations of her decision is equally thoughtful. She raises a question, 'In plain then, what forbids he but to know/Forbids us good, forbids us to be wise? (758–9) and expands, 'What fear I then, rather what know to fear/Under this ignorance of good and evil, /Of God or death, of law or penalty?' Adam and Eve have continually been advised by Raphael of their state of relative ignorance while they have also been promised enlightenment. It is evident from Eve's speech that she regards the rule of obedience as in some way part, as yet unspecified, of the existential puzzle which their own much promoted gift of reason will gradually enable them to untangle. They are aware that their observance of the rule is a token of their love and loyalty, but as Satan implies, such an edict is open to interpretation.

What can your knowledge hurt him, or this tree
Import against his will, if all be his?
Or is it envy, and can envy dwell
In heavenly breasts?

(IX: 726–30)

Eve's exchange with Satan inevitably prompts the reader to recall Adam's very recent account of his own with God and, indeed, his extended dialogue with Raphael. In each instance the human figure is naïve, far less informed than their interlocutor, while the latter both instructs and encourages his pupil to rationalise and speculate. (Eve is unaware of Satan's identity. He is disguised as a serpent and is, for all she knows, another agent of wisdom.) These parallels can be interpreted differently and the archetypal difference is evident between Christian and humanist readers. Of the former, Lewis argued that the parallels were meant to be recognised but were intended by Milton as a kind of re-enactment of the poem itself: the Christian reader – and in Lewis's view the poem was intended only for Christian readers – should perceive him/herself as a version of Adam and Eve and resist the temptation to overreach their perceptual and intellectual subservience to God's wisdom. Lewis held that the poem's moral of obedience and restraint has the 'desolating clarity' of what we are taught in the nursery. Children might be incapable of understanding the ethical and moral framework which underpins their parents' rules and edicts but they should recognise that these apparently arbitrary regulations are a reflection of the latter's protective love. Empson countered this as follows: 'A father may reasonably impose a random prohibition to test the character of his children, but anyone would agree that he should then judge an act of disobedience in the light of its intention' (1961: 161). Empson perceives the exchanges, particularly between Satan and Eve, not only as mitigating factors in Milton's particular account of the Fall but also as explanations of how the Fall was made inevitable by God himself. Both agree that the reader is prompted to question God's omniscient planning and strategies, while Lewis sees this as a warning and reminder that blind faith should be our only proper response and Empson that doubt informs Milton's own rendering of the story.

Eve does of course eat the fruit, and during lines 896–1016 she confronts Adam with her act. Adam's response and his eventual decision to follow Eve are intriguing because while the misuse, or misunderstanding, of the gift of reason was the significant factor for her Adam is affected as much by emotional, instinctive registers.

> I feel
> The link of nature draw me: flesh of flesh,
> Bone of my bone thou art, and from thy state
> Mine never shall be parted, bliss or woe.
> (IX: 913–16)

This is addressed 'to himself', and then to Eve he states that
> So forcible within my heart I feel

The bond of nature draw me to my own,
My own in thee, for what thou art is mine;
Our state cannot be severed; we are one,
One flesh; to lose thee were to lose myself.
                    (IX: 955–9)

And the episode is summed up by Milton:

She gave him of that fair enticing fruit
With liberal hand: he scrupled not to eat
Against his better knowledge, not deceived,
But fondly overcome with female charm.
                    (IX: 996–9)

These passages raise questions about chronology and characterisation. We already know from Book VIII (607–17) that Adam appreciates that the love he feels for Eve (partly physical) partakes of his greater love for God (mutual and transcendent) and we might wonder why and how Adam seems able to move so rapidly to a state of almost obsessive physical bonding with her: 'The link of nature', 'flesh of flesh', 'The bond of nature', 'My own in Thee', 'One flesh'. Moreover, during Milton's description in Book IV of Adam and Eve's innocent act of sexual liaison we were informed that the base, lust-fulfilling dimension of sex is a consequence of the Fall, and this is confirmed shortly after he too eats the fruit and they engage in acts 'of amorous intent' (IX: 1035). It seems odd, therefore, that Adam, still unfallen, seems to be persuaded to eat the fruit by the post-lapsarian instinct of pure physical desire.

One explanation of why Milton offers this puzzling, slightly inconsistent scenario could be implicit in his own rationale of Adam's decision; 'not deceived/But fondly overcome with female charm' (998–9). From this it would seem that her explanation of the act of disobedience is of virtually no significance compared with the sub-rational power of attraction that she shares, or will share, with the rest of her gender.

Charges of misogyny against Milton go back as far as Samuel Johnson and are generally founded upon the biographical formula that the failure of his first marriage to Mary Powell was the motive for his divorce tracts and that these personal and ideological prejudices spilled over into his literary writing. Since the 1970s more sophisticated feminist critics have argued that the distinctive, archetypal roles played out by Adam and Eve are less a consequence of Milton's personal state of mind and more part of a shared, patriarchal dialectic in which ongoing social conventions are justified and perpetuated through a mythology of religion and culture **[166–74]**.

Book X

Here the narrative of the Fall is continued, with God observing the act of disobedience and sending the Son to pronounce judgement on Adam and Eve. The death sentence is deferred and they, and their offspring, are condemned to a limited tenure of earthly existence, much of it to be spent in thankless toil and sorrow (103–228). There then follows a lengthy section (228–720) in which Satan and his followers have their celebrations ruined by being turned into serpents and beset by unquenchable thirst and unassuagble appetite – so much for victory. The most important part is from 720 to the end of the book, during which Adam and Eve contemplate suicide. Adam considers this in an introspective soliloquy.

> But say
> That death be not one stroke, as I supposed,
> Bereaving sense, but endless misery
> From this day onward, which I feel begun
> Both in me, and without me, and so last
> To perpetuity.
>
> (X: 808–130)

Adam is aware that self-inflicted death will involve a perpetuation, not a completion, of his tortured condition. This realisation prompts the circling, downward spiral of his inconclusive thoughts, until Eve arrives. She readily accepts blame for their condition. Adam is eventually moved by her contrition and they comfort each other. Crucially, the factor that enables Adam to properly organise his own thoughts is Eve's proposition that rather than kill themselves they should spare their offspring the consequences of their act and refuse to breed; 'Childless thou art, childless remain' (989). Adam points out that this would both further upset the God-given natural order of things and, most importantly, grant a final victory to Satan. He seems at last to be exercising his much promoted gift of reason in a manner that is concurrent with the will of God, which implies that reason is tempered by thoughtful restraint not through any form of enlightenment, but from punishment. This impression finds its theological counterpart in what is termed 'The Paradox of the Fortunate Fall'. This notion was first considered in depth by St. Augustine, and A.O. Lovejoy (1945 and 1960) traces its history up to and including *Paradise Lost*. The Fall is both paradoxical and fortunate because in the latter case it was a necessary stage in man's journey toward wisdom and awareness, while in the former it reminds us that we should not continually question and investigate God's will.

Again we are returned to the conflict between Christian and humanist readings of the poem. The Augustinian interpretation would be a reminder that we should not concern ourselves too much with the apparent inconsistencies and paradoxes sewn into the poem, while a humanist reading would raise the question of why Milton deliberately, provocatively accentuates such concerns.

At the end of the book (1041–96) we are offered the spectacle of Adam and Eve no longer pondering such absolutes as the will of God and the nature of the cosmos but concentrating on more practical matters, such as how they might protect themselves from the new and disagreeable climate by rubbing two sticks together. Is Milton implicitly sanctioning the Augustinian notion of investigative restraint or is he presenting the originators of humanity as embodiments of pathetic, pitiable defeat?

Books XI and XII

In these the angel Michael shows Adam a vision of the future, drawn mainly from the Old Testament but sometimes bearing a close resemblance to the condition of life in seventeenth-century England. Kenneth Muir (1955) argued that although the two closing books were essential to the scriptural scheme of the poem they are 'poetically on a much lower level'. What he means is that there is no longer any need for Milton to generate dramatic or logical tension: the future, as disclosed by Michael, has already arrived.

Adam is particularly distressed by the vision of Cain and Abel (XI: 429–60), the 'sight/Of terror, foul and ugly to behold/Horrid to think, how horrible to feel!' (463–5). Michael has already explained how, by some form of genetic inheritance, Adam is responsible for this spectacle of brother murdering brother. And we should remind ourselves that many of the first readers of this account had memories of brothers, sons and fathers facing one another across English battlefields; indeed its author's own brother was on the Royalist side.

These two are brethren, Adam, and to come

> Out of thy loins; the unjust the just hath slain,
> For envy that his brother's offering found
> From heaven acceptance; but the bloody fact
> Will be avenged, and other's faith approved.
>
> (XI: 454–8)

The tragic consequences of a perpetual rivalry between two figures who believe that theirs is the better 'offering' to God might easily be regarded as a vision of the consequences of the Reformation. The specific description of war (638–81) pays allegiance to the Old Testament and Virgil but would certainly evoke memories of when Englishmen, barely a decade earlier,

> Lay siege, encamped; by battery, scale and mine,
> Assaulting; others from the wall defend
> With dart and javelin, stones and sulphurous fire;
> On each hand slaughter and gigantic deeds.
>
> (XI: 656–9)

One wonders if Milton's own experience of the Civil War, the Cromwellian Commonwealth and the Restoration, when death and destruction were perpetuated by man's perception of God's will, was in his mind when he wrote these passages. Hill, the Marxist historian, (1977) is in no doubt that it was and he devotes a subsection to a political-historical decoding of Books XI and XII (380–90). Hill concludes that

> They [the books] represent Milton's attempt to be utterly realistic in facing the worst without despair. It seemed to be true that there was a cyclical return of evil after every good start ... God's people in England after 1660 must learn to escape from history as circular treadmill, must become free to choose the good, as the English people had failed to chose it during the Revolution.
>
> (386)

For Hill, Milton regarded the political swings and catastrophes of the previous three decades as a concentrated version of man's perpetual struggle and continual failure to build something better from his fallen condition. Moreover, Hill argues that the essential parallel between Adam's vision of the future and Milton's own of the recent past was that Milton perceived both as part of an extended process of man's 're-education and ultimate recognition of God's purposes.' (387) In short, the Cromwellian Revolution failed because man was not yet able to fully comprehend and engage with the legacy of the Fall.

Alongside the particulars of war and destruction Adam is shown more general, but no less distressing, pictures of the human condition. After enquiring of Michael if there are not better ways to die than in battle Adam is presented with the following.

A lazar house it seemed, wherein were laid
Numbers of all diseased, all maladies
Of ghastly spasm, or racking torture, qualms
Of heart-sick agony, all feverous kinds,
Convulsions, epilepsies, fierce catarrhs
Intestine stone and ulcer, colic pangs,
Demoniac frenzy, moping melancholy
And moon-struck madness, pining atrophy,
Marasmus, and wide wasting pestilence,
Dropsies, and asthmas, and joint racking rheums.
Dire was the tossing, deep the groans, despair
Tended the sick busiest from couch to couch;
And over them triumphant death his dart
Shook, but delayed to strike, though oft invoked
With vows, as their chief good, and final hope.
(XI: 479–93)

Disease, disablement, terminal illness and much pain will be inescapable and the only means by which their worst effects might be moderated is through abstinence and restraint: the pursuit of sensual pleasure brings its own form of physical punishment. Just prior to disclosing the 'lazar house' to Adam Michael informs him that he is doing so 'that thou mayst know/What misery the inabstinence of Eve/ Shall bring on men' (475–7) and yet again the reader feels a puzzling engagement with narrative chronology. At no point in Eve's book IX exchange with Satan does she even inadvertently disclose that hedonism plays some part in her desire to eat the fruit, but Michael clearly presents a causal relation between what she did and the self destructive inabstinence of man's fallen state. During his conversations with Raphael, before the Fall, Adam might well have enquired about such apparent discontinuities, but not now because as becomes evident in Book XII Michael's instructive regimen is informed by, and apparently achieves, a different purpose.

Most of Book XII charts a tour of the Old and parts of the New Testament – Noah, The Flood, the Tower of Babel, the journey to the

Promised Land and the coming of Christ – but its most important sections are towards the end when Adam is given the opportunity to reflect on what he has seen.

> How soon hath thy prediction, seer blest,
> Measured this transcient world, the race of time,
> Till time stand fixed: beyond is all abyss,
> Eternity, whose end no eye can reach.
> Greatly instructed I shall hence depart,
> Greatly in peace of thought, and have my fill
> Of knowledge, what this vessel can contain;
> Beyond which was my folly to aspire.
> Henceforth I learn, that to obey is best,
> And love with fear the only God, to walk
> As in his presence, ever to observe
> His providence, and on him sole depend.
>   (XII: 553–64)

Michael answers, approvingly:

> This having learned, thou hast attained the sum
> Of wisdom; hope no higher.
>   (XII: 575–6)

Without actually comparing his experiences with Michael with those before the Fall Adam is clearly aware that the cause of the Fall was his inclination to 'aspire' to an over-ambitious, extended state of 'knowledge'. One significant difference between Raphael's and Michael's methods of instruction is that while the former operated almost exclusively within the medium of language, the principal instrument of speculation and enquiry, the latter relies more upon empirical and tangible evidence, pictures. This is appropriate, given that Michael's intention is to present Adam with indisputable, ineluctable facts, matters not open to debate, and in doing so to reinforce the lesson that 'wisdom' has its limits; 'hope no higher'.

The question that has attended practically all of the critical debates on the poem is encapsulated in three lines at the centre of Adam's speech.

> Greatly instructed I shall hence depart,
> Greatly in peace of thought, and have my fill

Of knowledge.

(XII: 537–9)

The question is this: does Adam speak for the reader? And there are questions within the question. Did Milton intend the reader to share Adam's state of intellectual subordination to a mindset 'beyond which was [his] folly to aspire'? Are the tantalising complexities of the poem – the presentations of God and Satan, the intricate moral and theological problems raised in the narrative – designed to tempt the reader much as Adam had been tempted, and to remind us of the consequences? Or did Milton himself face uncertainties and did he use the poem not so much to resolve as to confront them? As Part III will show, these matters, after 300 years of often perplexed commentary and debate, remain unsettled.

Paradise Regained

Paradise Regained was published, along with *Samson Agonistes*, in 1671 and while there is considerable evidence that the latter was written much earlier **[91, 92–3]**, it is generally assumed that the former was composed during the four years following *Paradise Lost*. The anecdote which accompanies virtually every account of the poem involved the claim by Thomas Ellwood, a Quaker and friend of Milton, that he had prompted the great poet to write it 'Thou hast said much ... of *Paradise Lost*; but what hast thou to say of *Paradise found*?' (Ellwood 1714: 233–4). Ellwood's tale is unverified and its only significance is its implication that *Paradise Regained* was intended to present the first coming of Christ as the story of man's potential redemption from his fallen state.

Paradise Regained deals exclusively with the temptation of Christ by Satan in the wilderness. Luke, iv, 1–13 and Matthew iv, 1–11 are its New Testament sources. The most obvious thread of continuity between *Paradise Lost* and its successor involves the fact that while Eve and Adam could not resist temptation, Christ, similarly tempted by Satan, provides us with a lesson in resistance. Temptation is the poem's ostensible theme but, as will be shown, it has more complex resonances. *Paradise Regained* is comprised of four books and overall is roughly a fifth of the length of *Paradise Lost*.

Book I

The presentation of Christ as a literary character inevitably raises questions similar to those that attended the character of God in *Paradise Lost*, with the only difference being that Christ did indeed exist in mortal form. In his own account of his childhood Christ presents himself as precocious, learned.

> When I was yet a child, no childish play
> To me was pleasing, all my mind was set
> Serious to learn and know, and thence to do
> What might be public good ...
>
> (I: 201–4)

The obvious point of comparison in *Paradise Lost* is with Eve's relative state of naivety. Christ, now an adult, will it seems present a much more difficult prospect for Satan the tempter.

Satan himself we first encounter in hell addressing his compatriots (44–105) on his new mission, which is to unsettle, in some way destabilise, the condition of the recently humanised son of God, with 'well couched fraud, well woven snares' (97). Beyond that we are told nothing of Satan's specific plan or intention and caused to doubt that he has either. This image of Satan is almost the antithesis of the inventive, calculating, almost heroic presence who musters his troops and sets out for Eden at the beginning of *Paradise Lost*. His speech in *Paradise Regained* is reflective, considered but contains none of the rhetorical dynamism of *Paradise Lost* I, 254–64 **[96–7]**.

Christ, after forty days in the wilderness, is approached by Satan disguised as 'an aged man in rural weeds' (314) and during the 200 lines which close the book an exchange takes place. The crucial moment occurs during lines 337–56 when Satan suggests that since Christ is the Son of God he might transform the stones of the barren landscape into bread, and Christ replies, somewhat enigmatically, that existence on earth involves more important concerns than the assuaging of appetite. The passage has a double significance for the poem as a whole. It introduces the theme of temptation, and throughout the remaining three books Satan continually attempts to persuade Christ to use his superhuman powers to in various ways gratify or elevate his human state. More subtly, it initiates a subtext which will inform the fabric of the poem; the notion of identity. Throughout this opening exchange between Christ and Satan both pose questions regarding their respective roles, powers and states of mind. Satan's original suggestion regarding the stones and bread is regarded by some critics as the first of a selection from the seven deadly sins, but E.M. Pope (1947: 56–64) argues that this one can hardly rank as gluttony and suggests that it corresponds more with the Calvinist notion of our not fully understanding the nature of God, particularly in His corporeal state. Its somewhat ambiguous theological status contrasts with a more insistent impression that it functions as testing round for the broader issue of the existential status of the two figures. After Christ dismisses Satan's proposal and identifies him as the 'Arch-fiend' Satan embarks upon a lengthy autobiographical account of his activities and states of mind since the Fall of Adam and Eve. Christ would already know of this. It seems partly addressed as a kind of enquiry and at the end of the book Satan makes a request; 'permit me/To hear thee when I come.../And talk at least...' (483–5). Satan's principal objective would appear to be the open acquisition of knowledge.

Book II

During lines 121–234 we find Satan back in hell debating with his compatriots the next stage in their strategy of temptation. Belial suggests lust; 'Set women in his eye and in his walk' (153). Satan dismisses this, pointing out that while some mortals and indeed some demons in mortal form 'to the bait of women lay exposed' (204) (recalling obliquely the story of *Comus*), Christ is different. 'For beauty stands/In the admiration only of weak minds/Led captive' (220–2). There is no biblical counterpart to this episode and Milton's invention of it prompts the suspicion that it is inserted to emphasise the unfocused, inconclusive nature of the devils' debate. The entire scene obviously invites comparison with Book II of *Paradise Lost* in which the devils plot their assault upon earth. The cast is largely the same, as is the status of Satan as the wise, scholarly leader, but the mood has changed. Now the devils seem not only uncertain about policy but infused by a more general state of torpor and irresolution. Eventually Satan departs without apparently any clear strategy in mind and ultimately decides upon a more elaborate version of his Book I prompting of the instinct of appetite and sets before Christ a feast of even greater magnificence than the one set before the Lady by Comus (340–77). Again there is no biblical parallel for this (Pope 1947: 70–9, unconvincingly, suggests connections with the temptations of Adam and Eve) and Satan himself appears to be using the display more as the pretext for an enquiry than in any real expectation that Christ will break his fast. Indeed he begins with a question, 'Tell me if food were now before thee set,/Wouldst thou not eat?' (320–1) and seems unsurprised by Christ's continual refusal. The closing hundred lines of the book comprise what amounts to a theological debate between Satan and Christ on matters such as physicality, desire, appetite and, finally, ambition. It is ambition, worldly eminence and its attractions, which sets the agenda for Books III and IV.

Book III

Most critics regard this book as a reminiscence of Books XI and XII of *Paradise Lost* where Michael showed Adam the future of the human race. Here Satan offers a similar display to Christ with the difference that his sources from classical history and literature match those from the Bible. Christ is introduced to Alexander the Great, Scipio, Pompey and Julius Caesar (31–42) as an attempt on Satan's part to arouse some desire for worldly glory.

In the second half of the book Satan leads Christ 'up to a mountain high', shifts the frame of reference to Old Testament history, and has him behold Nineveh, Babylon, Persepolis, Bactra, Araxata, Teredon, Ctesipon (262–309). The parallels with Michael's disclosures to Adam are at once striking and confusing, given that while Adam is encountering the future, the not known, Christ, being omniscient, already has full knowledge of the display. Milton does not explain this, except by implication. By this point it is evident that Satan's ostensible policy, to tempt Christ into some act of worldly indulgence, is the framework for a more complex agenda. Satan hopes that the visions will provide the subject matter for a shared discourse on God's, and his Son's, perception of earth, the future of mankind, and by implication the part that Satan and his followers might play in this. Christ, while willing to engage in exchanges with Satan, is cautiously evasive. At the close of Book III he reflects on the visions which

> Before mine eyes thou hast set; and in my ear
> Vented much policy, and projects deep
> Of enemies, of aids, battles and leagues,
> Plausible to the world, to me worth naught.
> (III: 390–3)

They are 'worth naught' to Christ because they are the contingent activities of humankind, 'plausible' to man since man is their cause. Christ's 'time', when fractious contingencies will be replaced by atemporal absolutes, is, he reminds Satan, 'not yet come' (397).

Book IV

The first 285 lines of the book involve a continuation of Satan's attempt to in some way involve Christ in the human condition, with further presentations of the grandeur of Greece and Rome and, significantly, emphasis upon the intellectual-philosophical legacies of classical civilisation – along with Christianity, the bedrock of Renaissance culture. Christ responds to this dismissively, stating that the twin concerns of knowledge acquisition and speculative enquiry are like,

> Collecting toys
> And trifles for choice matters, worth a sponge;
> As children gathering pebbles on the shore.
>
> (IV: 328–30)

Christ implies what Michael had mercilessly forced upon Adam at the close of *Paradise Lost*; intellectual overreaching caused the Fall and man should recognise that faith is what remains.

The crucial episode of the book, and, many would argue, the essential point toward which the entire poem has been moving, occurs during lines 514–40. Satan finally speaks honestly of his state of mind, and the following passage is more frequently cited and debated than any other.

> I thought thee worth my nearer view
> And narrower scrutiny, that I might learn
> In what degree and meaning thou art called
> The Son of God, which bears no single sense;
> The Son of God I also am, or was,
> And if I was, I am; relation stands;
> All men are Sons of God...
>
> (IV: 514–20)

As line 520 shows, Satan has elected himself spokesman for the human condition and with this one gesture he and, by implication, Milton project the poem beyond its New Testament context. The dialogue between Satan and Christ of which much of the poem is comprised becomes a concentrated enactment of virtually all the strategies, uncertainties and aspirations that attend man's attempts to understand his situation and his relationship with God. Everything that Satan shows Christ is contingent, tactile, transient, the component features of man's fallen state and, as Michael reminded Adam, 'the sum/Of [human] wisdom' (*PL* XII: 575–6). Satan, like Adam, finally recognises this, effectively admits defeat in his attempt to engage Christ in some kind of expository discourse, and departs (*PR* IV: 535–40).

One is prompted to question Milton's purpose and objectives in writing *Paradise Regained*. It revisits and centralises key elements of *Paradise Lost*, particularly its predecessor's dalliance with the paradoxical relationship between man's thirst for knowledge of God and the self-denying ordinance of his fallen condition.

Pre-twentieth-century (i.e. pre-academic) commentators rarely mentioned the poem at. all, regarding it as a peripheral footnote to *Paradise Lost*, and for the Christian versus humanist centre-ground of twentieth-century criticism it offers nothing comparable with the heretical provocations of its predecessor. E.M. Pope (1947) and B.K. Lewalski (1966) are the poem's most frequently cited modern critics, not because like Lewis and Empson they reflect its divisive potential but for their commendable scholarly enterprises. They examine its sources and parallels within Milton's oeuvre and in biblical and classical texts. Critics of the Marxist and/or New Historicist inclination (Hill 1977, and Quint 1987) have considered it alongside *Paradise Lost*'s allegorical treatment of seventeenth-century politics, Satan's presentations of irresolvable religious and ideological conflict in Books III and IV particularly. It has, however, received some attention from critics who espouse the challenging implications of post-Saussurian linguistics : that language does not reflect and mediate reality but does, in part, create and sustain it (see Part III pp. 187–94 for a more extensive consideration of this). Belsey (1988: 95–104) suggests that its concentration upon the linguistic exchanges between Satan and Christ implicitly discloses a sense of doubt on Milton's part in an existential condition beyond what can be perceived and linguistically enacted (see also Myers 1987 and 1992).

Paradise Regained has created neither a critical consensus nor an outright division and for this reason it is an intriguing text. It is best read and perceived not as peripheral to *Paradise Lost* but as a reflection upon it. Satan does indeed bespeak the human condition, not in the quasi-heroic, embittered sense of his *Paradise Lost* manifestation but as a more subdued, puzzled figure. He might well be unredeemed, indeed unredeemable, yet at the same time his thirst for knowledge, his desire to share Christ's absolute wisdom, makes him almost stand outside his symbolic, archetypal status as the embodiment of evil. He becomes the querulous scholar, the theologian, the creation of a man who toiled for years on a text, *De Doctrina Christiana*, which was an endless exercise in questioning.

FURTHER READING

The critical works which engage with the most contentious and problematical features of Milton's poetry will be the subject of the following Part. There are, however, a number of publications which offer explanatory guides to the line-by-line specifics of the verse, including its particular frames of reference. Nicolson's *Reader's Guide* (1964) concentrates on the poetry but gives some attention to the prose pamphlets. Her method is explanatory and impartial, documenting the style of each poem, and explaining its references to religious, political, philosophical and historical issues. Blamires (1971) does the same with an even more detailed survey of *Paradise Lost*. Bradford (1992) provides a book-by-book guide through *Paradise Lost*, along with references to the major critical commentaries attending the poem.

Carey and Fowler (1968) is an edition of the poems and not a prose account of them, but their introductions and footnotes provide an at once comprehensive and economical guide to their contextual frameworks. Wolfe's 'Yale' edition (1953–82) offers an even more scholarly framework for Milton's prose.

PART III

CRITICISM

(a) INTRODUCTION

The purpose of this Part will be twofold. First, it will provide a guide through Milton criticism from the late seventeenth century to the present day, with comments on why critical disagreements have arisen and on how a critic's political-cultural affiliations and circumstances can affect their perspectives and opinions. Second, it will extend the debate beyond a critic's particular frame of reference and involve the reader in questions of analysis raised but not necessarily resolved by that critic.

There will be four principal sub-sections: the Seventeenth and Eighteenth Centuries; the Romantics, the Victorians, and the Twentieth Century. In the fourth of these, the most substantial, further sub-divisions will follow the particular trends and methodological practises of the various branches of modern critical theory, the more prominent of which, for Miltonists, being humanist-versus-Christian debates, Feminist Criticism and Marxist-Historicist Theories.

(b) THE SEVENTEENTH AND EIGHTEENTH CENTURIES

In the seventeenth century literary criticism was more an adjunct to literary writing than a genre in its own right; most of the comments on Milton's work during the four decades or so following *Paradise Lost* are contained in letters, poems and prefaces to works by others (see Shawcross I, 1970: 73–122). The review, which we understand as a contemporaneous evaluation of a work recently in print, did not exist. We know practically nothing verifiable of the opinions of Milton's contemporaries and our perceptions of the immediate impact of his literary writing is largely retrospective and speculative, founded upon anecdote and our gradually developed estimation of the late-seventeenth-century cultural fabric (see Rajan 1962).

One of the few exceptions is a short piece that appeared in the *Athenian Gazette* (the Restoration equivalent of a weekly magazine) on 16 January 1692, which addressed the questions of whether *'Milton and Waller were not the best English Poets? And which is the better of the two?'* Waller is now rarely mentioned outside specialised surveys of seventeenth-century literature and his classification then as at least Milton's equal offers some evidence as to the fickle relativity of critical opinion. The only significant points made in the *Gazette* piece (which remains undecided on who was the *'better of the two'*) involve *Samson*

Agonistes, which it regards as a 'terrible *Satyr* on *Women'* (which qualifies it perhaps at the first feminist response to Milton) and more importantly *Paradise Lost,* which apparently is 'inimitable' principally because of 'that antique Style which he uses' and which 'seems to become the Subject' (all references from Shawcross I, 1970: 98). Several points are made here and they effectively dominate seventeenth-century opinions on Milton. His style was 'antique' in the sense that it attempted to replicate in English the classical modes of Virgil and Homer; it was unrhymed and it employed grammatical formulae that, while correct, paid as much allegiance to Latinate constructions as to contemporary English conventions. Milton was attending to his 'Subject', the first attempt to write an Epic poem, comparable with its predecessors, on the Judaeo-Christian story of creation. The *Gazette's* contention that it was 'inimitable' was ironic since, while in 1692 there were no Milton imitators, his groundbreaking experiment in *Paradise Lost* would institute a new verse form for non-dramatic poetry, blank verse. (The best, most comprehensive survey of the stylistic influence of Milton is Havens 1922.)

Milton's style in *Paradise Lost* became an almost obsessive concern in eighteenth-century criticism. In virtually every commentary the writer appears to regard the meaning and range of the poem as obligatory and necessary topics while being unable to fully disentangle these from variously puzzled and anxious engagements with the way in which the material is dependent upon the style.

Charles Gildon (1694) is much quoted as an early commentator on *Paradise Lost* and our only source is an extant letter he wrote to a friend ('Mr. T.S.'). Here he writes of *'Antient* and consequently *less Intelligible* Words, Phrases, and Similies, by which he [Milton] frequently and *purposedly* affects to express his Meaning'. (Shawcross I, 1970: 107). Thereafter Gildon considers matters such as whether Eve should be regarded as more blameworthy than Adam, but he cannot quite detach himself from the impression that he is unsettled as much by the manner in which Milton has retold this familiar story as he is by the changes he might have made to it.

John Dryden, Milton's near contemporary, said little specifically about *Paradise Lost* but maintained throughout his critical writings that rhyme was a necessary feature of English non-dramatic verse, and, while respecting the beauty and significance of Milton's epic, regarded it as an aberration: 'rhyme was not his talent; he had neither the ease of doing it, no the graces of it' (1693, Shawcross I, 1970: 102), which is a rather obtuse dismissal of everything written by Milton prior to *Paradise Lost.*

John Dennis could make some claim to be one of the first serious literary critics in English, in that much of his work from the 1690s through to the 1720s involved prose discourses on English poetry, and he gave much attention to Milton. He was the first to consider in detail the possibility that *Paradise Lost* could significantly and deliberately alter standard perceptions of scripture, noting that the Satan of Book I is 'one whose Glory was not quite extinguished' and that Milton thought it 'necessary to give them [the Devils] something that was allied to Goodness' (Shawcross I, 1970: 112–3). In Dennis's view we are caused to feel an uneasy sense of identification with Satan and his fallen crew. Dennis also contends that Milton's use of blank verse enables him to balance the 'Spirit', 'Passion', 'Expression' and 'Harmony' of verse in a way that is diminished by the use of rhyme and suggests that Milton has brought the mechanics of English poetry much closer to ancient ideal of natural, spontaneous expression (Hooker I: 374–9) – and in this respect he preempts a number of the observations of the Romantics .

The idea, mooted by Dennis, that *Paradise Lost* offered a new model for the range and potentiality of English verse form became throughout the eighteenth century the basis for a number of critical and indeed creative issues. For example, from the 1730s through to the early 1800s a school of criticism known as the elocutionism conducted detailed close readings of English verse based upon their appraisals of poetry as a performed, spoken phenomenon. *Paradise Lost* featured prominently in the work of elocutionists such as John Mason (1749), John Rice (1765), Thomas Sheridan (1775) and Joshua Steele (1779) who found that it had created a precedent for all manner of experimental possibilities; in effect the creation of free verse two centuries before its official appearance (see Bradford 1992). Their findings were summed up by Samuel Johnson in the much quoted phrase, 'verse only to the eye', by which he meant that Milton's blank verse was essentially shapeless and only conformed to the conventions of regular poetry through its appearance on the page. What is certain is that *Paradise Lost* instituted what was effectively a new stylistic sub-category of English poetic writing. Before 1667 blank verse was thought suitable only for drama, but during the eighteenth century it came second to the heroic couplet as the most popular metrical formula for non-dramatic poetry. Its most famous eighteenth-century practitioners were Isaac Watts, Edward Young, James Thomson and William Cowper (see Havens 1922). One text which, notoriously, reflects the degree of puzzlement that surrounded what was in effect Milton's formal experiment in *Paradise Lost* is Richard Bentley's 'edition' of the poem (1732, see Shawcross II,

1972: 41). Bentley was so unnerved by Milton's radical use of syntax and unrhymed metre that he assumed that the poem had been mistranscribed by the blind poet's scribes and effectively rewrote it in a way that conformed to Bentley's own embarrassingly regimented expectations of correctness and regularity.

The questions of whether Milton had in *Paradise Lost* distorted scripture, and for what reason, were tackled by eighteenth-century commentators in a manner that was subdued, compared with that of their Romantic and post-Romantic successors. During the 1730s exchanges took place in *The Gentleman's Magazine* on the alleged divergences between Milton's poem and conventional, theological perceptions of the book of Genesis. A correspondent calling himself 'Theophilus' argued that God and Satan had been presented in a way that bordered upon heathenism while his adversary 'Philo-Spec' contended that Milton's extravagances were justified by his attempt to dramatise and make starkly immediate the issues of free will and redemption (see Shawcross II, 1972: 25, 93–8). However, these and other similar exchanges of the learned, scholarly type had no significant effect upon the general consensus that *Paradise Lost* was, for all its flaws and peculiarities, the first English epic.

The two critics who are still regarded as exemplars of eighteenth-century opinion on Milton are Addison and Johnson. Addison in 1712 published 18 papers on *Paradise Lost* in the weekly magazine *The Spectator* (Shawcross I, 1970: 147–221). These, collectively, constitute the first critical monograph on the poem. In the first six Addison deals with matters such as whether Milton's poem deserves to be classed, alongside Homer's *Iliad* and Virgil's *Aeneid*, as an epic (according to Addison it does) and traces the serious parallels and divergences between Milton's text and its Biblical and classical counterparts. In the following twelve articles he offers a book-by-book commentary on the poem.

What is remarkable about Addison's survey is its balance between constrained reverence and uncontentious triteness. He continually praises Milton's stylistic and imaginative skills but he says practically nothing about the, even then, controversial topic of Milton's poeticisation of a theological absolute, the Fall of man. It is as though Addison the journalist is responding to a cultural maxim: *Paradise Lost* has already become a literary monolith; do not undermine its status. For example, he touches upon the question of whether Satan is granted heroic status, and, instead of tackling the specifics of characterisation and language, he states that while *Paradise Lost* is an 'Epic or a Narrative Poem' it would be wrong, given its Biblical foundation, to even look for a particular hero (Shawcross: 166). Later, when looking in detail at Book IX, he deals with the exchange between Eve and Satan by commenting on 'the many pleasing Images of Nature which are intermixt in this Part of the Story' and nothing more (Shawcross, I, 1970: 206).

Samuel Johnson's writings on Milton, principally his 'Life of Milton' (1779) are much cited, for two reasons. Johnson is still regarded as the archetypal spokesman for eighteenth-century ideas on culture, language and literature, and his querulous estimation of Milton's writing stands in sharp contrast with the unburdened praise of the Romantics, writing barely two decades later.

Johnson did not like Milton. He paid allegiance to his talents and his courage, certainly, but throughout his surveys he qualifies praise with cautiously unemphatic doubt. Most eighteenth-century discussions of Milton centred on *Paradise Lost*, but Johnson broadened the spectrum. With 'Lycidas' he found that 'the diction is harsh, the rhymes uncertain and the numbers unpleasing' (Shawcross II, 1972: 293). 'L'Allegro' and 'Il Penseroso' are treated more generously, but again with qualifications; 'the colours of the diction seem not sufficiently discriminated' (295). On *Comus*: 'As a drama it is deficient. The action is not probable ... the figures are too bold, and the language too luxuriant for dialogue. It is a drama in the epic style, inelegantly splendid, and tediously instructive' (296–7). Johnson might be excused the charge of personal prejudice because his comments generally reflect the predominant literary conventions and opinions of the Augustan period. Much of Milton's early poetry, 'Lycidas' in particular, fell in with the baroque stylistic practices of the early seventeenth century. In the eighteenth century flamboyant and imaginative metrical devices and rhyme schemes had become an eccentricity, and Johnson's own statements on the Metaphysicals **[15–16]** as self indulgent in their figurative excesses is treated as the benchmark of contemporary opinion (see his 'Life of Cowley').

> [*Paradise Lost*] has this inconvenience, that it comprises neither human actions nor human manners. The man and woman who act and suffer, are in a state which no other man or woman can ever know. The reader finds no transaction in which he can be engaged; beholds no condition in which he can by an effort of imagination place himself; he has, therefore, little natural curiosity or sympathy (304).

As we have seen, eighteenth-century critics before Johnson were tentative, and in Addison's case evasive, on the issue of scripture rewritten as verse. Johnson, ever the epitome of Augustan logic and .

pragmatism, is blunt, stating that Adam and Eve before the Fall cannot ever be understood, even properly perceived, by the fallen reader. If Milton did intend his readers to question the moral logistics of our pre fallen state (and only Romantic critics and their successors have stated this emphatically) then Johnson either deliberately ignores or fails completely to apprehend this possibility. He reads the poem as a versified synopsis of the book of Genesis, nothing more, and is clearly puzzled as to why Milton undertook such a project. 'Being therefore not new [it raises] no unaccustomed emotion in the mind; what we knew before we cannot learn; what is not unexpected cannot surprise' (304). 'Paradise Lost', he claims, 'is one of the books which the reader admires and lays down ... Its perusal is a duty rather than a pleasure. We read Milton for instruction, retire harassed and overburdened, and look elsewhere for recreation...' (305).

Johnson clearly regards the poem as a redundant supplement to Christian awareness. It was immensely popular during the eighteenth century and went through a vast number of reprints (see Havens), but there is no reason to doubt that Johnson's estimation of it as the retelling of a fundamental story, albeit by an immensely gifted storyteller, is an accurate summary of its status within the contemporaneous cultural fabric. Shawcross's 'Critical Heritage' collections of seventeenth- and eighteenth-century commentators contain nothing that would overturn Johnson's perceptions. Some critics, such as Dennis, offer occasional comments on how daring and potentially unsettling Paradise Lost can be, but overall eighteenth-century critics regarded it with restrained puzzlement. It was accorded the status of the epic (Addison devotes much space to this) but since its Homeric and Virgilian predecessors were founded upon the pre-Christian perception of humanity and the cosmos as contingent and enticingly unpredictable, the question which underpinned most eighteenth-century readings (and explicitly addressed by Johnson) was of how and why Milton expected the reader to respond to an epic rendition of a story whose moral message, specifics and outcome were as accepted and familiar as life itself.

Johnson finishes his 'Life of Milton' with an unsettled and lengthy discussion of why exactly Milton chose to write Paradise Lost in a way that to him seemed eccentric; pseudo-Latinate syntax and blank verse. Blank verse had by 1779 become an established feature of English poetic writing, but Johnson seems to lament the fact that Milton had initiated this divergence from the strict regularity and discipline of rhyme (310).

Johnson agreed with his eighteenth-century peers that the style of Paradise Lost was revolutionary (and while many of them rejoiced in the fact, Johnson regretted it) and at the same time he was unsettled by the purpose of the poem. The possibility that it was an attempt to incite agnostic, radical opinions on standard notions of Christianity did not occur to him. The Romantics, as we shall see, enfolded both perspectives and found that the poem's stylistic peculiarities prefaced its far more disturbing presentation of Christian absolutes.

(c) THE ROMANTICS

It is generally agreed that during the late eighteenth- and early-nine-teenth centuries, the period dominated by the writing and ideas of the Romantics, perceptions of what Milton had intended and sometimes disclosed, particularly in *Paradise Lost*, changed radically.

William Blake was not a literary critic in the conventional sense; rather he disseminated his somewhat arcane and enigmatic ideas on literature through his own poetry and accompanying prose fragments. Milton he regarded as part mentor, part interlocutor. Blake conducted what amounted to a rereading of Milton's work, apparently on Milton's behalf. In *The Marriage of Heaven and Hell* (1793) Blake challenged the conventional Judaeo-Christian dichotomy between categories of good and evil, the heaven and hell of the title being the locative foci of each. He compares the Satan of the Book of Job, who tormented Job with physical pain with the Christ of *Paradise Lost* who carried the fire of God's wrath down into the abyss and helped to create hell. For Blake, Milton's Satan and Christ become interchangeable personae, each symbolising an extremity but at the same time exhibiting characteristics that we generally associate with the other. Blake's overall contention was the Milton in *Paradise Lost* was conducting an almost subliminal dialogue with himself, on the one hand attendant to the doctrinaire Christian theology that was inescapably part of his existence while on the other engaging with more intensely subjective inclinations that the medium of poetry allowed him to confront.

> The reason Milton wrote in fetters when he wrote of Angels and God, and at liberty when of Devils and Hell, is because he was a true Poet and of the Devil's party without knowing it.
>> (Wittreich 1970: 35. Unless otherwise indicated all page references for the Romantics on Milton will be from this edition.)

Most critics and editors agree that what Blake means here is not that Milton was a subliminal Satanist, but that despite himself he found that the rebellious, almost heroic condition of Satan and his followers seized his imagination, caused him to bestow upon them far more of the poetically inspired range of feeling and tragic grandeur than attended his presentation of God. Blake goes on to argue that the narrative shape of *Paradise Lost* was formed out of this tension, that the energy of the opening books, in which Satan features significantly, became restrained and eventually replaced by reason; hence the more subdued, reflective mood of the later books, particularly XI and XII.

Blake's own ruminations caused hardly any response at the time of writing (the 1790s) but have, retrospectively, been classed as early examples of the Romantic aesthetic. Most of the Romantic poets, Blake included, were variously inspired by the philosophical and aesthetic ideas of the Enlightenment and some – Wordsworth and Coleridge tenuously, Shelley blatantly – by the ideology of revolutionary politics that changed the history of Europe and the Americas at the turn of the eighteenth century. Essentially, the Enlightenment and the Age of Revolution involved a vast, complex undermining of the established presuppositions of post-medieval European politics, culture and religion. The monoliths of the hierarchical state, of God as the ultimate determinant of human action and fate, were challenged by ideas which allocated more esteem to the individual, to man as a figure who could exert singular power over his destiny and circumstances. Thus, for Blake and a number of his Romantic successors, Milton epitomised an early example of Enlightenment radicalism, steering his own course through the burdensome legacy of biblical and classical orthodoxy.

In 1804 Blake produced a poem called 'Milton', one of his longest and most obscure mythological works, in which Blake himself becomes imbued with the spirit of his predecessor who has descended to earth in order to save Albion (beset by the twin evils of the industrial revolution and intellectual-spiritual corruption) through the power of his imagination. Blake's engagements with Milton are, comparatively speaking, bizarre and eccentric, based as much upon his conviction that he was personally acquainted with him as upon a reading of his works. (H. Crabbe-Robinson recalls a conversation with Blake in which the latter disclosed that during one of his many exchanges with the dead poet's spirit he 'told me to beware of being misled by *Paradise Lost*. In particular he wished me to show the falsehood of his doctrine that the pleasure of sex arose from the Fall' (Wittreich 1970: 96).) However, Blake's emphasis upon the shaping power of Milton's imagination, particularly its ability to transcend doctrine and orthodoxy, became a benchmark of Romanticism.

Wordsworth's treatment of Milton was relatively uncontroversial and, it could be argued, unacknowledged in that the latter's two best known blank verse poems, 'Tintern Abbey' (1798) and *The Prelude*

(1850), involve an indebtedness to Milton's stylistic individuality in *Paradise Lost*, particularly in the deployment of enjambment and pseudo-latinate syntax, which goes beyond that of eighteenth-century blank verse poets (see Bradford 1992, and Havens). In the 1815 Preface to *Lyrical Ballads* Wordsworth cites *Paradise Lost* as a key example of how the Imagination 'shapes and *creates*' by 'consolidating numbers into unity and dissolving and separating unity into number, – alternations proceeding from, and governed by, a sublime consciousness of the soul...' (Wittreich 1970: 129), by which he means that Milton balanced formal improvisation against abstract structure ('number') in a way that enabled him to at once test and control the limits of language. Wordsworth implies here that *Paradise Lost* was an attempt to go beyond its apparent debt to scripture and this image of Milton as a radical spirit surfaced also in Wordsworth's poem 'London, 1802', which begins,

> Milton! thou shouldst be living at this hour:
> England hath need of thee...

and continues,

> raise us up, return to us again;
> And give us manners, virtue, freedom, power.

While the poem implies much more than it specifically states we can take 'this hour' to refer to both the industrial revolution and the continental war with France, and the qualities of 'virtue, freedom, power' to a vague combination of poetic inspiration and republican individuality. The Romantics, Shelley in particular, tended to select and appropriate impressions from Milton's work and allow them to obscure known facts about the man: republican he might have been but he was also an unswerving defender of civic power.

What Wordsworth implied Coleridge made more explicit. His treatment of Milton in *Biographia Literaria* mainly involves Milton as the exemplar of the 'Imagination' rather than the 'Fancy', meaning that his poetry challenged and transformed rather than merely beautified images and ideas (Wittreich 1970: 217–26). In his later essays and lectures Coleridge gives more attention to the particulars of Milton's work. In an 1819 lecture he states that Satan 'exhibits all the restlessness, temerity and cunning which have marked the mighty hunters of mankind from Nimrod to Napoleon ... around this character [Milton] has thrown a singularity of daring, a grandeur of sufferance and a ruined splendour, which constitute the very heights of poetic sublimity' (Wittreich 1970: 244). Without proposing particular allegorical links between this very human figure and Milton's immediate context Coleridge infers that the political turmoil of the period was as influential upon *Paradise Lost* as its biblical provenance (Wittreich 1970: 239–40). He concludes that Milton's epic carries more 'subjective character' than its predecessors, that 'the sublimist parts are the revelations of Milton's own mind' (245).

Shelley goes further and contends that 'Milton was, let it ever be remembered, a republican, and a bold inquirer into morals and religion' (Wittreich 1970: 532). This is from Shelley's 'Preface to *Prometheus Unbound*' (1819) in which he also compared his own hero, Prometheus, with Milton's Satan, 'The Hero of *Paradise Lost*' who, Shelley suggests, is often wrongly perceived by those who read Milton's poem 'with a religious feeling' (531). Shelley's perception of him becomes more evident in his *On the Devil, and Devils* (1819).

> Here is a Devil very different from the popular personification of evil indignity and it is a mistake to suppose that he was intended for an idealism of implacable hate ... Milton's Devil as a moral being is far superior to his God, as one who perseveres in some purpose which he has conceived to be excellent, in spite of adversity and torture.
>
> (Wittreich 1970: 534–5)

Shelley was an avowed rebel, a supporter of political radicalism and an atheist, and he argues, very subtly, that Milton followed the same inclinations but was prevented 'in a country where the most enormous sanctions of opinions and law are attached to a direct avowal of certain speculative notions...' (Wittreich 1970: 535) from directly proclaiming his views. Instead, according to Shelley, Milton worked within the framework of classical mythology and Christian doctrine and undermined both. He 'restored' [Satan] to society' (Wittreich 1970: 535), made him a participant in the spectrum of moral and political contingency that was the seventeenth century.

Not all of Milton's Romantic critics focused upon *Paradise Lost* as a personal-political allegory. Some, particularly those famed more for their prose than their verse, broadened the focus but at the same time maintained the quintessential tendency of the period: the reading of Milton within what was rapidly becoming a humanist, almost secular, context.

Thomas De Quincey was an exceptional literary critic, capable of transforming a reader's perception of a work through a combination of meticulous close-reading and expansive ratiocination; he did so with Milton. His *Life of Milton* (1838) provided one of the most shrewd accounts of the man and the period then available, but he saved his best observations on Milton's writing for later works such as *On Milton* (1839). In this he asks the questions 'Who and what is Milton?' and takes issue with Johnson, who, in De Quincey's view, was so entrenched in the critical and political orthodoxies of his period (particularly the perception of Milton as a regicide) that his opinions became clouded and prejudiced. De Quincey argues that the question can only be properly addressed when we recognise that *Paradise Lost* lifts itself beyond matters such as political and theological contingency, transcends even the mythology of the classical epic and becomes 'a central force amongst forces' (Wittreich 1970: 478), meaning that it deals with the absolutes of existence, choice and identity in a way that obliges us to challenge all ingrained knowledge and preconceptions. Later (in *The Poetry of Pope*, 1848) De Quincey expands on this, stating that it is a poem about *'power* – that is exercise and expansion to your own latent capacity of sympathy with the infinite ...' (Wittreich 1970: 492). By 'infinite' he does not refer to the classical or Christian notions of the superhuman but to the individualised concept of an awareness that transcends intellectual orthodoxy, an ongoing Romantic pretext and an experience that De Quincey himself sought with the assistance of opium.

William Hazlitt is, amongst his early nineteenth-century peers, the critic who most resembles his twentieth-century counterparts, in that most of his readings are founded upon detailed scrutiny of language and characterisation, exercises in what the New Critics valued as making the text speak for itself, irrespective of the reader's subjective inclinations or his or her perception of contextual influences. For example, he was the first to concentrate closely on Satan's speeches in Book I not simply as rhetorical exercises but as linguistic reflectors, creations of an imagined speaking presence. As a consequence he judges Satan as 'the most heroic subject that was ever chosen for a poem' whose 'love of power and contempt or suffering are never once relaxed from the highest pitch of intensity' (384–5). And again we encounter the Romantic tendency to project Milton beyond his particular context into the timeless zone of the poetic.

Hazlitt also gave a good deal of attention to Milton's earlier verse, particularly 'Lycidas' (355–8): 'The gusts of passion come and go like the sounds of music borne on the wind' (366), by which he means that the poem's structure and mood appear to replicate the fluctuating emotional registers of death and loss. Coleridge too had praised the way in which the varying metrical structures and sound patterns of this poem seemed responsive to an unbalanced state of oscillation between the tragic, the immediate and the reflective (258). Their observations are largely consistent with a general sense of approval amongst the Romantics of Milton as a lyric poet, perhaps because forms such as the ode had been revived during this period as appropriate media for a blending of improvisational impressionism and reflection – unlike the eighteenth-century elevation of rational order as the maxim for poetic design, implicitly supported by Johnson in his own depredations of Milton's lyric poems.

The perceptions of the Romantic poets and critics, by virtue of their radical difference from those of their Augustan predecessors, raise a question which attends all Milton criticism: is it possible to construct a dispassionate, impartial model of Milton's intentions and their textual manifestations? Literary response will inevitably be influenced by the affective, intuitive registers which literature provokes, and even when the reader becomes the critic and attempts to deal objectively with his/her feelings about a poem other factors, concomitant to that person's frame of mind and circumstances, will play their part in the casuistry of interpretation. The Romantics were affiliated to the Enlightenment ethos of radical, unorthodox, often revolutionary thinking (albeit with varying degrees of sincerity and commitment) and celebrated poetry as the medium in which such ideas could best be explored. They elected Milton as a precursor of their intellectual condition. Were they discussing aspects of Milton previously undisclosed or were they allocating to him elements of themselves?

Robert Southey was a close friend of Coleridge and Wordsworth (he and Coleridge married sisters) and initially shared many of their beliefs and enthusiasms, but he earned himself a degree of contemporaneous notoriety by then adopting extremely conservative views on writing and politics. In the 1821 preface to his *Vision of Judgement* (a poem describing the admission of the dissolute monarch George III to heaven) he lashed out against what he saw as a depraved and distorting feature of Romantic thinking and writing.

> The school which they have set up may properly be called the Satanic school; for though their productions breathe the spirit of Belial in their lascivious parts, and the spirit of Moloch in those loathsome images of atrocities and horrors which they delight to represent, they are more especially characterised by a Satanic spirit of pride and audacious impiety, which still betrays the wretched feeling of hopelessness werewith it is allied.
>
> (Hunter IV 1978: 124)

To an extent, Southey was using Milton as a lever against the political, religious and moral radicalism of his, Southey's, peers, Shelley in particular, but this is underpinned by the valid point that much Romantic criticism does indeed treat *Paradise Lost* as a poem which goes against its stated remit, is potentially heretical, and promotes Satan as a figure with whom some of its readers might identify. Wittreich (1970) has argued that the so-called Satanic School of Romanticism is a myth, licensed mainly by twentieth-century critics of the non-Christian, liberal-humanist persuasion, and while it is true that the Romantics rarely go so far as to celebrate Milton's Satan as a moral exemplar it cannot be denied that the image of him as a rebel with the courage to take arms against apparently insuperable power is a centralising feature of the majority of Romantic criticism. Nor can we disregard the parallels between this reading of Satan and the radical nature of Romantic ideology.

The notion that Milton criticism is informed by historical-political relativism would be explored within the broader theoretical framework of twentieth-century reader-response criticism **[161–2]** but even those who view the general principles of reader-centred theory with caution or scepticism cannot question the fact that the Romantics scrutinised Milton's work in a manner that was variously partial, subjective and ideologically weighted.

Wittreich, who edited the 1970 selection of Romantic criticism on Milton, later (1979) produced a monograph on the same subject. Newlyn (1993) considers the effect of Milton upon the broader cultural ethos of the Romantic period.

(d) VICTORIAN CRITICISM

Milton criticism of the post-Romantic period of the nineteenth century, the era generally termed Victorian in literary-historical discourse, is similarly affected by contemporaneous, collective moods and states of mind. The essay which established the core agenda for this period was published in 1825, twelve years before Victoria's accession of the throne, but its author would become one of the acknowledged spokesmen for mid-Victorian bourgeois consciousness. Thomas Macaulay's 'Milton' was originally commissioned as a review of the recently discovered *De Doctrina Christiana* **[43–6]** but what appeared in print was a general survey of Milton as an exemplar for the virtues of hard work, high principles and single minded endurance so venerated by the Victorian middle classes. Like his Romantic near-contemporaries, Macaulay admired Milton's Satan, but for different reasons. For Macaulay Satan was a version of Milton: 'his [Satan's] spirit bears up unbroken, resting on its own innate energies, requiring no support from anything external, nor even from hope itself' (Hunter IV, 1978: 130), just as Milton had endured the trials and tribulations of the post-Cromwellian era. Macaulay studiously avoids an engagement with theological–philosophical issues that for the Romantics and a number of their predecessors attended *Paradise Lost*. Instead he heaps praise upon Milton the poet in a manner that can best be described as bland hyperbole, peppering his essay with terms such as 'images of beauty and tenderness', a 'healthful sense of the pleasantness of external objects', 'the most rugged and gigantic elevations' and saves his real message for a celebration of Milton the man, 'the statesman, the philosopher ... the champion and the martyr of English liberty'.

> His conception of love unites all the voluptuousness of the Oriental harem, and all the gallantry of the chivalric tournament, with all the quiet affection of an English fireside?
>
> (130)

The quality which for Macaulay sets Milton apart from other great writers is 'the battle which he fought for the species of freedom which is the most valuable, and which was then the least understood, the freedom of the human mind.' The qualifying clause 'and which was then the least understood' is the vortex of Macaulay's piece. The principles of freedom of speech and religious liberty which Macaulay espoused (he would become, as well as one of the century's most eminent historians, a politician of the moderate reformist type) he apportions to Milton, and his suggestion that Milton, and by implication other Cromwellians, in some way anticipate the parliamentary and social democracy of mid to late-nineteenth-century Britain is, to say the least, questionable. However, Macaulay's reinvention of Milton as a standard bearer for his own beliefs typifies much Victorian Milton criticism. It was not that later nineteenth-century critics shared Macaulay's ideological standpoint – many did not – but throughout the century Milton's life, writing and perceived ideals were variously trimmed and shaped to suit contemporaneous issues and trends.

As its title indicates, Joseph Ivimay's *John Milton: His Life and Times, Religious and Political Opinions* (1833) was more concerned with Milton the radical than Milton the poet. Ivimay mounts a diatribe against Johnson's *Life of Milton* in which he argues that its author's 'ultra toryism and bigotry' blinded him to Milton's true character and achievements. Like Macaulay, Ivimay pays dutiful allegiance to the quality of Milton's verse but his central agenda involves him as a republican and advocate of liberty. Ivimay, a Baptist preacher, regarded Milton's attachment to the Independents and his prose writings as forerunners to the birth of Wesleyan non-conformity. Ivimay was also a supporter of the Chartist movement, the early nineteenth-century precursor to socialism, and cited Milton's prose work, particularly *The Tenure of Kings and Magistrates* and *The Ready and Easy Way to Establish a Free Commonwealth,* as relevant to the Chartist objective of creating in nineteenth-century England an updated, democratic version of the Cromwellian republic. Similarly, in the 'Introduction' to his edition of *The Prose Works of John Milton* (1835), John Fletcher argues that the 'inward prompting' which would make Milton's poetry powerful and controversial was a still not fully appreciated contribution to his political and religious thinking, his prose.

Throughout the mid-to-late-nineteenth-century Milton's poetry was treated as a monument to the venerated principles of classical learning, Christian resolve and English ambition. Tennyson, in his sonnet on Milton, extols him as the 'mighty mouthed inventor of harmonies', 'the God gifted organ voice of England' and in *Alfred, Lord Tennyson, A Memoir by His Son* the laureate speaks of him as the most sublime of all poets, the supreme exponent of the 'grand style' (an epithet that would thereafter attach itself regularly to celebrations of Milton's style, as the title of Christopher Ricks's famous 1963 study indicates). Milton's influence upon Tennyson's verse is dealt with in many critical studies of the latter (see Ricks 1972): *Idylls of the King,* where Arthur's splendid city is broken and destroyed by the bestial lusts and intellectual failure of man, often echoes Michael's presentations to Adam in the closing books of *Paradise Lost; In Memoriam* was thought to be a perfect blending of Christian and poetically emotive registers of loss, and 'Lycidas' was often cited as its precedent; and many of Tennyson's early blank verse pieces inherit the stylistic debt already owed to Milton by Wordsworth.

Gerard Manley Hopkins, in his *Letters* to Robert Bridges and R.W. Dixon, acknowledges Milton as a major influence upon his own radical, iconoclastic experiments with sprung rhythm and counterpoint. He praises the irregular metre of *Samson Agonistes* as one of the few examples in the language of improvised movements breaking down abstract metrical conventions, 'the *native rhythm* of the words used bodily imported into verse' (1 August 1877). 'In *Paradise Lost* and *Regained*, in the last more freely, it being an advance in his art, he employs counterpoint more or less everywhere, markedly now and then' (5 October 1878). 'Counterpoint' means an interplay between unpredictable rhythmic-intonational movements and a regular framework such as the iambic pentameter. Notably, given Hopkins's own poeticisation of Christian belief, he says nothing of Milton's.

Within the high Victorian cultural fabric Milton became a statuesque subject of respect, dutiful awe and, when not regarded as a commanding precedent, indifference. The radical energy that had fuelled Romanticism, and inspired the Romantics' veneration of Milton as their precursor, had been replaced by a more conservative attendance to the immediate political, religious and ethical concerns of a nation no longer challenged by revolution. David Masson's biography of Milton bespeaks the contemporaneous mood. His *Life of Milton* comprised seven lengthy volumes and appeared gradually from 1859 until its completion in 1894. It is a voluminous masterpiece of scholarship. All recorded facts, relevant texts and contextual details – or at least those available to Masson – are included. It tells us everything, but it says virtually nothing. Controversy, particularly religious controversy, is accounted for in a manner which more than implies that Milton is irretrievably part of the past. The living Milton who spoke so eloquently to the likes of Blake, Shelley, even Ivimay, has been replaced in Masson by a life record.

Matthew Arnold is frequently cited as the prime spokesman for a literary-critical consensus of later Victorianism. His major contribution to contemporary cultural debate centred upon his distinction between Hebraism and Hellenism (in *Culture and Anarchy*, 1869), the former being the unimaginative deference to religious codes of obedience, conduct and thought, the latter being the free play of the intellect within and around Christianity. Arnold regarded Milton as a Hebraist, limited and confined by his Puritan affiliations. His opinions on Milton feature frequently in his major works of criticism, but his most blunt appraisal is a short essay called 'A French Critic on Milton' (Hunter IV 1978: 344) in which he concurs with Edmund Scherer that Milton's political and religious commitments injured him as a poet: 'he had natural affinities with the Puritans. He has paid for it by his limitations as a poet'. Scherer, and Arnold, regard *Paradise Lost* as a Puritan polemic, 'a false poem, a grotesque poem, a tiresome poem', a poem whose aspirations to epic status are self-destroyed by its use as a dialectical instrument of Puritanism. Within a century, perceptions of Milton's image had changed from that of the dangerous, radical poet to that of the poet whose talents were restricted by his ideological conformity. This testifies to Milton's power as a multi-faceted, ever provocative figure. More objectively, we should note that while Arnold seems to differ from Macaulay on the relevance of Milton to contemporary life, both select, both apportion significance to aspects of his life and work that suit their own conceptions of an ideal.

The essay by Arnold most frequently cited and reprinted as a reflection of his opinions is the piece on 'Milton' (1888) (see Dyson and Lovelock 1973: 67–9). Its accredited status is both inaccurate and appropriate. It is a published version of a speech that Arnold gave, celebrating the completion of a window in St. Margaret's Church, Chiswick, dedicated to Milton's wife Margaret. As befitted the occasion, Arnold did not repeat his earlier demolition of Milton. Instead he praised his style, celebrated him as the true English language inheritor of classical grandeur. This accurately sums up the late Victorian view of Milton: a brilliant stylist; but, as a spokesman for issues of contemporaneous significance? – dated, sometimes selectively useful, but largely irrelevant.

(e) MODERN CRITICISM

Twentieth-century criticism of Milton differs from what preceded it in one particular respect. The vast majority of its practitioners are academics and even those writers who are not professionally attached to universities, such as T.S. Eliot and A.N. Wilson, reflect their influence. The effects of this degree of corporate affiliation have been many and various, but several factors stand out.

Milton scholarship has proceeded in a way that reflects the academic principles of impartiality and comprehensiveness. The Columbia University Press edition of the complete *Works* (ed. F. Patterson *et al.*, 18 vols, 1931–38) was followed by the Longman edition of *The Poems* (ed. Fowler and Carey 1968). The massive *Complete Prose Works* (Yale University Press, ed. D.M. Wolfe *et al.*, 8 vols, 1953–82) took almost thirty years to complete and *A Variorum Commentary on the Poems of John Milton* (Columbia University Press, 1970–) is at time of writing three decades into achieving the enormous objective of its title. Along with these monuments to scholarly endeavour there have been dozens of other more slight and affordable contributions to the general aim of enabling the twentieth-century reader to attain foot-of-the-page knowledge of the literary, linguistic and historical contexts of Milton's works. Scholarship by definition is an unbiased, disinterested undertaking, but it is also accumulative. Two of the earliest annotated editions of *Paradise Lost* reflect the editor's problem of distinguishing between fact and opinion. Patrick Hume (1695) did an excellent job of glossing

Milton's classical and biblical borrowings but by 1749 Thomas Newton found himself having to deal with Richard Bentley's (1732) eccentric emendations and effectively took part in the debates (on whether Milton had altered the book of Genesis) that these provoked (see Oras, 1930 for an account of the problems encountered by Milton's early editors, and Shawcross for extracts). Consequently the twentieth-century editor faces the task of balancing a knowledge of the original writings and their cultural-linguistic contexts against more than two centuries of shifting perspectives on these, up to and including the modern debate. In Fowler and Carey, for example, we will encounter footnotes on Newton's editorial comments (1749) alongside references to Virgil, the Old Testament and William Empson's controversial critical reading (1961). Milton's status as an academic subject or field of enquiry is troubling for academics because, as pre-twentieth-century commentary indicated, he is capable of provoking all manner of theological and political controversies which cut across his reputation as a poet and can be as relevant to the 1960s as they were in the 1660s.

Beyond the sphere of editing Milton, modern critical writing on his work can be broken down into two categories. The first was predominant from the early years of this century up to the mid-1960s. Many of its practitioners would have claimed to be individualists, unrestricted and unconfined by collective aims or methodologies, but the academic writing of this period was in truth affected by the principles and conventions of New Criticism. It was designated 'New' because of its recently acquired status in the universities, and it had three main objectives: (i) to evolve a method of critical writing that had academic, neo-scientific respectability and thus to distance itself from the belletristic partialities of pre-twentieth-century 'amateur' criticism; (ii) to identify a self-defining canon of major texts and authors; (iii) to map out the contours, borders and routes of literary history. Milton created problems for all three. With regard to (ii) and (iii) he was difficult to categorise. His early verse was, chronologically and stylistically, related to the epoch of the late-Renaissance, baroque, lyric poetry, but it was difficult to place him in a particular school. The Metaphysicals generally used poetry as a medium for speculation and enquiry, as an exploration of the accepted fundamentals of life and existence: Milton's early verse, while stylistically flamboyant, maintained, often reinforced, Christian orthodoxies. His later work, *Paradise Lost* and *Paradise Regained* particularly, has little if anything in common with the post-Restoration trend towards political and social satire, Augustanism. The late seventeenth century was regarded as a significant turning point in literary history (T.S. Eliot famously perceived it as the beginning of the so-called 'dissociation of sensibility' **[154–5]**, but Milton seemed to transcend both the periodised specifics of pre- and post-Restoration writing and the change itself. Nor is it possible to claim that as an individual he founded or instituted a particular tradition. It was true that blank verse and its stylistic patterns become, after *Paradise Lost*, accepted conventions of non-dramatic poetry, but while poets as diverse as Thomson, Wordsworth and Tennyson show in some of their work the imprint of Miltonic technique they are certainly not perpetuating the sub-genre of the Christian epic. So, for academics who wished to specify or work within clearly defined generic and historical zones, Milton proved to be a slippery presence.

With (i), the maintenance of a critical method that was impartial and balanced, Milton created further problems. His literary fame was guaranteed by *Paradise Lost*, a poem which engaged with absolutes of belief and human identity in a way that challenged the boundaries between literary and non-literary writing. We have already considered the conflict between Lewis and Empson and will look at it in more depth below. They exemplify a more pervasive difficulty with Milton criticism. When does a literary text become a statement or a declaration and how should this blurring of borders be dealt with in literary criticism, particularly when the critics are dealing as much with their own non-literary beliefs and ideals as they are with literary aesthetics?

The second category of twentieth-century Milton criticism has been brought about by the most turbulent and perplexing period in the history of the British and US literary studies; the post 1960s proliferation of critical theories which owe as much allegiance to external intellectual and ideological factors as they do to the study of literature itself. The problems with Milton encountered by the New Critics have not gone away and they have been supplemented by the fact that the modern (i.e. recent) critical theory has massively extended the spectrum of literary studies. For example, feminist literary criticism grew out of a broader movement which challenged and investigated the historically ingrained social, cultural and political ascendancy of men over women. Feminist critics treat elements such as characterisation, narrative voice and plot structure not simply as formal or aesthetic conventions but as in various ways symptomatic of gender roles perceived, and often ratified, by particular authors in particular periods. Milton's pre-eminent text centred upon the story of the first man and the first woman and, as one might expect, feminist critics have further blurred the boundaries between literary and non-literary discourse, literary criticism and gendered dialectic. Similarly, deconstruction originated in radical French philosophy and is as much concerned with the absolutes of language and identity as it is with literary–critical scrutiny: *Paradise Lost* is a particular account of the provenance of language and human identity and in it, as a consequence, the distinguishing features of literature and philosophy begin to disintegrate, at least for the deconstructionist. Marxist literary critics, like their feminist counterparts, see literature as part of an assembly of discourses, all of which, for the Marxist, carry traces of the dynamics of political and economic history. Milton lived and wrote within, indeed participated in, one of the most contentiously debated periods of British history. Inevitably, Marxists regard his verse not just as art but as an aesthetic dimension of an historical-ideological phenomenon.

Practically all literary writers have been scrutinised by practitioners of the various branches of critical theory but Milton has created an extra problem because he exists uneasily at the axis between literary and non-literary writing, aesthetics and politics, the distracting pleasures of poetry and the ingrained absolutes of belief, subjective identity and ideological affiliation.

Lewis, Empson and the pre-theory critics

As the publication dates of their respective, proactive books indicate, C.S. Lewis (1942) and William Empson (1961) were by no means the initiators of twentieth-century Milton criticism. I begin with them because they variously exemplify, articulate and dichotomise the issues underpinning the work of their predecessors and set an agenda for the complex issues to be addressed by their successors.

Lewis (1898–1963) was a literary critic, an academic and an amateur theologian. He wrote critical monographs, novels and fantasy stories for children, all of which are shot through with his almost evangelistic dedication to Christianity. His *Preface to Paradise Lost* (1942) is important because it takes issue with what Lewis regarded as the agnostic, impartial drift of early twentieth-century academic criticism. In it Lewis insists that *Paradise Lost*, while immensely important as a literary work of art, should be treated foremost as a Socratic dialogue, designed to test the reader's faith and to remind the reader that while questions can be asked about our origins, state and destiny, these questions can only be properly addressed when underpinned by a substratum of unquestioning faith. For example:

> But *Paradise Lost* records a real, irreversible, unrepeatable process in the history of the universe... The truth and passion of the presentation are unassailable. They were never, in essence, assailed

until rebellion and pride came, in the romantic age, to be admired for their own sake. On this side the adverse criticism of Milton is not so much a literary phenomenon as the shadow cast upon literature by revolutionary politics, antinomian ethics, and the worship of Man by Man. After Blake, Milton criticism is lost in misunderstanding.

(Lewis 1942: 133)

Lewis's manifesto seems clear enough. The Romantics misread *Paradise Lost* and misinterpreted Milton as man and poet; modern, academic readers and critics should not fall into the same trap, particularly since radical questionings of Christian faith are far more comprehensive and endemic in the mid-twentieth century than they were in the early nineteenth.

More specifically Lewis tackles controversial features of the poem, such as the heroic status of Satan. 'Satan is the best drawn of Milton's characters. The reason is not hard to find. Of the major characters whom Milton attempted he is incomparably the easiest to draw' (Lewis 1942: 100). Why? Because Satan engages our basest instincts, Milton's included. 'Hence all that can be said about Milton's "sympathy" with Satan, his expression in Satan in his own pride, malice, folly, misery and lust, is true in a sense, but not in a sense peculiar to Milton. The Satan in Milton enables him to draw the character well just as Satan in us enables us to receive it' (Lewis 1942: 101). Lewis argues that Satan is not so much a literary presence as device, a second strategy of temptation. For Lewis *Paradise Lost* extends Eve's moment of transgression into our post-lapsarian world and embodies a message: don't do it again. Don't be taken in by the grand, persuasive rhetoric of a rebel – rebellion is coterminous with misinterpretation. Lewis rereads Satan's speeches of Books I and II, attends to the meticulous New Critical conventions of 'close reading' (Lewis 1942: 110–2) and then takes a step back.

> To adore Satan, then, is to give one's vote not only for a world of misery, but also for a world of lies and propaganda, of wishful thinking, of incessant autobiography. Yet the choice is possible. Hardly a day passes without some slight movement towards it in each of us. That is what makes *Paradise Lost* so serious a poem.
>
> (Lewis 1942: 102)

Despite the fact that Lewis was writing in the mid-twentieth century he gives the impression that Milton is his immediate correspondent, engaging him with matters of timeless relevance.

William Empson in *Milton's God* achieves a similar level of immediacy, but for Empson the dialogue involves issues that are timebound, conditional, contentious and always open to question. Empson's style throughout the book is impatient, sometimes facetious and gives the general impression that on the one hand he feels that he is writing to similarly inclined, enlightened individuals while engaging with opinions of other critics and academics that are self-evidently absurd.

He offers rather patronizing praise to the unorthodox Romantics in the opening chapter – Blake and Shelley particularly – and implies that he has even more to say. On Satan he looks closely at the famous speeches of Book I and claims that while these do indeed stir in the reader a feeling of identification with, even admiration for, courage in defeat they also operate at a more complex level. Satan and his crew are enduring and battling with relativist uncertainty gratuitously imposed by God. They are as much our intellectual counterparts as our fallen heroes.

> Whether the rebels deserve blame for their initial doubt of God's credentials, before God had supplied false evidence to encourage the doubt, is hard for us to tell; but once they have arrived at a conviction they are not to be blamed for having the courage to act upon it. I hope I will not be told that this moral doctrine is sentimental because it was invented by Shelley; it has been an essential bit of equipment since the human mind was first evolved.
>
> (Empson 1961: 46–7)

Empson, his reader, Satan and of course Milton are participants in a constant struggle to make sense of what they perceive and experience and its meaning, if it has any at all. To a degree, Empson shares Lewis's view that Milton intended the poem to be read as a complex revisiting of Adam and Eve's experience of temptation, but Empson regards this not as a prompter to and lesson against mental misbehaviour, but rather as an invitation on Milton's part to share his condition of speculative questioning. Empson continually examines the logical inconsistencies of the plot – in his view Raphael's intervention and scholarly instructions effectively caused the Fall (Empson 1961: 147) – and perceives these neither as Milton's errors nor reminders of how the absolute truth of scripture is prone to human misinterpretation, but as an encouragement to think, to purposively question the themes and the narrative of the Old Testament.

Empson regards Milton' state of mind following the Civil War and its aftermath as comparable with that of mid-twentieth-century man.

He punctuates his survey with anecdotes, often drawing on his own experiences teaching in China just before World War II and his return to Britain following the Japanese invasions of continental Asia, and the implied parallels are clear enough. World War II has caused humanity to rethink its grandiose aspirations to moral and intellectual enlightenment, and most significantly to question all creeds, political or religious, which make claims to all-encompassing superiority. Milton, he more than implies, has a message for us: the human tendency to question, compare and reflect is our best guarantee of collective equanimity and wisdom, irrespective of God's plans and intentions.

Empson often nods toward 'recent critical trends' and while he makes condign, nominal references to Lewis, Leavis and Eliot, he seems to assume on his reader's part a considerable knowledge of what had been going on. What had?

The first extended 'modern' survey of Milton was published by Sir Walter Raleigh in 1900. Raleigh was one of the first generation of academic critics, holding Chairs in English in Glasgow, Liverpool and eventually Oxford. His *Milton* is a thorough, sensitive monograph, but scrupulously uncontentious. He considers the intellectual and political context of Milton's writing and acknowledges the Romantics as critics yet his method is unintrusive; he tells us much and says very little. His description of Milton as a 'monument to dead ideas' sums up his approach. Raleigh's chapter on 'Style' is the one part of the book that has enthusiasm and this is a fair reflection of the general drift of academic-scholarly studies of Milton in the early decades of the last century. George Saintsbury, another academic, gave great precedence to Milton in his monumental *History of English Prosody* (1906–10) and Robert Bridge's *Milton's Prosody* (1893, revised 1921) is a meticulous survey, partly inspired by Bridges's friendship with Hopkins. What emerges from these studies is a consensual awareness of Milton as having individually altered the history of English versification by inventing in *Paradise Lost* a new sub-genre of non-dramatic blank verse. Articles on Milton appeared in recently founded academic journals, such as the *PMLA*, on all manner of editorial and scholarly issues; early conventions of printing and punctuation, Milton's borrowings from the Old Testament and classical sources, his parallels with other Renaissance writers and texts variously obscure and canonised etc. (Greenlaw, 1917, is an excellent example of this.) Detailed as these often were, and frequently useful to later editors of Milton, their thematic benchmark included a continuation of Raleigh's view that Milton was a great writer with a stature undiminished by the passage of time, but, except for those with a particular interest in the seventeenth-century theology, now curiously irrelevant.

The lengthy preamble to Lewis versus Empson began with T.S. Eliot. Eliot's most controversial article on Milton appeared in 1936 but he had already posed intriguing questions about Milton's place in literary history in his more famous piece on 'The Metaphysical Poets' (1921). Here Eliot presents the Metaphysicals, John Donne particularly, as true poets in that they deliberately, ambitiously used the conventions of verse to unsettle our ordered perceptions of reality **[15–16]**. In the later seventeenth century however a 'dissociation of sensibility set in'; poets began to discriminate between intellectual, sensual and emotive registers rather than create a dynamic interplay between them, as the Metaphysicals had done. And who were the two principal culprits in this alteration in literary history which, Eliot implies, has had an overbearing influence on all English poetry up to the end of the nineteenth century? Dryden and Milton. This is an odd pairing. They were contemporaries, certainly, but while Dryden was acknowledged as one of the founding presences of Augustanism, the transparent, neo-journalistic mode of writing which dominated eighteenth-century verse, Milton resisted easy categorisation. In Eliot's view they shared guilt because while both, with different consequences, were gifted stylistic craftsmen they also showed an equally 'dazzling disregard of the soul'. What exactly he meant by this, in Milton's case, became evident in his 1936 essay in which he conducted a systematic prosecution case against Milton as the monumental example of dissociated sensibility.

> A dislocation takes place, through the hypertrophy of the auditory imagination at the expense of the visual and tactile so that the inner meaning is separated from the surface, and tends to become something occult, or at least without effect upon the reader until fully understood. To extract everything possible from *Paradise Lost*, it would seem necessary to read it in two different ways, first solely for the sound, and second for the sense.
>
> (Dyson and Lovelock 1973: 77)

According to Eliot, then, Milton maintains a continual separation between the stylistic effects of his verse and its meaning. Eliot does not provide concrete evidence of how this is achieved – 'That I feel would be the matter for a separate study...' Instead, he deftly shifts the emphasis toward the meaning itself.

So far as I perceive anything, it is a glimpse of a theology that I find in large part repellent, expressed through a mythology which would have been better left in the Book of *Genesis* upon which Milton has not improved.

(Dyson and Lovelock 1973: 77)

The question we have to ask here is whether this thesis would have been taken seriously had it not been promoted by a man who, in 1936 and thereafter, was the dominant presence in contemporary English verse, and to address it we should also consider Eliot's background and affiliations. He does not explain why he finds Milton's theology 'repellent' but the fact that when he wrote this he had become attached to High Church Anglicanism (Anglo-Catholicism, the modern counterpart to the seventeenth-century Royalist allegiance) offers more than a suggestion. Moreover, Eliot had been a central figure in literary Modernism. Modernism spanned a broad spectrum of beliefs and opinions, but Eliot in particular had espoused the contention that one of the intrinsic faults of much pre-Modernist writing was that it employed literary devices as vehicles for statements and not as instruments to unsettle the reader and cause him/her to reconsider the very nature of language and the world.

Eliot's case was seconded by a man whose influence upon twentieth-century academic criticism was immense, F.R. Leavis.

It needs no unusual sensitiveness to language to perceive that in [Milton's] Grand Style, the medium calls pervasively for a kind of attention, compels an attitude towards itself, that is incompatible with sharp concrete realisation.

(Dyson and Lovelock 1973: 80)

Leavis was never famed for his self-parodic inclinations, but here his apparent admission to 'no unusual sensitiveness to language' makes one wonder about an under-employed talent. He characterises the style of *Paradise Lost* in terms of 'the routine gesture, the heavy fall', 'the foreseen thud', 'the inescapable monotony', 'the routine thump'. Leavis's anti-Miltonic thesis follows Eliot's almost to the letter and his implicit claim to disinterested close-reading is equally questionable. Leavis, throughout his career as a critic, had involved himself in the creation of a canon of important texts and writers and his criteria for inclusion were influenced principally by his self-created ideal of literature as a moral, intellectual and rationalistic bulwark against cultural degeneration. He did not regard Milton as an amoralist or an intellectual vandal, but like Eliot he was troubled by his rewriting of the conventions of English verse. Leavis regarded Shakespeare as one of the team, an imaginative exemplar of 'the English use, the essential spirit of the language, of its characteristic resources' while Milton was a distraction from the Great Tradition, a perversity.

During the 1920s and 1930s Milton was treated as the uninvited visitor to the party. For the Modernists, Eliot especially, he was a strange anachronism; radical and unusual, but neither an exemplar of pre-Modernist tradition nor an obvious precedent for revolt. Certainly he was a rebel, at least stylistically, but one who embodied and promoted ideals with which few early twentieth-century critics, writers and intellectuals felt comfortable. At the same time, however, Milton continued to raise questions which were contentious in a period when perceptions of Christianity were divided, even among critics who espoused it. Lewis, for example, engages with Eliot (9–12) and raises the issues of what poetry is and what it should do. In Lewis's view poetry cannot be separated from matters of faith and spiritual identity. He implies that even if we do not like Milton, whether for religious or cultural reasons, we should respect his adherence to endurable faith, his inspirational, aesthetic bedrock.

The Eliot-Leavis attack on Milton contributed to what is generally known as the 1930s–1940s 'Milton Controversy' (see the Introduction to Dyson and Lovelock 1973). One of the more subdued, reflective contributions was E.M.W. Tillyard's book (1930). Tillyard poses the question of what *Paradise Lost* is about and answers that it 'has no means been settled' (237). He takes up where the Romantics left off and, while acknowledging the status of Satan and God, looks more closely at Adam and Eve as Milton's models for, progenitors of, the human condition – inquiring but hopelessly uninformed, imaginative but eventually damned by their opportunities to intellectual freedom. Tillyard does not quite espouse the humanist perspective of Empson, but his book is infused by an implied notion of Milton as pre-emptor, the first literary doubter of Christian philosophy.

The book that crystallised these partialities and fluctuations in Milton criticism was A.J.A. Waldock's (1947). Waldock's work is in many ways a lengthy preface to Empson (and Empson acknowledges the debt), considering in detail the critical debates that had attended *Paradise Lost* since publication and treating the poem itself in a manner that is consistent with the detached analytical protocols of New Criticism. Waldock regards its historical-political context and its religious registers as factors which contribute to its intrinsic structure: *Paradise Lost* becomes a gigantic network of poetic devices and narrative patterns whose operations and their consequent effects can be disclosed by rigorous and historically informed close reading. Waldock found that the poem's fabric is alive with tensions, not so much inconsistencies as antithetical states of mind, symptomatic of Milton's own, which continually pull the text in different directions. The most fascinating feature of the poem, in Waldock's view, is the fact that Milton had selected a topic which would progressively and incessantly provoke his own apparently unsettled condition: the explanation of the beginning of everything.

> In a sense Milton's central theme denied him the full expression of his deepest interests. It was likely, then, that as his really deep interests could not find outlet in his poem in the right way they may find outlet in the wrong way. And to a certain extent they do; they find vents and safety-valves often in inopportune places. Adam cannot give Milton much scope to express what he really feels about life: but Satan is there, Satan gives him scope. And the result is that the balance is somewhat disturbed; pressures are set up that are at times disquieting, that seem to threaten more than once, indeed, the equilibrium of the poem.
>
> (Waldock 1947: 24)

One example of the poem's unsettled equilibrium is the sometimes unsteady relationship between the reported speech of the characters and Milton's third-person commentary, particularly during Book I when it appears as though Milton needs to warn the reader against sympathising, identifying with the emotive registers of Satan's speeches [96–7]. Waldock: 'He will put some glorious thing in Satan's mouth, then anxious about the effect of it, will pull us gently by the sleeve, saying (for this is what it amounts to): "Do not be carried away by this fellow: he *sounds* splendid, but take my word for it ...."' (1947: 77–8).

Waldock is habitually cited in studies of Milton and in the prefaces to collections of essays, but always briefly. He sits in the shadow of Empson because while his survey is meticulous and detailed it is inconclusive; he looks at how characterisation – Adam's role compared with Satan's for example – is determined by the tensions underpinning the poem. Empson takes his premise a stage further and concludes that Milton did indeed emerge from the shifting complexities of the text as a figure with identifiable affiliations, particularly regarding Satan as a vanguard for the attractions and uncertainties of intellectual liberty.

Perhaps the most puzzling feature of Milton criticism during the four decades following Eliot's essay is the manner in which critics treat the relationship between style and meaning. Eliot in 1946 revisited the themes of his 1936 piece and cautiously retracted a number of his earlier condemnations. (He also takes to task Middleton Murry who in *Heaven and Earth* had attacked Milton as a doctrinaire ideologue lacking the true imaginative spirit of the literary writer.) Now he presents Milton as an aberration, a writer of 'peculiar greatness'; 'As a poet ... probably the greatest of all eccentrics'. What he means is that Milton attempted to do too many things: create the first English epic, rewrite the Old Testament, explain the human condition, and at the same time distance himself from the conventions and habits that characterised English poetry. Eliot argues that these giant aspirations deserve our respect but that Milton guaranteed his own ultimate failure because of his obsession with stylistic uniqueness.

> We must, then, in reading *Paradise Lost*, not expect to see clearly; our sense of sight must be blurred, so that our *hearing* may become more acute. *Paradise Lost*, like *Finnegans Wake* (for I can think of no work which provides a more interesting parallel: two books by great blind musicians, each writing in a language of his own based upon English) makes this peculiar demand for a readjustment of the reader's mode of apprehension. The emphasis is on the sound, not the vision, upon the word, not the idea ...
>
> (Dyson and Lovelock 1973: 82)

Eliot here has driven himself into a corner. The comparison with *Finnegans Wake* is demonstrably invalid, even absurd: *Paradise Lost* might be a complex, demanding exercise in poetics but it is not incomprehensible. Johnson (who, ironically, Eliot cites as an ally) disliked *Paradise Lost* precisely *because* he understood it. Essentially Eliot disliked Milton but found himself, as one of the most eminent poets and critics in English, clutching desperately at straws to legitimise and justify his personal animosity: he went for style.

Two critics effectively brought to a head – summarised, specified and re-examined – the confusing agenda of mid-twentieth-century Milton criticism: Christopher Ricks and Stanley Fish. Both, albeit in very different ways, founded their discussions upon the troubling relationship between what Milton wrote and the way he wrote it.

Ricks's *Milton's Grand Style* (1963) is still regarded as one of the most important pieces of Milton criticism ever produced. His opening chapter is called 'The Milton Controversy', which he sums up shrewdly.

> The Milton controversy, then, is triangular. Leavis and Lewis agree as to what a poem is, but differ as to what a poem should be, and

so as to how good it is. Leavis and (say) Empson agree as to what a poem should be, but differ as to what a poem is, and so as to how good it is. Meanwhile Lewis and Empson agree as to how good the poem is, but differ about what it is and what a poem should be.

(Ricks 1963: 10)

The axis for these antinomies, their pervasive element, is the question of the empirical nature of *Paradise Lost*; what it is and how it functions as a text. To an extent Ricks orchestrates this to justify his approach, but as his book gets into its stride it justifies itself. Ricks's method has often been regarded as a very sophisticated example of New Critical close-reading but it is more complex than that. He does conduct detailed analyses of particular passages from all the books of *Paradise Lost*, but these are selected because they have also been used as the foundation for other critical estimations of Milton, going back as far as Addison and including the work of Ricks's contemporaries. Ricks conducts a kind of Socratic dialogue, citing the passage, looking at how a particular critic reached their conclusion and then considering how and why Milton caused them to do so.

For example, he spends seven pages (Ricks 1963: 40–7) in the company of Donald Davie, whose book *Articulate Energy* (1955) was probably the most celebrated exercise in New Critical stylistics and whose essay in a more recent collection, *The Living Milton* (1960), involved the specific reading of *Paradise Lost*. Ricks is concerned with Davie's treatment of Milton's use of syntax, particularly the way in which the verse form of *Paradise Lost* creates emphases and ambiguities in a manner that would not be possible in regular, prosaic sentences.

There is a passage in Book I where Milton describes the defeat of Satan

> Him the Almighty Power
> Hurld headlong flaming from th'Etherial Skie
> With hideous ruine and combustion down
> To bottomless perdition, there to dwell
> In Adamantine Chains and penal fire,
> Who durst defy th'Omnipotent to Arms
>
> (*PL*, I: 44–49)

Ricks considers Davie's reading of this, noting particularly the latter's comments on how Milton's placing of 'Him', 'Down' and 'To' creates in the reader the sense that 'our own muscles are tightening' as we witness Satan's experience (Ricks 1963: 41). Ricks does not question the accuracy of Davie's interpretation. Instead he tackles his comment that such effects in Milton are 'rather the exception than the rule' (Ricks 1963: 42) and goes on to reinforce his own general argument, his overall thesis, that *Paradise Lost* is a fabric of very different stylistic effects which alter in accordance with characterisation and narrative context. Ricks subtly implies that Milton is deliberately, systematically causing the reader to overreact (as he contends that Davie has done in commenting on the rarity of this particular effect) and that, in the end, *Paradise Lost* continually demands that we question our first response and look again at how this relates to matters such as our preconceived idea of what Milton was trying to do. (Davie, as Ricks notes on p. 40, is a supporter of Leavis.)

Ricks might seem to be concentrating mainly on Milton's method rather than its effect but his overall objective is to show that *Paradise Lost*, almost uniquely, is a text in which the mechanics of writing are incessantly related to such matters as belief. It does question the fundamentals and orthodoxies of Christian thinking, much as the Romantics had argued, but not by direct statement or dramatised episode; rather it uses poetic devices to deliberately unsettle the reader's expected response and, since this will always be attended by the biblical absolutes that underpin the poem, the reader's more personal sense of certainty. Does Ricks himself reach a conclusion? In an elegantly evasive manner he does.

> It seems to me that there is a very close analogy between the successes of the style and the wider successes of the poem. The more closely one looks at the style, the clearer it seems that Milton writes at his very best only when something prevents him from writing with total directness... as a rule it seems that his greatest effects are produced when he is compelled to be oblique as well as direct.
>
> (Ricks 1963: 147–8)

Ricks seems to be saying that Milton deploys his most impressive, and consequently troubling, command of poetics and style as both a substitute for and an enactment of his own innate feelings of doubt about what the events he describes actually signify.

There are parallels between Ricks and Stanley Fish: both base their broader arguments upon the minutiae of Milton's text and play subtle games with the dynamics of reading and interpretation. But they reach different conclusions and, within the spectrum of twentieth-century criticism per se, Ricks remains in the traditional, New Critical camp (reading the text closely to discern the author's ultimate motive or state of mind), while Fish often crosses the border into the field of more recent critical fashion, combining empirical, exegetical method with an attendance to an all-encompassing theory of language, literature and interpretation.

Fish is generally associated with reader-response or reception theory, a broad school of criticism which gives as much attention to the circumstances and state of mind of the particular reader as it does to the assumed objective of the author. The following is from Fish's *Surprised By Sin* (1967), on Satan's first perception of Adam and Eve in Book IV.

The Fiend
Saw undelighted all delight, all kind
Of living Creatures new to sight and strange:
Two of far nobler shape

(IV: 285–8)

Nobler than what or whom? Strange and new to whom? The questions may seem unnecessary in view of the narrative situation: the creatures are new to Satan, and among them Adam and Eve stand out 'erect and tall'. But in fact it is the reader in addition to Satan who is the stranger in Paradise, although he may not realise it until the description of Eve presents a problem he can solve only at his own expense:

She as a veil down to the slender waist
Her unadorned golden tresses wore
Dishevell'd, but in wanton ringlets wav'd
As the Vine curls her tendrils, which implied
Subjection.

(IV: 304–8)

Fish goes on to argue that Milton has led the reader into a cunningly laid trap (100–1). We, like Satan, are strangers in Paradise, and we are obliged to acknowledge this by conceding that the terms 'dishevell'd' and 'wanton' reflect our post-lapsarian condition; we cannot witness female beauty without carrying elements of corruption and eroticism into this experience. At this point in the narrative of the Fall we could hardly regard Eve as either wanton or dishevelled, but we cannot prevent ourselves from imposing our corrupt state of mind upon a lost condition of pure innocence. Satan before Book IV had not encountered any form of humanity, let alone its female dimension. Perhaps our sense of collusion with Satan is even more disturbing than we first imagined. The reader, in responding to Milton's double pattern of images, is thus confirmed in his state of corruption by effectively pre-empting Satan's lascivious designs. Fish again:

> The relationship between the reader and the vocabulary of Paradise is one aspect of his relationship with its inhabitants. Just as the fallen consciousness infects language, so does it make the unfallen consciousness the mirror of itself ... Fallen man's perceptual equipment, physical and moral, is his prison; any communication from a world beyond the one he has made for himself reaches him only after it has passed through the distortions of his darkened glass.
>
> (Fish 1967: 103–4)

Fish states his case at the beginning of the book. 'Milton's method is to recreate in the mind of the reader the drama of the Fall, to make him fall again as Adam did (Fish 1967: 1). Fish's putative reader is important here because throughout the book he continually points out that, in effect, the late seventeenth-century reader and his/her twentieth-century counterpart are reading different poems. The words on the page are the same but they will, he argues, register differently for a person for whom God and the story of creation are incontestable absolutes (Milton's contemporaries) and for someone who must, irrespective of their own affiliations, perceive fundamentalist Christianity alongside its revisionist counterparts, humanism and atheism – the late-twentieth-century condition. Consequently Fish's thesis offers a radical perspective upon the critical debates that had attended Milton, particularly since the Romantic period. It is not that either Lewis or Empson are correct or incorrect in their respective perceptions of Milton as true Christian and potential doubter; more that their readerly conditions determine their interpretations – Lewis, the seventeenth-century throwback, Empson the querulous, sceptical agnostic.

Fish's standpoint is immensely important because its premise is carried over into a number of other influential schools of criticism of the last three decades. For example, feminist critics have frequently pointed out that criticism and reading cannot be regarded as abstract, impartial undertakings, that men and women will, by virtue of their societal and biological differences, read the same text differently **[166–74]**.

For the time being, however, particular credit should be given to Fish for raising the profile of Milton's shorter poetry in modern criticism. Milton's lyric, non-dramatic verse, written mostly before the Civil War, was dealt with by mid-twentieth-century critics in a manner that is best described as perfunctory: Milton's reputation as a literary figure, a presence within the historical canon, seemed to be coterminous with *Paradise Lost*.

One of the classics of New Critical thinking and methodology was Cleanth Brooks's *The Well Wrought Urn* (1947). The title comes from Donne and the focus of the study is the early seventeenth-century lyric poem. Brooks carries forward Eliot's 1921 assessment of the Metaphysicals as the magicians of figurative language, 'constantly amalgamating disparate experience'. Brooks extrapolates this to a general theory: 'the language of poetry is the language of paradox' (Brooks 1947: 3). By 'paradox' Brooks meant the poetic tendency to address complex intellectual or empirical problems and rather than attempt to resolve them, as might be expected in prose discourse, use them as a springboard for further speculations on the nature of language, thought and identity. For New Critics such as Brooks the Metaphysicals offered the perfect playground for close-reading, puzzles aplenty which the sophisticated critic could analyse, assess and indeed celebrate as testaments to the uniqueness of poetic writing. Young Milton, while a near contemporary of the Metaphysicals, presented a problem because the figurative tendencies and metrical habits that allied his early poems with the sub-genre of the baroque, late Renaissance lyric were largely concessions to ongoing fashion and at odds with a presence in the text who had something particular and non-paradoxical to say. Brooks devotes a chapter to 'L'Allegro' and 'Il Penseroso' and in this he gives the impression that his treatment of Milton is more an obligation than an enthusiastic choice. He is aware, for example, that modern critics must in their dealings with the notion of 'liberty' as celebrated in 'L'Allegro' pay due attention to the ideological significance of the concept in relation to Milton's later involvement in politics (Brooks 1947: 43). Brooks asks if the 'Jest and youthful jollity/Quips and cranks and wanton wiles' of the fun-loving country-folk should be treated as blamelessly hedonistic liberty or as the ominous antithesis of a countryside soon to be soaked in blood, and effectively leaves the question unanswered. He deals with the poems in an oblique, distracted manner not because of any critical shortcomings on his part but because they disrupt his agenda. Compared, for example, with Donne's 'The Exstasie' or Marvell's 'The Garden', where natural imagery becomes the foundation for flamboyant casuistry and metaphor, 'L'Allegro' is a catalogue of observations and controlled reflections.

The best mid-twentieth-century study of Milton's early verse is Leishman's, published posthumously in 1969 and comprised of essays written over the previous thirty years. What Leishman does is to recreate for the young Milton a comprehensive literary context. He does not claim to have verifiable knowledge of all that Milton would have read, from classical Greek texts to contemporaneous writing, but, given that the educational curriculum of the time is well documented and Milton's own voracious appetite for knowledge and culture acknowledged, he can make valid assumptions. Instead of following the New Critical technique of concentrating mainly upon the internalised complexities of the poem Leishman broadens the perspective and considers the accumulated mindset of other texts, devices and styles that would have influenced Milton as he produced his own work. For example, the famous much debated lines from 'Lycidas'

> But that two handed engine at the door,
> Stands ready to smite once, and smite no more
> (TP: 130–1)

have been treated as a bizarre and puzzling metaphor (what exactly does 'the engine' symbolise?). Leishman, rather than attempting to decode the image in terms of the perceived objectives or stylistic character of the rest of the poem, makes use of his own considerable knowledge of early seventeenth-century discourse, poetic, scholarly and theological, in which 'engine' was frequently used as substitute for 'sword' (Leishman 1969: 275–6).

Leishman does not avoid the hands-on technique of close-reading – he is a shrewd and sensitive decoder of poetics – but he continually stabilises this with an almost encyclopaedic knowledge of the literary and intellectual context of Milton's writing. Rosamond Tuve's book (1957) is similarly meticulous and informative in its treatment of Milton's shorter poems as part of early-seventeenth-century literary culture: his linguistic mannerisms, indigenous and classical frames of reference are noted and particularised. Both critics imply, through their approach, that Milton's early verse is at once anachronistic and purposive, attendant to many of the conventions of its period yet produced by a man with a separate agenda. Louis Martz in a 1965 essay argued that Milton's *Poems 1645* was a calculated gesture on its author's part, its contents evincing a 'light and dancing posture that we do not usually associate with John Milton ... the entire volume strives to create a tribute to a youthful era now past' (Martz (1965) 1980: 5). Martz contends that Milton, then aged 37, was attempting to formulate his posthumous literary reputation and destiny by publishing a collection of pieces that would thereafter be treated as mere rehearsals for a much more significant project.

Thomas Corns (1982) similarly argued that the 1645 collection was a deliberate attempt on Milton's part to write his own literary biography, to create an intriguing contrast between his ongoing, polemical prose writings and the more adventurous, less focused poetry of his youth.

The common feature of those discussions of the early verse, from Brooks to Corns, is the impression that Milton by various means distanced himself from both orthodoxy and fashion, consciously and pre-emptively separated himself from contemporary convention as a rehearsal for what would eventually become *Paradise Lost*.

Fish, however, followed his study of *Paradise Lost* with a number of examinations of the shorter poems which do not so much to offer further disclosures of their intended meanings as reconsider them as readerly experiences. In 'What it's like to Read "L'Allegro" and "Il Penseroso"' he concentrates on the former poem and considers in detail the critical consensus that it was written carelessly, its random, sometimes discontinuous, catalogue of daytime pleasures testifying perhaps to Milton's temperamental discomfort with non-intellectual experience (Fish 1980: 113–23). He does not disagree with the findings of these critics (Brooks, Tuve and Leishman are cited); rather he shifts the perspective from the interpretative, explicatory mode to that of the effects created within the process of reading. He pays particular attention to a minor but vigorous critical debate that surrounds lines 45–6.

> Then to come in time of sorrow
> And at my window bid good morrow,
> *(TP: 45–6)*

He points out that critics had offered four potential answers to the question of who or what exactly does come to the window: the lark; dawn; the poet; mirth personified (Fish 1980: 117). Fish argues that this catalogue of possibilities tell us as much about modern criticism as it does about Milton's intention; that critics, particularly New Critics, are caught up in a process known as naturalisation, the objective of which is to resolve poetic ambiguities and arrive at a conclusive, paraphrased meaning. He contends that to do proper justice to the experience generated by literature we should concentrate more upon the dynamic effects of reading the text than upon our search for a final, underpinning solution.

'L'Allegro' and 'Il Penseroso' are the reader: that is they stand for modes of being which the reader realises in response to the poems bearing their names. The formal and thematic features of each poem are intimately related to its meaning, not because they reflect it but because they *produce* it, by moving the reader to a characteristic activity.

(Fish 1980: 132)

Fish suggests that 'L'Allegro' is deliberately less co-ordinated, more superficial than 'Il Penseroso' because Milton is not so much specifying or defining mirth and daytime pleasure but using the texture of poetry to recreate its inconclusive, transient nature. Similarly he looks at 'Lycidas' (Fish 1980: 162–5) and *Samson Agonistes* (1980: 272–4) as texts in which the fabric of poetic devices creates effects upon the reader which are at once irresolvable yet consistent with the prevailing mood of each poem. He does not reach a specific conclusion about Milton but his coverage implies that the early, shorter poems involve a kind of stylistic saturation not evident among Milton's contemporaries, exercises which draw the reader into a complex network of effects and responses which are ultimately and deliberately irresolvable.

Fish differs from traditional, predominantly New Critical, Miltonists in a number of ways, but he can be cited as an early representative of late twentieth-century critical theory for one important reason: he allies himself with a general theory of literary interpretation – in his case reader response or reception theory – at the expense of the specifics and individuality of a particular writer and his work. Consequently the remainder of this section will be subdivided into distinct categories of theoretical approach. We will begin with the most complex, variegated and contentious of these.

Feminist criticism

Feminist literary criticism evolved out of the network of social, cultural and political movements which gained prominence in the 1960s, carry the collective designation as feminism, and which sought to re-examine and alter the prevailing and implicitly accepted ideology: that the mores, rituals, hierarchies and conventions of society, along with their representational media, are dominated by the self-focused thinking and practical governance of the male. The literary-critical branch of this phenomenon had two principal perspectives: the representation of gender difference within a male-dominated literary canon; and the condition, perceptions and states of mind of women writers and readers, as compared with those of their male counterparts.

Milton was a self-selecting but by no means easily manageable subject for feminist critics: his most important work was, after all, based upon a representation of the original man and woman.

We will begin with an essay by one of the first and most influential feminist critics, Sandra Gilbert's 'Milton's Bogey':

> In a patriarchal Christian context the pagan goddess Wisdom may, Milton suggests, become the loathsome demoness Sin, for the intelligence of heaven is made up exclusively of 'Spirits Masculine' and woman like her dark double Sin, is a 'fair defect/Of Nature' (X, 891–2)... for sensitive female readers brought up in the bosom of a 'masculinist', patristic, neo-Manichean church, the latent as well as the manifest content of such a powerful work as *Paradise Lost* was (and is) bruisingly real. To women the unholy trinity of Satan, Sin and Eve, diabolically mimicking the holy trinity of God, Christ and Adam, must have seemed even in the eighteenth and nineteenth centuries to illustrate [the] historical dispossession and degradation of the female principle.
>
> (1978: 373–4)

An enormous number of claims are made here. First, Milton is operating within a '"masculinist" patristic' framework, cultural and religious. In his representation of Eve he dramatises and reinforces the ingrained perception of woman as, in various ways, allied to the more dangerous and degenerate human tendencies. Consequently *Paradise Lost* has functioned for women readers and, significantly, for women writers as a dominant, even threatening, cultural monolith. Gilbert argues that the poem remained largely unchallenged in its literary presentation of the archetypes of male and female characteristics up to the beginning of the twentieth century. Women writers of the nineteenth and twentieth centuries (Gilbert emphasises the work of the Brontës and Virginia Woolf), found themselves dealing not only with non-literary social codes of gender stereotyping but also with a literary text which claims to describe, indeed verify, the origins of these socio-cultural abstracts. So, according to Gilbert, women both as literary subjects and as readers of literature were continually shadowed by the presence of Eve, the archetype of naiveté, gullibility, vulnerability and dangerously unsophisticated instinct. Gilbert's essay extends the structuralist-sociological model of Landy (1972) who looks at the characters of *Paradise Lost* in terms of the traditional, Western, family. Christ is the decent, conventional sibling while Satan is the deviant 'son of God' who enters a pseudo-social relationship with Eve (he is in a general sense her 'seducer' in Book IX), which in turn results in the perpetration of Satanesque deviance in Eve's seduction of Adam and the creation of humanity.

Christine Froula (1983) gives more emphasis than her predecessors to the close-read minutiae of *Paradise Lost*. She concentrates on Book IV, particularly the passage (461–91) in which Eve discloses her first memories of existence to Adam **[104–5]**. Froula examines the contrast between the image of Eve herself provided by her reflection in the lake (silent, but visible) and her first encounter with another presence, the voice of God (vocal, but invisible).

> The fable of Eve's conversion from her own visible being in the world to invisible patriarchal authority traces a conversion from being in and for herself to serving a 'higher' power – from the authority of her own experience to the hidden authority of the Tree of Knowledge.
>
> (Froula 1983: 156)

The fact that the voice of male authority is unattended by a physical presence, and is by implication timeless and transcendent, while her own self image is that of an attractive, silent object prefigures, so Froula argues, an entire tradition involving the patriarchal governance of language, with the female as the silent subject. She closes the essay with a citation of the famous passage in Book III (40–55) **[101–2]**, where Milton himself reflects upon his own blindness as perversely beneficial, allowing him undistracted access to 'Celestial light', the inspiration for the poem. Milton, being male, would of course regard this as his destiny.

Gilbert, Landy and Froula give special emphasis to Milton's characterisation of Eve, his presentation of her as the vital axis in the narrative of the Fall, and they supplement this with her role beyond the poem as in various ways symbolic and paradigmatic, the original woman as perceived by the patriarchal establishment. Diane McColley (1983) takes issue with this. McColley too looks closely at the Book IV passage in which Eve speaks of her reflection in the lake (McColley 1983: 74–86). She does not engage directly with Froula (their pieces were published almost simultaneously), but the contrast between their readings is striking. According to McColley the scene takes the reader with Eve through a pattern of response that is a mimetic model, both for the art of marriage and for the art of reading. Like Eve, the reader pauses to see his own reflection, but that is not the end of the interpretative process, nor of Eve's experience.

(McColley 1983: 75)

McColley goes on to argue that Eve's self-evident appreciation of the lake experience as part of her process of understanding narcissism prefigures her broader characterisation as a figure just as intelligent, thoughtful and responsible as Adam. True, in a practical sense she plays a secondary role to Adam's – he is the one who engages directly with Raphael, for example – but Milton's treatment of her in this way can hardly be regarded as unusual evidence of patriarchal authority: he could neither be expected to rewrite Genesis completely nor to personally reschedule the seventeenth-century notion of the woman's social role. McColley, throughout her book, interprets Eve as a figure who mentally and linguistically transcends gender differentiation. She operates independently, as a means of drawing the reader into the complex narrative and psychological dynamics of the fall. McColley's method draws partly upon Fish's in that she continually reminds us that twentieth-century readers, feminists included, should pay particular attention to the cultural-historical context in which Milton was working; not as an excuse for his alleged misogyny, rather as background for a proper understanding of how his Eve rises above her historical circumstances as a representative of the Christian/human condition and not only its gender-divided dimension.

McColley's book is certainly not a reactionary, anti-feminist tract; rather it represents a sub-tradition of critical writing where the largely late-twentieth-century interpretative strategies evolved by feminism are balanced against more impartial, historicist readings. Lewalski (1974) and Webber (1980) also belong in this category: both articles involve assessments of how the ideology of feminism as a broader movement can cloud, sometimes deliberately obscure, the objective detail of literary scholarship.

Aers and Hodge (1981) conduct a survey of Milton's treatment of gender and marriage, both in *Paradise Lost* and in his prose pamphlets, particularly the divorce tracts. Their method is unprecedented because they combine a feminist agenda, which they do not unquestioningly endorse, with a Marxist perspective [174–82]. They begin by noting that the modern 'neo Christian' critical school (Lewis, succeeded by Patrides 1966, and Halket 1970) is cautiously selective both in its eulogising of Milton as a bedrock of the old orthodoxies of religious belief and in its implicit support of his related endorsement of the pre-twentieth-century gender roles. They argue that the neo-Christians are wrong on both counts; that Milton continually questioned Christian doctrine (and here they praise Empson), including its theological paradigms of male and female. They argue that on the one hand he endorsed 'a revolutionary political and religious life which is also sexually radical' but that 'nor should we ignore Milton's inevitable complicity with orthodox sexist ideology... there are limits to how far even a heroic individual can transcend his background and education, in thought and practice' (Aers and Hodge 1981: 84). Here, their Marxist methodology comes into play because they argue that Milton was subject to the ideological confusion that surrounded the immense transformations and dynamic tensions of seventeenth-century politics and culture – in Marxist terms the dialectic of historical change. His intellectual, indeed his subjective, engagements with issues such as Christian orthodoxy and gender were continually prey to an ever-changing socio-political foundation. Their argument is convincingly substantiated by their citations from Milton's writing. In *Paradise Lost* for example Milton seems to be uncertain of his own state of mind.

Aers and Hodge point out that it is difficult to extrapolate from the poem an allegiance either to the ideology of male supremacy or to more enlightened, non-sexist perceptions; they concentrate particularly on Adam's exchange with Raphael, mostly about the former's relationship with Eve, in Book VIII (531–59) where the emphasis shifts continuously between orthodox seventeenth-century attitudes and the uncharted sphere of non-gendered absolutes (Aers and Hodge 1981: 72–5).

As Joseph Wittreich comments, the title of his book *Feminist Milton* (1987) is 'bold, deliberately so' (ix). He does not argue that Milton pre-empted late-twentieth-century feminist ideas, not exactly. Instead he re-examines a definition of the feminist enterprise – the deconstructing of '"dominant male patterns of thought" while "reconstructing female experience previously hidden or overlooked"' – and goes on to propose that in the light of this Milton could be seen as 'not just an ally of feminists but their early sponsor' (ix). His evidence is taken mainly from the extant writings of women of the eighteenth and early-nineteenth centuries. In these he claims to find that while Milton was not widely celebrated by women as an emphatic proponent of enlightened ideas he functioned as a stimulus, an incitement to pro-active thinking and speculation. He claims, for example, that Mary Shelley's late novel *Lodore* (1835) describes the title character's attempt to educate his daughter Ethel so that she will embody the dignified subservience of Eve but that, ironically, Ethel's experience of *Paradise Lost* enables her to identify with Eve as something else, a figure at least with the potential for independent thought and action (Wittreich 1987: 80–1).

Wittreich's thesis is complicated. It involves the process of deconstruction **[187–9]** which also he sees as being anticipated by Milton in that *Paradise Lost* asks to be read 'with a suspicious eye on the poem and its narrative' (Wittreich 1987: 67); the text will always have the ability to unsettle pre-scheduled, even ongoing, assumptions about its overall allegiance or intention. In this respect Wittreich carries forward elements of Aer's and Hodge's argument; indeed he states that there is a case for 'distinguishing between the essential and the culturally relative in *Paradise Lost*' (Wittreich 1987: 68), meaning that while the poem was not at time of publication regarded as radical in its presentation of women it was sufficiently oblique and multi-layered to enable the likes of Mary Shelley to treat it in retrospect as a springboard for radicalism.

Also, Wittreich submits a case that is antithetical to Gilbert's: she saw Milton as a sexist monolith, a restraint to subsequent women writers; he reinterprets restraint as provocation and oblique encouragement. 'The human condition [as Eve and Mary Shelley's Ethel discover] is not to move from paradise to paradise but to be in exile, in prison. There we find our paradise – or not at all' (Wittreich 1987: 81).

Probably the most sophisticated critic of Milton in the feminist zone is Mary Nyquist. In a 1987 essay she begins by addressing a question that has been central to feminist readings of *Paradise Lost*: 'Why does Milton's Eve tell the story of her earliest experiences first in Book IV? Why, if Adam was formed first, then Eve, does Adam tell *his* story to Raphael *last* in Book VIII?' (Nyquist 1987: 88). This is significant because the order of events is decided by Milton (no specific chronology operates in Genesis) and implies a great deal: she defers to Adam as a figure of authority, while he moves up the scale of being and discourses with Raphael; hers involves an instinctive, naively transparent account (Froula and others concentrate on this) while his is both more learned and educative. Nyquist goes against Froula's proposition that Eve, irrespective of Milton's intention, is an empowering presence, operating both in the shadow of Adam yet essentially alone, and argues that contemporary ideological forces should be considered; specifically seventeenth-century ideas on marriage. She takes into account Calvin's thesis, Milton's own comments in the divorce tracts and the political pamphlets, and Mary Astell's *Reflections upon Marriage* (1706), assembles a fabric of contending attitudes to marriage and concludes that 'Adam is revealed as articulating the doctrine of marriage' while 'Eve is portrayed enacting its discipline' (Nyquist 1987: 97): in short, Adam theorises (with Raphael) and Eve takes on a role involving both subservience and (domesticated) independence. In the light of this Milton emerges as a thoughtful, quasi-liberal conservative.

Nyquist herself represents, sometimes self-consciously, a significant development in feminist treatments of Milton. She employs a neo-Marxist discussion of contemporary ideology, similar to Aers and Hodge, and often draws upon the deconstructionist work of Jacques Derrida **[187–9]**. Her approach is eclectic and she argues in her 1988 essay that feminism can only maintain a relevant and valid role in Milton studies if it operates alongside other textual, historical and theoretical approaches:

> Yet if the various discourses that have, historically, sought mastery over the text were themselves to be placed in intertextual relation with it, *and* in conflictual relation with any feminist counter-readings, as I have tried to do here, then *Paradise Lost* as a text whose meaning is somehow pre-given or authoritatively present would be lost to history by being given up to it. Intervening in that history, a feminist reading of the text we have been looking at would refuse to stabilise or recuperate it, thereby appropriating *Paradise Lost* by happily letting it go.
>
> (Nyquist 1988:182)

What Nyquist appears to be saying, in the convoluted manner that has become customary in literary theory, is that the way forward for feminist Milton critics involves a kind of dynamic pluralism. Following her advice, then, one might examine a book written shortly after the first feminist essays appeared, Edward Le Comte's *Milton and Sex* (1978). Le Comte is aware of ongoing discussions (he cites Landy and Lewalski) and he presents himself as a more impartial commentator, despite his maleness. His book is amusing and provocative; he presents Milton less as a patriarchal, mysoginistic presence and more as someone who is both confused and fascinated by the female condition and state of mind (Milton's several marriages are referred to). Le Comte presents the relationship between Adam and Eve (Le Comte 1978: 94–100) as the prototype for perpetual and self-destructive battles between two people who do not properly understand each other, men and women. Satan comes across as a kind of incompetent marriage guidance counsellor who confuses their mutual and self-perceived images even further.

Le Comte's book is not an anti-feminist diatribe – the movement was then in its infancy – but it says, partly by example and implication, a great deal about the ever contentious issue of Milton and gender. Le Comte's method is unfashionable – even the New Critics had questioned the assumption that a writer could be known via his words – in that he reconstructs from Milton's poetry and prose, and from biographical evidence, an image of the man, a mixture of tensions: instinctive and erudite, ideologically affiliated and perversely individual, as much fascinated and perplexed by his material as in full control of it. Significantly, Le Comte gives generous space to Milton's shorter poetry (the mainstream feminists concentrate almost exclusively on *Paradise Lost*); *Comus* for example (Le Comte 1978: 15–23).

Comus, as Le Comte and many others point out, can be perceived as a rehearsal for *Paradise Lost*, particularly the Book IX exchanges between Eve and Satan **[112–14]**. Most feminist readers perceive Satan as the archetypal male, with the temptation scene carrying obvious overtones of seduction. The question which Le Comte prompts, but does not explicitly address, is why feminist critics have not given more attention to the Lady of *Comus* within their treatment of Milton's gendered archetypes.

She is a version of Eve, the parallels are obvious, but at the same time she is the most powerful moral, intellectual and reflectively self-assured figure in the masque. Continually she undermines Comus's rhetorical strategies with transparent logic and unadorned individuality. Doing so she also undermines a literary convention, that of the male speaker and silent female addressee of the Metaphysical lyric: Donne's 'The Flea' and 'The Exstasie' and Marvell's 'The Garden' are the most prominent examples. She answers back, pro-actively, challenging the language-based core of Comus's self-assumed dominance **[72–4]**. Interestingly, the feminist critics, Gilbert particularly, focus upon literary language as a gender-biased ideological discourse enshrining male dominance, but they do not give space to *Comus*.

Apart from Le Comte's somewhat idiosyncratic piece there are a number of other critical studies which address the reader to the topic of Milton and gender, yet which it would be inaccurate and perhaps unfair to classify as mainstream feminist writing. Halkett (1970) examines the divorce tracts and *Paradise Lost* as reflective of their author's singular perception of marital relationships, without finding evidence of partiality fuelled either by personal experience or disposition. Turner (1987) examines the divorce tracts in relation to the libertine tradition of Rochester, Casanova and de Sade, and argues that while Milton deliberately provoked the fundamentalist morality of the Presbyterians his intention was to evolve a non-abstract code for gender relationships. Significantly, Turner also proposes that this exercise – contentious, contingent and with innumerable Biblical resonances – was the primary inspiration for *Paradise Lost*. Patterson (1990) covers similar territory to Turner's, particularly on the tracts, and, while engaging with the theoretical realms of feminism, Marxism and psycho-analysis, keeps the focus of her writing upon the particulars of Milton's state of mind and circumstances.

Feminist theories of Milton cover a vast range of issues. Historical context is important, given that Milton's engagements with gender in his writing have to be considered in relation to the seventeenth century, male-dominated perception of woman as an honoured sub-species, as much desired and feared as listened or spoken to. Just as significant is the fact that while the gender of the reader will not alter the words on the page, it will seriously affect their discursive and personally registered understanding of them. In the end, however, the debate centres upon Eve, specifically her first words in Book IV and her exchange with Satan in Book IX, and the prevailing questions are these: How and for what reason does Milton alter scripture? Does he create Eve as an embodied justification for personal, male and therefore hegemonic standardisa-tions of womankind: the original woman, instinctive, intellectually active and vulnerable, unpredictable and, as Genesis proved, dangerous? Or does he presents her as almost heroic: far more an individual than Adam, more imaginative and therefore the easiest, most tragically inclined target for Satan's destructive machinations?

Three lines from Book IX centralise these issues. Eve, as much to herself as in reply to Satan, states 'What fear I then, rather what know to fear/Under this ignorance of Good or Evil,/Of God or death, of law or penalty?' (*PL*, IX: 773–5). Economically, just prior to the Fall, she addresses all of the questions that would attend the consequences of the Fall, questions which carry over into the existential plight of non-believers: what do I know, what can I know, of the best and the worst of experience, and what of their consequences in this life or thereafter? Surely, these are ungendered, human questions, and the other question of why Milton, in a poem which addresses the state of humanity, should give them to a woman raises even more – unanswered as yet by the feminists or anyone else.

History and politics

The theory which dominates twentieth-century studies of the historical and political contexts of literature is Marxism. Marx and Engels themselves gave slight attention to literature and history, but critics have grafted theories of interpretation onto the Marxist model of post-feudal Western society, and the best short survey of their enterprises is by Forgacs (1982). The point upon which all Marxist critics focus, though rarely agree, is that literature belongs within the broader concept of ideology. This term has undergone a vast number of definitions but it is generally held to mean the collective, socially and politically determined, representation of ideas and experience as opposed to the material reality upon which experience is based. Specified as such, ideology might seem to be virtually the same thing as language and their differences are not so much intrinsic as determined by the different ways in which they are analysed. The ideological import of a statement or a text is exposed by the examination its socio-political registers, sometimes implied, sometimes hidden, and rarely, except in the case of self-consciously political theses, openly disclosed. Marxists regard all linguistic discourses as subject to the contextual pressures and inferences of contemporary history. A legal document produced in the beginning of the nineteenth century might not seem to engage with the industrial revolution and an abstract philosophical tract produced 80 years later might appear to have little to say about the historical apex of Victorian capitalism. However, Marxists will decode the ideological significance of such texts by going beyond the words on the page and examining the historically determined context in which they were produced: they will be treated as symptomatic of the way in which institutions such as the legal profession or the academy are influenced by prevailing economic and political conditions. According to Marxist theory everything said or written at a particular point in history is affected by that period's predominant ideology, which in turn reflects the prevailing economic and political condition, sometimes dynamic and unsettled, of a particular region or state.

Marxist literary critics have been troubled and divided by several questions. Is literary history determined by its economic-political counterpart? (The massive socio-economic changes brought about by the industrial revolution in relation to the political-intellectual radicalism of Romanticism is an obvious case in point.) To what extent is a literary writer consciously aware of the political resonances of his/her writings? (Is the Modernists' avoidance of a direct engagement with turbulent contemporary political issues a political statement in itself or symptomatic of self-serving middle class indifference?)

Milton provides an immensely rich source for Marxist speculation. He witnessed, was involved in, a revolution unprecedented in Europe: the monarchy was replaced by a republic. While traditional historians of the Civil War saw Cromwellians as inspired by religious and ethical principles, Marxists perceive them as symptomatic of the rise and extended power base of the bourgeoisie, the newly emergent middle class, who a century later would be the foundation for the industrial revolution. In the mid-seventeenth-century, England, compared with the rest of Europe, experienced the most rapid exchange of what remained of the feudal monarchical system for something else, involving the contesting interests and political affiliations of a more complex socio-economic fabric. Milton was part of this and he was a writer. He therefore participated in the ideology of change. But how?

Christopher Hill's *Milton and the English Revolution* (1977) is the most influential and widely debated attempt to answer this question. Hill is a Marxist historian, but throughout the book he keeps his immense learning and related affiliations in check (Marx is mentioned briefly, three times). Instead he tries to offer Milton a voice, to present him as a figure who pre-empted Marx, a thinker for whom socialism and civil libertarianism, then unnamed, were prescient, fundamental principles.

In his Introduction Hill trawls through the history of Milton criticism: the Romantics dallied with his radicalism but didn't really understand him, the Victorians effectively censored and neutralised his political import. The mid-twentieth-century critics either wasted time on questions such as when exactly he composed *Samson Agonistes* or updated and adopted him as a spokesman for less than popular Christianity. Hill favours critics such as Waldock, Empson and Ricks, the ones who present Milton as an individualist, almost anarchistic in his overturning of religious and stylistic conventions. However, while they celebrate his literary endeavours Hill attempts to examine these as political gestures, elements of an albeit unformed revolutionary ideology.

> *Paradise Lost* is a poem, not a historical document. The surface meaning is not necessarily to be taken at its face value, as though it were a series of statements in prose ... But *Paradise Lost* should not be taken out of history. It is possible simply by 'reading the poem' to find in it meanings which seem unlikely to have been consciously intended by Milton ... Our problem is to decide whether Milton *had* intentions other than his professed aim of justifying the ways of God to men.
>
> (Hill,1977: 354)

An old cliché seems apt here, since Hill wants to have his cake and eat it. Hill cannot prove empirically that *Paradise Lost* was more than a dutiful reinterpretation of Genesis, nor that this was Milton's intention, but he will demonstrate that it was. He does this in two ways. First of all he rereads Milton's non-poetic writings in terms of their partially subdued ideological import. His pro-Cromwellian tracts are treated as compromises, taking inspiration from the extreme revolutionary inclinations of the Levellers and the Diggers, while deferring to the pragmatic conservatism of the government, Milton's sponsors. Then Hill transfers this assumed state of necessary compromise to a reading of *Paradise Lost*, and his decoding of the 'Satanic Parliament' of Book II is intriguing. For example the following passage, quoted by Hill, is Milton's description of Satan's followers.

> O shame to men! Devil with devil damned
> Firm concord holds, men only disagree
> Of creatures rational, though under hope
> Of heavenly grace: and God proclaiming peace
> Yet live in hatred, enmity and strife
> Among themselves, and levy cruel wars,
> Wasting the earth, each other to destroy:
> As if (which might adduce us to accord)
> Man had not hellish foes enow besides,
> That day and night for his destruction wait.
>
> (II: 496–505)

Hill interprets this as follows: 'The Satanic Parliament gave Milton the chance to stress what was most lacking in 1658–60 – unity among the members of the Good Old Cause' (Hill 1977: 369). Also, Hill interprets a passage from Book VI, which ostensibly refers to Satan, as Milton's perception of Charles II in exile.

> Plotting how he may seduce
> Thee also from obedience, that with him
> Bereaved of happiness thou mayst partake
> His punishment, eternal misery.
>
> (VI, 901–4)

Hill's political-allegorical readings are generally less straightforward than this. He argues that on the one hand Milton identified with Satan's act of rebellion against God – the parallels between this and the republican revolt against absolutionist monarchy are clear enough – while also perceiving him as prone to the kind of despotism that enabled Cromwell and his senior officers to suppress the more radical elements of the republican cause. As a Marxist, Hill is concerned rather to highlight the contradictions in Milton's ideology than to resolve them. He perceives these as reflective of the 'dialectical' character of history and society: that is, the opposed and dynamic forces which attend the progress of Western society from feudalism to capitalism. At the same time, however, he often allows the mask of the orthodox Marxist theory to slip and presents Milton as a special case, someone for whom only insurmountable obstacles prevented from becoming a modern radical before his time.

> Milton was *sui generis*, wedded and glued to no forms, the great eclectic. But he was open to the left and closed to the right – intolerant of papists though embracing all varieties of Protestantism, merciless to the Philistine aristocracy and priests but merciful to the excluded vulgar, linking himself with the radicals just as far as his strong sense of the necessity of bourgeois society would permit.
>
> (Hill 1977: 470)

Andrew Milner's book (1981) is partly a critique and partly an extension of Hill's study. At one point he describes Hill as a 'perplexed middle-of-the-road-liberal' (Milner 1981: 209) by which he means that Hill is insufficiently rigorous in his treatment and application to Milton of radical post-Marxist ideas. Milner adopts the approach formulated by the Marxist theorist Lucien Goldmann (see Forgacs) which regards the literary work as the expression not so much of the author's consciously formed ideas as a reflection of the collective ideology of the social class to which he belongs. According to Milner Milton identified with the Republican ascendancy, the Cromwellian Independents who would eventually dominate post Civil War England and whose power-base enabled them to defeat both the querulous 'Presbyterians and the radical Levellers' [40–2]. This group, argues Milner, provided the foundation for the late eighteenth and nineteenth-century bourgeoisie; rationalist, individualist, meritocratic, humanist.

In the light of this contextualist thesis Milner conducts a rigorous close reading of *Paradise Lost* and decodes it as a manifesto for the middle-class notion of rational individuality. For example, he derides a catalogue of Miltonists for their misguided attempts to explain the precise cause of the Fall: pride (Lewis), intellectual ambition (Tillyard), gratuitous disobedience (Waldock), sex (Saurat) (Milner 1981: 164–5). Milner, citing particularly Raphael's and Michael's discourses, contends that Milton clearly presented the Fall as caused by the subordination of reason by instinct and passion and, more significantly, that this accords with his commitment to a newly emergent middle-class ideology of individuality constrained by educated rationalism.

Milner revises Hill's perception of Satan as a misguided revolutionary. He gives particular emphasis to the exchange between Satan and Abdiel in Book VI in which the former claims that his side promotes liberty above servility and the latter replies:

> Unjustly thou deprav'st it with the name
> Of servitude to serve whom God ordains,
> Or nature; God and nature bid the same,
> When he who rules is worthiest, and excels
> Them whom he governs. This is servitude,
> To serve the unwise, or him who hath rebelled
> Against his worthier, as thine now serve thee,
> Thy self not free, but to thy self enthralled;
> (VI: 174–81)

Abdiel's speech is in Milner's view 'the Miltonic theory of politics' (Milner 1981: 161). Satan is in servitude to his own passions, obeying the tyranny of the unworthy, while a meritocratic system involves the full justification of the government of the worthy over the unworthy: in short, the self-perpetuating class structure of capitalism.

It is intriguing to contrast Milner's reading with Michael Wilding's (1996). Wilding claims that Adam and Eve's day-to-day existence in paradise corresponds with Marx's idealised concept of labour, explained in *Capital* (1867) as 'a necessary condition of human existence ... independent of the forms of human society' (Wilding 1996: 28): for unfallen Adam and Eve work is an element of the agreeable fabric of existence. Hell, however, is 'materialist, technological, sophisticated, hierarchical and militaristic'. Wilding cites Milton's description of Mammon's role in the building of Pandemonium (Book I: 678–92) as a prediction of the industrial revolution and high capitalism. The lines 'Men also ... Ransacked the bowels of their mother earth/For treasures better hid' (686–8) are taken by Wilding as prophesying the role of mining in the industrial revolution; 'Hell represents a pre-vision of what the earth was to become, with its mines, buildings, parliament, military and false philosophers' (Wilding 1996: 30). Wilding goes on to suggest that the passage in Book IX (1100–18) where the recently fallen Adam and Eve suffer shame and feel the need to clothe themselves refers to the early stages (and eventual consequences) of British and European colonialism, which caused the similarly uncorrupted peoples of India and America to participate in the corrupt and degenerate culture of

179

their oppressors (Wilding 1996: 31). In another essay Wilding argues that the rural labourers of 'L'Allegro' are given 'a dignity and an aesthetic beauty' in contrast to the lazy landowners, gentry and aristocrats who also feature in the poem (1987: 44).

So, while Milner perceives Milton as the forerunner of high capitalist, bourgeois consciousness Wilding presents him as an early instance of socialist class-consciousness, a subversive prophet of the injustices of capitalism; which raises the question of how two critics with similar methodologies (both are Marxist affiliated) can reach completely antithetical conclusions following their surveys of the same material? They do so because while Marxism and related socio-political models can deal confidently with verifiably linked historical phenomena – economic facts and statistics, political occurrences and their written records etc. – Milton's writings, his poetry in particular, are self evidently oblique and shifting in their relevance to Milton's own political creed and contemporary circumstances. Abdiel's speech (Milner) and Mammon's enterprises (Wilding) can plausibly be interpreted in the way that each of these critics did; plausibly but not verifiably. Verification is replaced by the manner in which each critic chooses to select features of Milton's work and then relocate these within the ideological dynamic of the period.

This problematical tension between the core discipline of socio-historicism and its more fragile, variegated and, to a degree, subjective counterpart in literary interpretation underpins all Marxist readings of Milton. Indeed it presents problems for all attempts to interpret his work in accordance with its historical-political context. For example, in 1943 M. Ross, who was not a Marxist, was perplexed by the conflicting parallels between God as a monarchical figure in *Paradise Lost*, Milton's anti-monarchist opinions, Satan's failed and evil revolution and Cromwell's failed and honourable one. Whiting (1964) and Bennett (1977) treated Satan and the devils as evocations of Charles I and the Cavaliers, founding their arguments upon the image of Satan as usurper whose resentment of the Son's elevation through the heavenly hierarchy parallels Charles's perception of himself as a kind of mortal deity. Others, such as Fallon (1984) and Revard (1980) found correspondences between Satan and Cromwell. Cromwell is the failed revolutionary, whose attempt to replace kingship with republicanism turned out to be an unrealizable objective, just as Satan's own ambitions would be eternally constrained by the omnipotence of God. Fact and interpretative hypothesis always seem to intersect in unpredictable ways.

Kendrick (1986), a Marxist, can't quite seem to make up his mind as to whether Milton was a free-thinking liberal or subject to the materialist ideology of the emergent middle-classes, or both. His assertion that 'It was by identifying the soul's powers with those of the free commodity that Milton felt himself free' (Kendrick 1986: 13) could mean that either Milton predicted socialism ('free commodity' signifying collectively available, as in paradise) or simply projected himself, via pre-fallen Adam and Eve, beyond the growing culture of materialism as an assuagement of guilt. Kendrick does not finally decide on one or the other.

Norbrook (1984) considers the political resonances of Milton's early poetry and concludes that in 'Lycidas', 'the joy of poetic composition is bound up with the exercise of the political imagination' (Norbrook 1984: 62); meaning that the radical structure of the poem, along with its constantly shifting focus, is predictive of the soon to be experienced political climate. Well, perhaps, but Norbrook feels the need to predicate his readings upon an interpretative hypothesis, that the early poems 'make their political points not so much by direct comment as by modification of generic expectations... After the dissolution of Parliament in 1629 orthodox channels of political debate were still more strictly controlled.' (Norbrook 1984: 48). This can be translated as: Milton's early stylistic experiments were political gestures, necessarily disguised because of the repressive atmosphere of the reign of Charles I. Again we encounter a managed relationship between indisputable historical facts and literary-critical speculation.

Barker (1984) examines *Areopagitica* in relation to the theories of French writer Michel Foucault (1926–84). Foucault is difficult to categorise within the sub-spheres of modern theory; he certainly engages with the Marxist notion of history, while combining this with post-Freudian concepts of individuality and subjectivity **[182–6]**. Barker treats *Areopagitica* as symptomatic of the evolving and consequently uncertain modern sense of identity which, in the mid-seventeenth century, was caught between feudalism and capitalism. *Areopagitica's* engagement with censorship is assessed by Barker as involving perceived tensions between institutional control, surveillance and threatened individuality.

Marxism during the 1980s and 90s would experience, some would say suffer, the fate of all other sub-categories of literary theory. It would be swept into a less easily specified theoretical zone where different non-literary ideas – linguistics, psychoanalysis, politics, feminism et al – would begin to merge and intersect. This is generally known as post-structuralism, and is dominated by the overarching and unsettling machinations of deconstruction, an activity invented by Jacques Derrida. The best example of Marxist-poststructuralist writing on

Milton is Fredric Jameson's essay (1986) and we will defer treatment of it until the section after next.

One book which deserves mention beyond the Eurocentric political readings is Evans' *Milton's Imperial Epic* (1996) which considers *Paradise Lost* as, partly a direct allegory upon, partly a sublimated engagement with the colonial expansion of England in the seventeenth century. Evans considers parallels between texts dealing directly with the Plantation of Virginia early in the century and reaches some intriguing conclusions regarding the relation between God as an Imperial presence, his subjects, Adam and Eve, and Satan and his crew as dispossessed natives. For example,

> Exiled from their 'native seat' (I: 634) in Heaven, the Devil and his followers can thus be cast by Milton in the role of the dispossessed Indians eager to avenge themselves on the newcomers who have been 'by our exile/Made happie' (X: 484–5).
>
> (Evans 1996: 105)

Psychoanalysis

Freudianism is the predominant doctrine of modern psychoanalysis. Central to Sigmund Freud's model of the conscious and subconscious registers of the mind is the Oedipus complex: the culturally suppressed desire of the child – generally perceived to be male – for the mother in rivalry with the father. This desire is transferred, via pressures of convention, from the conscious mind or ego to the unconscious realm of the id at the behest of the father figure or superego. According to Freud we resolve these conflicting pressures in a number of ways, sometimes by consciously confronting them (one purpose of psychoanalytical 'talking cures') or by reallocating their forces in other forms of coded expression, obsession or involvement – literary writing incorporates all three.

In Milton Studies psychoanalytic criticism is almost solely represented by William Kerrigan's book (1983). In Kerrigan's view, Milton's Adam and Eve represent for their author the original primal scene, at once a version of his own parents and an expansion of this personal register into the shared human conundrum: they were the first people, parentless themselves, but the originators of sexuality and procreation. Kerrigan analyses all of the speakers in *Paradise Lost* as enactments of Milton's shifting perspective upon his conscious and subconscious registers. Particularly important is the passage at the beginning of Book III where Milton self-consciously announces his own speaking presence and reflects upon his gigantic undertaking in writing the poem.

> The poet sings, 'in shadiest covert hid', his mind a place symbolic of the bower where nightingales celebrated the union of Adam and Eve. In the song arising here we find the entire transformational history of this space in psychic life. The composing of the song demands and receives co-operation among the various relationships or states of the ego that have achieved organisation in this space, moving back from the Father and the father-as-superego to contact the pre-oedipal mother, moving back to contact the potency of the oedipal father.
>
> (Kerrigan 1983: 189)

Kerrigan seems to be arguing that Milton's shift to the reflective and personal at the beginning of Book III involves him in a marking out of the psychic territory of the poem. What Kerrigan calls the 'various relationships or states of the ego' constitutes the use of the main figures of the Genesis story variously as projections of and substitutes for Milton's own psychic universe. All of them – Adam, Eve, God, the Son, Satan, Raphael, Michael – at different points in the narrative assume roles that we identify with the family relationships that are part of or are affected by the Oedipus complex. One example of how these roles continually alter and reform themselves occurs in Book VIII when Adam gives an account of his exchange with God which eventually results in the creation of Eve **[111–12]**. In Kerrigan's view Adam's assertion that God is not alone, is in fact always accompanied by the Son, initiates a process of psycho-sexual interchange; Adam's relationship with Eve becomes the equivalent of the relationship between God the Father and Christ the Son. 'At the prompting of God we place Christ in the position of Eve. The allegory of Satan, Sin, and Death, read as a parody of the Godhead, also encourages us to entertain a relationship between Christ and the woman' (Kerrigan 1983: 187).

Kerrigan subjects the entire poem, in terms of the psycho-sexual and pseudo-familial relationships between each of its characters, to a psychoanalytical decoding, treating it as an enactment of the dynamic relationship between Milton's ego and his unconscious state. In his Introduction he states that

> I would like to recover something of the original urgency of the encounter between religion and psychoanalysis. If psychoanalysis would guard us against the primitive illusions of religion, perhaps

religious affirmations would guard us against the civilised illusions of a self-authenticating ego.

(Kerrigan 1983: 7–8)

In Kerrigan's opinion Milton should not be treated as many, particularly pre-twentieth century, literary writers have been by psychoanalytical critics; virtually as patients for whom such 'primitive illusions' as religion are substitutes for some type of repressed imbalance between the ego and the unconscious. Rather, Milton's poeticisation of religion ought to be examined, as Kerrigan intends to do, as the operation of his superego, that element of his ego with the critical, judging function. As Kerrigan reminds us, psychoanalysis, with its attendant model of our conscious and unconscious states, was unknown in the seventeenth century and Milton cannot quite be regarded as a figure who pre-empts Freud. At the same time, however, his decision to re-examine the closest seventeenth-century counterpart to modern perceptions of the mind, the religious distinction between empirical and supernatural states, should be analysed as a self-fixated psychoanalytical experiment.

The psychoanalytic theorist who arguably has influenced late twentieth-century literary criticism as much as Freud is Jacques Lacan. A comprehensive understanding of Lacan's ideas requires some familiarity with poststructuralist notions of language, which will be looked at in the next section. For the moment it should be noted that while Freud dealt with the unconscious, particularly in its manifestation via dreams, mainly in terms of visual images and pre-linguistic inclinations, Lacan shifted the emphasis toward the dependency of our conscious and unconscious states upon language. He contended in his famous essay on 'the mirror stage' (see Wright 1982: 154–6), that reality, including our perception of ourselves, is not something that we first know and are then able to name but that the naming process, the acquisition of language, prefigures and enables our engagement with reality. Before we are able to make use of such basic pronouns as 'I' and 'you' we have no proper ability to distinguish ourselves from others. Consequently, the symbolic manifestations of our ego and our unconscious state are effectively determined by language. Claudia Champagne (1991) conducted a Lacanian survey of *Paradise Lost* and gave particular attention to the passage in Book IX where Adam has to decide whether or not to fall with Eve **[114–15]**. Generally the section in which he vocalises his need to remain with her (908–79) is interpreted as a magnanimous gesture of love and self sacrifice; he is also willing to die with her. Champagne (1991: 130) cites Lacan's theory that our perception of other people, even those to whom we are most closely, emotionally, attached, is grounded in the necessity of being able to share with them the existential, epistemological field of language. Adam is obliged to chose between two people who occupy principal roles in his linguistic sphere, God and Eve. He chooses Eve, according to Milton, 'Against his better knowledge, not deceiv'd,/But fondly overcome with Female charm' (IX: 998–9). In Champagne's view Adam's ability to distinguish between these two linguistic presences, one 'Symbolic' (he never actually *sees* God), the other tactile and capable of causing physical attraction, means that 'he is not psychotic, as Lacan's definition of psychosis makes clear. The psychotic never accedes to the realm of the Symbolic, never represses his own individual desire, never acknowledges the authority of the Father's law' (Champagne 1991: 131). Satan, however, while also refusing to accept the word of the Father, acts out what 'Lacan calls psychotic "foreclosure"' (Champagne 1991: 131).

Champagne's essay prompts a number of questions, not so much addressed to the specifics of Lacanian or Freudian readings as more overarching and attendant upon the ever more complex practice of literary theory in general. Principally, what exactly are the objectives and consequent disclosures of Champagne's essay? She concludes that at the end of Milton's poem 'Adam is no longer alone, no longer alienated from God or from Eve because of the Son's perfect love and obedience. This harmony, then, of love and obedience is that "paradise within thee, happier far" upon which Milton's epic is hinged' (Champagne 1991: 132). This summation sounds very similar to commentaries by Christian readers of Milton from the eighteenth century to Lewis. Certainly, Champagne has reached it via an analysis of the main characters, chiefly Adam, according to Lacan's perplexing model of language and the unconscious, but what is not clear is whether her principal focus is upon, in descending order of significance, psycho-analytic theory, language and literary representation, or the particular questions raised by John Milton in a poem about the creation and destiny of man. Kerrigan goes some way toward crediting Milton and his work as special cases, particularly important in their challenging engagement with psychoanalytical issues, but again we are left wondering whether his book is about Milton or about psychoanalysis.

In another Lacanian reading of Milton, Richard Halpern (1987) concentrates upon the 'Nativity Ode' **[61–3]**. He premises his account upon Lacan's 'mirror stage' thesis. In this the acquisition language is compared with a hypothetical moment at which the human being first recognises a reflected image of him/herself in a mirror; with language we can be present within and articulate ourselves in the pronominal

'I'. Lacan considers how this moment enables us to exist within a multiplicity of mental narratives, stories about who we are or can be. Halpern suggests that Milton's writing of the 'Nativity Ode' is symptomatic of a mature version of this, that in placing the poem within his first collection of 1645 'he appropriates the occasion of Christ's birth to announce his own poetic nativity and to anticipate the maturation of his own powers ... Christ enables Milton to mediate his own relationship with literary history by providing a model for that history and for his place within it' (Halpern 1987: 6). So, for Milton the writing and public presentation of this poem involves a recognition and an ambitious projection of his self-perceived identity, a moment of poetic birth in which he implicitly compares his own self with that of that redemptive power of Christ. What Halpern is saying here is that Milton's poetic ambitions are bound into a complex fabric of mental projections and narratives; Milton is using language, poetic language, to explore his part-sublimated, part-conscious sense of identity.

Again we have to consider the relationship between the complex theoretical premise upon which this reading is based and, to put it bluntly, an empiricist interpretation of the poem and its historical/autobiographical context. The premise assumes that for three hundred years interpreters have not recognised the psychoanalytical resonances of the poem because they have not read Lacan, or Freud; and that without this enlightening perspective a crucial element of Milton's writing – indeed of all writing – will not be evident. As with Kerrigan and Champagne the taxing issue here is the balance between a theoretical, explanatory discipline and Milton as a self-determined individual, conscious of his intentions and state of mind. To an extent this issue also prefigures feminist and Marxist readings of Milton; the implication of both being that Milton's feelings and thoughts about gender and politics can best be articulated and understood within an analytical-methodological framework that is all-encompassing and for which Milton the poet is one amongst an almost limitless number of case-studies, literary and non-literary, particular and generic.

Literary criticism was, and for some still is, a self-defining activity, grounded upon the intensive study of the literary text and involving a detailed knowledge of its writer, its stylistic character, its assumed purpose, and its historical-generic context. The debates that took place between Lewis, Empson, Eliot, Leavis and Ricks were founded upon these preconditions. The question, which will be addressed in the following section, is this: have the old disputations on what Milton really meant been subsumed, made irrelevant, by a vast theoretical programme involving its own self-determined fields of thinking and writing?

Poststructuralism and deconstruction

Deconstruction is an extension of the linguistic theories of Ferdinand de Saussure (1857–1913) propounded in his *Course in General Linguistics* (1915). Saussure argued that language is not so much a medium that enables us to reflect reality but more an autonomous structure of relations through which, to some extent, we construct reality. For instance the panorama of colours from, in English, blue to grey is divided very differently in Welsh and in French. Do the Welsh, the French and the English see things differently or, as Saussure argues, do our different language systems impose different perceptual frameworks upon us? Jacques Derrida pursued the more disturbing implications of this concept of language as refractory system rather than transparent medium and founded the technique of deconstruction. Deconstructionists believe that language determines the limits and the structure of our temporal and spiritual awareness. God is a word, a signifier that we understand and, indeed, worship not because of its verifiable relation to a tangible entity (who has seen God?) but because it is the nexus, the meeting point of other words and concepts. God is omnipotent, omniscient, benevolent yet finally unknowable. He is the synthesis and summation of a continuum of signifiers and concepts whose validity depends upon their relation to other signifiers and concepts. We understand good because we also understand evil, and we can embody these abstract ideas in presences such as God and Satan. To deconstruct a text is to demonstrate how it subverts its own claim to reflect or mediate prelinguistic reality, to show how it creates an artificial or fictional pattern of reality by relying upon the differential structure of language.

As far as Milton criticism is concerned there are no all-inclusive, self-defining examples of deconstruction, not in the sense that we can identify particular books or articles as exclusively incorporating a Marxist or a feminist approach. Instead we encounter in 1980s and 1990s uses and acknowledgements of Derrida's ideas on language often as supplements to other tactical or ideological approaches to Milton. Hence the proposed pairing of deconstruction with poststructuralism: that latter term is used to describe the influence of Derrida's ideas upon all branches of literary theory and criticism.

The closest that anyone has come to a comprehensive deconstructive survey of Milton is Rapaport (1983). To properly describe, let alone explain, the panorama and complexity of Rapaport's survey would require another chapter: what can be said is that the book regularly involves encounters between Rapaport's perceptions of Derrida and

Milton. One of the more accessible occurs at pages 38–41, considering the last two books of *Paradise Lost*. Here, 'Milton clearly shows how the sin that Adam and Eve commit initiates the Fall of language, causes signifiers and signifieds to break their natural bonds' (Rapaport 1983: 38). 'Signifier' and 'signified' are Saussurean terms; the former referring to the actual, material sign, the word uttered or on paper, the latter to the prelinguistic object or concept that the sign is held to represent. Saussure argued that their relationship is arbitrary and customary, that there is no natural relationship between the two, but that our ingrained familiarity with language causes us to presume that there might be: when we use or think of the signifiers 'mother' or 'father', for instance, they seem innately bound into our particular perception of their signifieds.

Rapaport suggests that in Books XI and XII Milton pre-empts Derrida, albeit within a limiting theological framework. He argues that the Fall causes Adam and Eve to first encounter the arbitrary relation between signifiers and signifieds.

> Nature first gave Signs, imprest
> On bird, Beast, Air, Air suddenly eclips'd
> After short blush of morn
>
> (XI, 182–4)

> That is to say, things are no longer signifieds but signifiers; things are not archetypes but only copies of archetypes ... things have faded, and all that remains is their residual semiotic significance.
>
> (Rapaport 1983: 39)

Much is implied here. Before the Fall, so Rapaport argues, things, objects and ideas were in some way organically related, almost blended, with their linguistic representations. One of the consequences of the Fall was that language became only arbitrarily related to prelinguistic reality – which is consistent with the orthodox Christian view that the Fall caused humanity to be denied any proper knowledge of ultimate truth, God.

Rapaport raises, but leaves unanswered, several questions. Is Milton a deconstructionist? This seems unlikely, given that deconstruction involves the assumption that language per se is an arbitrary structure. If this is the case, then how did Adam and Eve communicate with God, Raphael and Satan before the Fall, before the arbitrariness of language became part of their punishment? Maybe Milton is reminding us that, given our fallen condition, we can never properly understand what occurred before that. If so, his decision to represent these occurrences *in* language seems perverse and self-contradictory. This spiral of irresolvable conundrums informs Rapaport's book, and the fact that they remain unresolved testifies to his Derridian affiliation: the resolution of such questions is an objective and an illusion, sustained by our foolish belief that language can mediate truth.

Terry Eagleton (1987) takes up where Rapaport left off. Eagleton is an example of post-structuralist eclecticism, probably more faithful to Marxism than to any other branch of modern theory.

> If the bourgeois ideological need to narrate, explain, apologise threatens in its discursive realism to undo the very rhetorical frames in which it is staged, this is at once to its detriment – for such magnifying, universalizing forms are as Marx points out a bourgeois revolutionary requirement – and the sign of a certain deconstruction of traditionalist culture at the hands of a progressive bourgeois rationality. Milton's Protestant commitment to sense and discourse, his refusal of the idolatry of the apodictic image, his secularising faith in rational causality: all of these impulses subtly assert themselves over the very symbolic forms of which they stand in need. Traditional culture, reverently summoned to illuminate the present, finds itself in that very act appropriated, swerved from, rewritten in heretical terms.
>
> (Eagleton 1987: 346–7)

For Eagleton the linguistic-philosophical core of deconstruction becomes a useful supplement to his thesis that Milton embodied the dialectical conflict between bourgeois rationality and the ingrained, religion-based presumptions of the society that bourgeois consciousness was rapidly colonizing. This 'historically determined clash of semiotic codes' offers in Eagleton's view an explanation of *Paradise Lost*'s stylistic character.

> The clash of semiotic codes in *Paradise Lost* highlights with peculiar visibility what we might call the "materiality" of the poem's forms; and nowhere is this materiality more evident than in its language. The remorselessly logocentric Leavis, for whom the signifier, emptied of any action or substance of its own, must be no more than the obedient bearer of a signified, can see little in the "Miltonic music" but an external embellishment, clumsily at odds with the springs of sense. When T.S. Eliot remarked that you needed to read

the poem twice, once for the sound and once for the meaning, he too had been struck by its contrived dislocation of the unified sign, the sonorous excess of language over meaning, the way in which the poem's language works athwart the "natural" texture of the senses and so fails to repress its own artifice. Nothing could be further from the swift fusion of the Metaphysical conceit than the calculated self-conscious unfurling of the epic simile, with all its whirring machinery of production on show. As Habakkuk gives way to Locke, the materiality of the signifier in English discourse is on the point of yielding to the naturalised representational sign of bourgeois empiricism, which will serve the ideological ends of middle-class rule extremely well. Milton's rhetoric puts up a last-ditch resistance to this shackling of the sign, irreducible as that rhetoric is to the "natural" rhythms of a speaking voice.

(Eagleton 1987: 347)

At its core, Eagleton's survey of the style of *Paradise Lost* involves the much debated opinions of Eliot and Leavis **[154–6]** recycled as 'logocentric' hunts for the elusive signified. This gives way to his own diagnosis of the poem as caught somewhere between 'bourgeois empiricism' and whatever preceded it. Apart from being slightly puzzled about what exactly Eagleton is trying to say one is caused to wonder whether, to borrow one of his terms, 'the whirring machinery' of pseudo-deconstruction – material signifiers, emptied signifieds, remorseless legocentrism etc. – tells us anything about Milton that we don't already know from the more accessible writings of Eliot, Leavis, Lewis, Empson and Hill.

Frederic Jameson's (1986) essay, without citing Derrida, employs a Derridean model of language and identity. He states that

What is unsatisfactory about *Milton's God* is the retention of a framework in which the organizing perspective remains the biographical Milton, as author and individual subject with his opinions, flaws, weaknesses and strengths, and the like.

(Jameson 1986: 49)

On the one hand Jameson praises Empson's book for its 'hatred of religion and superstition' (Jameson 1986: 48) and its disclosure of a sceptical subtext beneath Milton's rewriting of Genesis, while at the same time he contests Empson's presumption that the words of *Paradise Lost* disclose the particularities of Milton as an individual with a discernible state of mind. Instead Jameson argues that, irrespective of

Milton's intention or true inclinations, his 'symbolic act is alienated from itself, turns against itself, ends up producing the opposite of what it originally intended' (Jameson 1986: 49). Although Jameson does not cite Derrida he adopts the Derridean position that prelinguistic intent or inclination will always be subservient to the arbitrary, controlling function of language. He does this, like Eagleton, as a supplement to his generally Marxist thesis.

Belsey (1988) posits the contradictory, self-deconstructive feature of *Paradise Lost* as an element of all attempts to represent or engage in language that which is held to transcend language, the presence and nature of God.

> Thus all cultures and all narratives proclaim a single meaning-which-is-truth, conspire to justify the ways of God. And yet at the heart of the project there lies impossibility. Whatever words are invoked to define him, God cannot be contained there. He is beyond difference itself, able to be defined only in a succession of negatives: 'Immutable, immortal, infinite' (III: 373), 'invisible' (III: 375), 'inaccessible' (III: 377). God is different from everything we know, and therefore 'unspeakable', 'beyond thought' (I: 156, 159).
>
> (Belsey 1988: 39)

Belsey's discussion centres upon her notion of 'difference', an anglicised version of Derrida's concept of *différance*. Derrida's spelling of 'ance' instead of 'ence' indicates the contrast (in French) between 'differing' and 'deferring', his point being that ultimate, final prelin-guistic meaning is continually 'deferred' through language's ability to transfer elements or versions of it from one semantically related word to another; 'differing' words. Belsey draws upon, without citing, Derrida's thesis of *Writing and Difference* (1978) that 'the absence of (a presence, or) a transcendental signified (or final prelinguistic meaning) extends the domain and play of signification infinitely'; Belsey adapts this to Milton's engagement with the ultimate 'transcendental signified', God, which, she argues, he is only capable of defining 'in a succession of negatives'.

Derrida's thesis is in itself controversial and debatable, and Belsey's adaptation of it to *Paradise Lost* even more so. She more than implies that Milton was struggling to overcome the 'impossibility' of repre-senting God in language. However, as a Christian, albeit even a sceptical one, he would surely have been fully aware of the fact that the nature of God is beyond the comprehension, let alone the linguistic capabilities, of fallen humanity. (One should note that while pre-fallen Adam speaks with God the Father, after the Fall he only ever encounters the word of Christ, who as everyone is aware will temporarily become human.) Belsey's next point is grounded upon her perhaps misguided assumption. Milton's 'remedy', as she puts it, is to continually invoke song and music throughout the poem as a kind of substitute for language. 'Music is irreducible, opaque, pure inscription. It is sound, pattern: it "charms the sense"' (Belsey 1988: 39). What she seems to be suggesting here is that music suspends the endless chain of signification that constitutes language. This might be the case with wordless music, but Milton's invocations of it (the best known being his request that the 'heavenly Muse' 'Sing' through him I: 6) are always predicated upon the traditional Renaissance convention that metrical language, poetry, is a type of music.

Belsey's survey, like Rapaport's, rests upon the implied contention, borrowed from Derrida, that humanity has been engaged in the self-deluding enterprise of causing language to do that which by its very nature it cannot do, to provide transparent access to some ultimate, transcendent pre-linguistic truth, and that *Paradise Lost* is a prime example of this self-deconstructing activity. The flaw in this, generally elided by Derrida and his followers, is that for many writers and thinkers, Christians included, the precondition that language is a limited, self-referential continuum, incapable of mediating ultimate truth, was an accepted fact. One of the reasons why Milton, unlike many other major writers, has remained relatively immune from the full-blown ministrations of the deconstructors is that he unsettles their all-encompassing presumption about the nature of literary, and indeed non-literary, writers; that they are all either oblivious or deluding themselves with regard to the philosophical-existential limitations of language. Milton frequently tested the effects of poetic language upon the beliefs and ingrained prolusions of his readers, but he did so as someone who was fully aware of the boundaries of this process.

Many regard Geoffrey Hartman as the paradigmatic deconstructor, one who has caused the empiricist scholarship of Anglo-American literary criticism to wither under the radical scrutiny of French intellectualism. Significantly he wrote, deconstructively, of Milton only once, in an essay reprinted in *Beyond Formalism* (1970). In this he returns again and again to the term 'Balmy Sweat' (VIII: 255); this the 'Beams the Sun/Soon dried', all during Adam's first waking moments after his dream-encounter with God. Hartman continually refers to the way in which the alliterative-assonantal concentrations of language here seem, for no obvious reason, to interfere with its mediating function. Hartman does not attempt to resolve the questions raised by this (reaching conclusions is for deconstructors a self-deluding enterprise). Rather he employs his estimable scholarly and interpretative resources and circles, plays upon, the problem. He suggests, but only suggests, that there might be some parallel between Milton's occasional swamping of the referential function of language by its concrete substance and the more systematic version of this in Joyce's *Finnegans Wake* (Hartman 1970: 156): that perhaps both were, in different degrees, surrendering to the governance of language itself over its misperceived function. A more conventional critic might have pointed out to Hartman that the use of alliterative-assonantal effects in the passage cited was intended by Milton to underline the contrast between Adam's exchange with God and his return to the very human realm in which language is comprised of distracting devices. But to do so would invoke the assumption that Milton knew what language is capable and incapable of doing; and that would unsettle the deconstructive programme.

Milton was not a deconstructor. He was a Christian poet who was probably given to doubt the very basis of his beliefs, and as such he at least attended to the same agenda as poststructuralism – what exactly constitutes the real, the assumed and the represented. *Paradise Lost* invokes the transcendental signified, encourages us to search for what Derrida calls 'the metaphysics of presence' only to confront us with the origins of our position in the domain of infinite play and signification – the doubts and anarchic uncertainties of deconstructive method are a consequence of our first misuse of reason and language. Deconstruction might well be the tower of Babel in its modern, secular manifestation.

> each to other calls
> Not understood, till hoarse, and all in rage,
> As mocked they storm; great laughter was in heaven
> And looking down, to see the hubbub strange
> And hear the din; thus was the building left
> Ridiculous, and the work Confusion named.
>   (XII: 57–62)

Would it stretch credibility to read this as a very shrewd anticipation of what would happen to *Paradise Lost* in its journey through post-seventeenth-century history? True, we could not argue that Milton offered his poem, perhaps in the manner of Beckett, as the source of 'hubbub strange' and 'Confusion', but it has certainly been the focus, the catalyst for the seemingly endless 'calls/Not understood' between critics and literary theorists.

The builders of the Tower of Babel thought they might obtain access to the source of absolute certainty and stability by building a tower to heaven. The tower and its appalling, almost farcical consequences is, at least in the Old Testament, a literal fact, but it is also a metaphor for what Derrida calls 'aporia'. Aporia, in a literal translation from the Greek, is the track that leads nowhere, and this phenomenon has been deployed by deconstructionists to show that each text, each claim to truth, will eventually subvert its own grounds and coherence and disperse its apparent meanings into indeterminacy. *Paradise Lost* provokes and incites aporia. No single critical formula will ever account for its interweavings of what we know and recognise and what we will never fully understand. Attempts finally to explain will result in the same cacophony of voices and proclamations that attended the building of the tower. Milton's 'solution' is to abandon speculation and return to faith, but perhaps he knew that his readers would never, to paraphrase Adam, 'have their fill of knowledge... beyond which was their folly to aspire'. Suspending for a moment any doubts we might have regarding the existence of an afterlife, might we assume that the great laughter in heaven prompted by the building of the tower has been joined by the otherwise sombre voice of John Milton as he observes the progress of his poem?

(f) CONCLUSIONS

It has been indicated that modern literary criticism on Milton is governed by two overarching categories, which can be designated as Intentionalist and Theoretical. The Intentionalists are not so naively self-assured as to claim that Milton's writing transmits an exact version of his state of mind as he wrote or uttered the words we have on paper. Lewis and Empson differ radically, antithetically on this, but despite their differences they share the assumption that they are reading, listening to Milton. The theoreticians, however, desubstantiate the Intentionalist image of Milton as an individual human presence; they treat him as one element of a broader interpretative fabric in which matters of gender, politics, philosophy, linguistics, psychology are mapped out. The borderlines between these two critical categories are sometimes blurred: Hill often suspends his Marxist orthodoxies and allows in a very subjective impression of Milton as a querulous individual, and Lewis just as frequently juggles with the unquestioning certainties of his own belief and the troublesome potentialities of Milton's. Nonetheless it is evident that there is an intrinsic difference between critics who debate the true nature of the effects that Milton intended to create and those who treat him as a subject, whose words are symptomatic of something they understand better than he did.

FURTHER READING

The above section focuses upon the most groundbreaking and controversial examples of Milton criticism; it is not a comprehensive, bibliographical survey. The following is a selection of other critical works which variously extend aspects of the above critical fields, provide detailed accounts of contextual and peripheral issues, and offer introductory guides.

Theology and religion

All critical works on Milton engage inevitably with religious issues; the following concentrate almost exclusively on these. Patrides (1966) provides a reasonably comprehensive and uncontentious account of Milton's place within the various traditions of Christian theology. Kelley (1941) focuses specifically upon *De Doctrina Christiana* as the theological foundation for issues raised in *Paradise Lost*; Sewell (1939) also concentrates on these two texts. Stroup (1968) looks at how the formal and ceremonial aspects of organised religion are treated in Milton's poetry. Barker (1942) and Fixler (1964) examine the political and historical dimensions of Milton's attachment to radical Protestantism. Riggs (1972) considers *Paradise Lost* as the vehicle for Milton's particularised perception of Christianity. The most complex and extensive study of the intersections between Milton's literary and theological radicalisms is the collection of essays by Patrides, Adamson and Hunter (1971). Schwartz (1988) considers Milton's theology within the context of poststructuralism.

Style and form

Stein (1953) predates Ricks (1963) as a detailed New Critical revaluation of Milton's poetic style but lacks Ricks's breadth and interpretative panache. Sprott (1953) provides an updated, revised account of Milton's versification and prosody, Bridges (1921) being his most influential predecessor. Emma (1964) offers a comprehensive modern linguistic survey of Milton's syntax and grammar and an even more sophisticated account is provided by Corns (1990). Burnett (1981) is a reasonably accessible guide to the style and versification of *Paradise Regained*, *Samson Agonistes* and the shorter poems. Treip (1970) examines the way that Milton's punctuation sets his verse apart from contemporary non-literary conventions. Prince (1954) looks at the influence of Italian verse upon Milton's poetry, particularly regarding style. Bradford (1987) considers the relation between the innovative versification of *Paradise Lost* and deconstruction. Ferry (1963) examines the narrational presence in *Paradise Lost* in a manner that we more often associate with studies of fiction.

Context and politics

The following examine Milton's relationship with seventeenth-century politics and thinking without attending to the agenda established by the Marxists.

Geisst (1984) conducts an extensive and largely objective survey of the politics of Milton's prose writings. Spencer Hill (1979) considers in detail the political contexts of Milton's writing and argues that his republican radicalism came very late, that the Puritan of the 1650s was a very different figure from the poet of the 1630s. Richmond (1974) follows the straightforward argument that the failure of the Cromwellian republic, which for Milton had once involved a Platonic ideal, was the principal precondition for *Paradise Lost*: the Fall was a political allegory. Rowse (1977) take the same line. Svendsen (1956) compares Milton's treatment of this world and beyond with seventeenth-century advances in science.

Student-targeted surveys, reference books and collections

As indicated above, Milton criticism of the seventeenth and eighteenth centuries is collected in Shawcross's *Critical Heritage* (2 vols, 1970) and that of the Romantic period in Wittreich (1970). Dyson and Lovelock's *Casebook* (1973) includes a relatively brief selection of seventeenth to nineteenth-century criticism, and concentrates upon the period between Eliot (1936) and Fish (1965) (i.e. mainly New Criticism): curiously Empson is omitted. The collections edited by Patrides (1967) and Rudrum (1968) include criticism from roughly the same period: Rudrum includes Empson. Two more recent collections, which reflect the influence of feminist, Marxist, psychoanalytical and deconstructive criticism, are Patterson (1992) and Zunder (1999). Kermode (1960) and

Nyquist and Ferguson (1987) also reflect, respectively, the New Critical and the more recent theoretical drift of Milton criticism and the essays in each were specifically commissioned for this purpose. Stocker (1988) provides a brief but reasonably comprehensive survey of mid to late-twentieth-century criticism on *Paradise Lost*.

Nicholson (1964), on all the poetry, and Blamires (1971), on *Paradise Lost*, are respectable guides to the primary texts, though dated in their treatment of critical method. Belsey (1988) and Davies (1993) are brief student-targeted introductions to Milton which incorporate new theoretical approaches, and Bradford (1992) offers a short book-by-book survey of *Paradise Lost*.

The most comprehensive reference guide to Milton is Hunter's (1978) seven-volume *Encyclopaedia*, while Danielson's (1989) shorter *Companion* contains more on recent critical theory.

CHRONOLOGY

1608   John Milton (JM) born 9 December in Bread Street, London.
1620   JM enters St. Paul's School, where he will begin his friendship with Charles Diodati.
1625   JM admitted to Christ's College Cambridge, where some of his first published poems will be written.
1630   Edward King (later the subject of 'Lycidas') elected to fellowship at Christ's.
1632   JM takes M.A. and retires to Horton for several years of private study. 'On Shakespeare' published.
1634   *Comus* performed.
1637   *Comus* published.
1638   *Lycidas* published. JM sails for France (May). Arrives in Italy (August–September), attends Barberini concert and meets, amongst others, Galileo and Frescobaldi. Charles Diodati dies (August).
1639   JM goes to Geneva and meets John Diodati, Calvinist theologian and uncle of late Charles. Returns to England (July).
1641   JM begins to publish political and religious pamphlets, including *Animadversions* and *Of Reformation*.
1642   JM marries Mary Powell who, later that year, returns to her family near Oxford, probably because of the recently begun Civil War. (Her family were Royalist, while JM and much of London favoured the Parliamentarians.) *Apology for Smectymnuus* published.
1643   *Doctrine and Disipline of Divorce* published.
1644   *Of Education* and *Areopagitica* published.
1645   *Tetrachordon* and *Colasterion* published. Wife Mary returns.
1646   *Poems ... 1646* published. Daughter Anne born.
1647   Father dies, leaving JM a 'moderate estate'.
1648   Daughter Mary born.
1649   JM appointed Secretary for Foreign Tongues in the victorious Cromwellian government. *Tenure of Kings and Magistrates* published (February) shortly after the execution of Charles I. *Eikonoklastes* published.
1651   *Defensio pro populo Anglicano* published. Son John born.
1652   Deaths of wife Mary, daughter Deborah and son John. Becomes totally blind.

1655 JM semi-retires from Secretaryship and returns to private study, possibly involving early planning for *Paradise Lost* and *De Doctrina*.

1656 Marries Katherine Woodcock.

1657 Daughter Katherine born.

1658 Wife dies.

1659 Cromwell dies. *A Treatise of Civil Power* published.

1660 *Ready and Easy Way to Establish a Free Commonwealth* published shortly before the Restoration of Charles II as monarch. JM's books burned in public (August) and JM arrested (October). Released (December) following the intervention of Marvell and others.

1663 JM takes house in Bunhill Fields, London, where he will produce most of his later writings, with the practical assistance in dictation of his remaining daughters and others. Marries Elizabeth Minshull.

1667 *Paradise Lost* published.

1670 *History of Britain* published.

1671 *Paradise Regained* and *Samson Agonistes* published, the latter thought by some to have been written during the 1650s.

1673 *Of True Religion* published, *Poems, etc. upon Several Occasions...* published, including many of JM's political sonnets from the 1640s and 1650s.

1674 Second edition of *Paradise Lost* (now 12 rather than 10 books) published. JM dies in Bunhill house and is buried in St. Giles, Cripplegate, on 12 November.

BIBLIOGRAPHY

Aers, D. and Hodge, B., '"Rational Burning": Milton and Sex and Marriage' (1981), References from Zunder (1999).

Barker, A.E., *Milton and the Puritan Dilemma*, Toronto: University of Toronto Press (1942).

Barker, F., *The Tremulous Private Body: Essays on Subjection*, London: Methuen (1984).

Belloc, H., *Milton*, London: Cassell (1935).

Belsey, C., *John Milton. Language, Gender, Power*, Oxford: Blackwell (1988).

Bennett, J.S., 'God, Satan and King Charles: Milton's Royal Portraits', PMLA 92 (1977) pp. 441–57.

Blamires, H., *Milton's Creation*, London: Methuen (1971).

Bloom, Harold, *The Anxiety of Influence*, Oxford: Oxford University Press (1973).

Bradford, R., 'Milton's Graphic Poetics', in Nyquist and Ferguson (1987).

Bradford, R., *Paradise Lost. An Open Guide*, Buckingham: Open University Press (1992).

Bradford, R., *Silence and Sound. Theories of Poetics from the 18th Century*, London: Associated University Presses (1992).

Bridges, R., *Milton's Prosody*, Oxford: Oxford University Press (1921).

Brooks, C., *The Well Wrought Urn. Studies in the Structure of Poetry*, London: Methuen (1968, first published 1947).

Brown, C., *John Milton. A Literary Life*, London: Macmillan (1995).

Burnett, A., *Milton's Style*, London: Longman (1981).

Bush, D., *John Milton. A Sketch of His Life and Writings*, London: Weidenfeld and Nicolson (1964).

Champagne, C., 'Adam and his "Other Self" in *Paradise Lost*: A Lacanian study in Psychic Development', in Zunder (1999).

Corns, T., 'Milton's Quest for Respectabiltiy', *Modern Language Review* 77 (1982).

Corns, T., *Milton's Language*, Oxford: Blackwell (1990).

Danielson, D. (ed.), *The Cambridge Companion to Milton*, Cambridge: Cambridge University Press (1989).

Darbishire, Helen (ed.), *The Early Lives of John Milton*, London: Constable (1932).

Davie, D., 'Syntax and Music in *Paradise Lost*', *The Living Milton*, ed., F. Kermode, Oxford: Oxford University Press (1960).

Davies, S., *Milton*, London: Harvester (1993).

Derrida, J., *Writing and Difference*, Chicago: Chicago University Press (1978).

Dyson, A.E. and Lovelock, J. (eds), *Milton: Paradise Lost. A Casebook*, London: Macmillan (1973).

Eagleton, T., 'The God That Failed', in Nyquist and Ferguson (1987).

Eliot, T.S., 'Milton I' (1936); 'Milton II' (1947), in *On Poetry and Poets*, London: Faber (1957).

Eliot, T.S., 'The Metaphysical Poets' (1921), in *Selected Essays*, London: Faber (1961).

Ellwood, T., *History of the Life of Thomas Ellwood*, London (1714).

Emma, R.D., *Milton's Grammar*, The Hague: Mouton (1964).

Empson, W., *Milton's God*, London: Chatto (1961).

Evans, J. Martin, *Milton's Imperial Epic*, Ithaca: Cornwell University Press (1996).

Fallon, R.T., *Captain or Colonel*, Columbia: Missouri University Press (1984).

Ferry, A., *Milton's Epic Voice: The Narrator in Paradise Lost*, Cambridge, MA: Yale University Press (1963).

Fish, S., 'What its Like to Read *L'Allegro* and *Il Penseroso*' (1975), in *Is There a Text in This Class?* Cambridge, MA: Harvard University Press (1980).

Fish, S., *Surprized By Sin: The Reader in Paradise Lost*, London: Macmillan (1967).

Fixler, M., *Milton and the Kingdoms of God*, Northwestern University Press (1964).

Fletcher, H.F., *The Intellectual Development of John Milton*, Illinois: Illinois University Press (1956).

Forgacs, D., 'Marxist Literary Theories', in *Modern Literary Theory*, (eds) A. Jefferson and D. Robey, London: Batsford (1982).

French, J.M. (ed.), *Life Records of John Milton*, New Jersey: Rutgers University Press (1949–58).

Froula, C., 'When Eve Reads Milton: Undoing the Canonical Economy' (1983). References from Patterson (1992).

Geisst, C., *The Political Thought of John Milton*, London: Macmillan (1984).

Gilbert, S., 'Patriarchal Poetry and Women Readers: Reflections on Milton's Bogey', *PMLA* 93 (1978), pp.368–82.

Graves, Robert, *Wife to Mr. Milton*, London: Cassell (1942).

Greenlaw, E., 'A Better Teaching Than Aquinas' *Studies in Philology*, 14 (1917), pp. 196–217

Halkett, J., *Milton and the Idea of Matrimony*, New Haven: Yale University Press (1970).

Halpern, R., 'The Great Instauration: imaginary narratives in Milton's "Nativity Ode"', in Nyquist and Ferguson (1987).

Hanford, J., *John Milton, Englishman*, New York: Crown (1949).

Hartman, G., 'Adam on The Grass with Balsamora' (1970) in Zunder (1999).

Havens, R.D., *The Influence of Milton on English Poetry*, Cambridge, MA: Harvard University Press (1922).

Hayley, W., *Life of Milton*, London (1794).

Hill, Christopher, *Milton and the English Revolution*, London: Faber and Faber (1977).

Honigman, E.A.J. (ed.), *Milton's Sonnets*, London: Macmillan (1966).

Hooker, E.N. (ed.), *The Critical Works of John Dennis*, 2 Vols, Baltimore: John Hopkins Press (1939–43).

Hopkins, G.M., *Selected Letters*, ed. C. Phillips, Oxford: Oxford University Press (1990).

Hunter, W.B. (ed.), *A Milton Encyclopedia*, 7 Vols, London: Associated University Presses (1978).

Ivimay, Joseph, *John Milton: His Life and Times, Religious and Political Opinions*, London (1833).

Jameson, F., 'Religion and Ideology: A Political Reading of *Paradise Lost*' (1986). References from Zunder (1999).

Johnson, S., *Lives of the Poets*, 1779–81; references from reprints in *Oxford Anthology of English Literature*, Vol. I, ed. Kermode, F. *et al.*, Oxford: Oxford University Press.

Kelley, M., *This Great Argument*, New Jersey: Princeton University Press (1941).

Kendrick, C., *Milton. A Study in Ideology and Form*, New York: Methuen (1986).

Kermode, F. (ed.), *The Living Milton: Essays by Various Hands*, London: Routledge (1960).

Kerrigan, W., *The Sacred Garden*, Cambridge, MA: Harvard University Press (1983).

Landy, M., 'Kinship and The Role of Women in *Paradise Lost*', *Milton Studies* 4 (1972), pp.3–18.

Le Comte, E., *Milton and Sex*, London: Macmillan (1978).

Leavis, F.R. *Revaluation*, London: Chatto (1936).

Leishman, J.B., *Milton's Minor Poems*, London: Hutchinson (1969).

Levi, P., *Eden Renewed. The Public and Private Life of John Milton*, London: Macmillan (1996).

Lewalski, B.K., 'Milton on Women – Yet Once More', *Milton Studies* 6, (1974), pp.3–20.

Lewalski, B.K., *Milton's Brief Epic*, Providence (1966).

Lewis, C.S., *A Preface to Paradise Lost*, Oxford: Oxford University Press (1942).

Lovejoy, A.O., *The Great Chain of Being: A Study in the History of an Idea*, New York: Harper and Row (1960).

Macauley, T., *The Works of Lord Macauley*, ed. Lady Trevelyan, Vol. 5, London: Longman (1875).

Martz, L., 'The Rising Poet, 1645' (1965), in *Poet of Exile: A Study of Milton's Poetry*, New Haven: Yale University Press (1980).

Masson, D., *Life of Milton*, 7 Vols, London (1859–94).

McColley, D., *Milton's Eve*, Champagne: Illinois University Press (1983).

Milner, A., *John Milton and the English Revolution*, London: Macmillan (1981).

Milton, John, *The Complete Prose Works of John Milton*, ed. D.M. Wolfe, 8 Vols, New Haven: Yale University Press (1953–82).

Milton, John, *The Poems*, eds J. Carey and A. Fowler, London: Longman (1968).

Milton, John, *The Works of John Milton*, ed. F.A. Patterson, 20 Vols, New York: Columbia University Press (1931–40).

Muir, K., *John Milton*, London: Longman, Green & Co (1955).

Myers, W., *Milton and Free Will: An Essay in Criticism and Philosophy*, London: Croom Helm (1987). References from Patterson (1992).

Newlyn, L., *Paradise Lost and the Romantic Reader*, Oxford: Oxford University Press (1993).

Nicolson, M., *A Reader's Guide to John Milton*, London: Thames and Hudson (1964).

Norbrook, D., 'The Politics of Milton's Early Poetry', (1984). References from Patterson (1992).

Nyquist, M. and Ferguson, M. (eds), *Re-Membering Milton. Essays on the Texts and Traditions*, London: Methuen (1987).

Nyquist, M., 'Fallen Differences, Phallogocentric Discourses: Losing *Paradise Lost* to History' (1988). References from Patterson (1992).

Nyquist, M., 'The Genesis of Gendered Subjectivity in the Divorce Tracts and in *Paradise Lost*', in *Re-Membering Milton*, eds Nyquist and Ferguson, London: Methuen (1987). References from Zunder (1999).

Oras, A., *Milton's Editors and Commentators from Patrick Hume to Henry John Todd 16959–1801*, Tartu (1930).

Oras, A., *Milton's Blank Verse and the Chronology of His Major Poems*, Gainsville: University of Illinois Press (1953).

Parker, W.R., *Milton. A Biography*, Oxford: Oxford University Press (1968).

Patrides, C.A. (ed.), *Approaches to Paradise Lost*, London: Edward Arnold (1968).

Patrides, C.A., Adamson, J.H. and Hunter, W.B., *Bright Essence. Studies in Milton's Theology*, Salt Lake City: University of Utah Press (1971).

Patrides, C.A., *Milton and the Christian Tradition*, Oxford: Oxford University Press (1966).

Patterson, A. (ed.), *John Milton: Longman Critical Reader*, London: Longman (1992).

Phillips, E., *Life of Milton*, (1694). References from Darbishire (1932).

Pope, E.M., *Paradise Regained, the Tradition and the Poem*, Baltimore (1947).

Prince, F.T., *The Italian Element in Milton's Verse*, Oxford: Oxford University Press (1954).

Quint, D., 'David's Census: Milton's Politics and *Paradise Regained*', in Nyquist and Ferguson (1987).

Rajan, B., *Paradise Lost and the 17th Century Reader* (1947). Referenes from Dyson and Lovelock (1973).

Raleigh, W., *Milton*, London (1900).

Rapaport, H., *Milton and the Post Modern*, Lincoln: University of Nebraska Press (1983).

Revard, S.P., *The War in Heaven*, Ithaca, NY: Cornell University Press (1980).

Richmond, H., *The Christian Revolutionary: John Milton*, Berkeley: University of California Press (1974).

Ricks, C., *Milton's Grand Style*, Oxford: Oxford University Press (1963).

Ricks, C., *Tennyson*, London: Macmillan (1972).

Riggs, W.G., *The Christian Poet in Paradise Lost*, Berkeley: University of California Press (1972).

Ross, M., *Milton and Royalism*, Ithaca: Cornell University Press (1943).

Rowse, A.L., *Milton the Puritan*, London: Macmillan (1977).

Rudrum, A. (ed.), *Milton. Modern Judgements*, London: Macmillan (1968).

Saintsbury, G., *A History of English Prosody*, 3 Vols, London (1906–10).

Schwartz, R., *Remembering and Repeating: Biblical Creation in Paradise Lost*, Cambridge: Cambridge University Press (1988).

Sewell, A., *A Study of Milton's Christian Doctrine*, Oxford: Oxford University Press (1939).

Shawcross, J.T. (ed.), *Milton. The Critical Heritage*, Vols I and II, London: Routledge (1970 and 1972).

Smart, John (ed.), *The Sonnets of Milton*, Glasgow (1921).

Spencer Hill, J., *John Milton: Poet, Priest and Prophet*, London (1979).

Sprott, S.E., *Milton's Art of Prosody*, Oxford: Oxford University Press (1953).

Stein, A., *Answerable Style*, University of Minnesota Press (1953).

Stocker, M., *Paradise Lost: The Critics' Debate*, London: Macmillan (1988).

Stroup, T.B., *Religious Rite and Ceremony in Milton's Poetry*, Lexington: University of Kentucky Press (1968).

Svendsen, K., *Milton and Science*, New York: Greenwood Press (1956).

Tillyard, E.M.W., *Milton*, London: Chatto and Windus (1930).

Tillyard, E.M.W., *The Miltonic Setting, Past and Present*, Cambridge: Cambridge University Press (1938).

Treip, M., *Milton's Punctuation and the Changing English Usage*, London: Methuen (1970).

Turner, J.G., *One Flesh: Paradisal Marriage and Sexual Relations in the Age of Milton*, Oxford: Oxford University Press (1987).

Tuve, R., *Image and Themes in Five Poems By Milton*, Oxford: Oxford University Press (1957).

Waldock, A.J.A., *Paradise Lost and its Critics*, Cambridge: Cambridge University Press (1947).

Webber, J.M., 'The Politics of Poetry: Feminism and Paradise Lost', *Milton Studies* 14 (1980), pp.3–24.

Wedgwood, C.V., *Milton and His World*, London: Lutterworth (1969).

Whiting, G.W., *Milton's Literary Milieu*, New York: Russell and Russell (1964).

Wilding, M., 'Milton's Early Radicalism' (1987) in Patterson (1992).

Wilding, M., 'Milton's Radical Epic', in *Writing and Radicalism*, (ed.) J. Lucas, London: Longman (1996).

Wilson, A.N., *The Life of John Milton*, Oxford: Oxford University Press (1983).

Wittreich, J. (ed.), *The Romantics on Milton*, Cleveland: Case Western Reserve University Press (1970).

Wittreich, J., *Feminist Milton*, Ithaca: Cornwell University Press (1987).

Wittreich, J., *Milton's Tradition and his Legacy*, California: Huntingdon Library (1979).

Wright, E., 'Modern Psychoanalytic Criticism' in *Modern Literary Theory*, eds A. Jefferson and D. Robey, London: Batsford (1982).

Zunder, W. (ed.), *Paradise Lost. New Casebooks*, London: Macmillan (1999).

INDEX

CPSIA information can be obtained at www.ICGtesting.com
Printed in the USA
BVOW09s0405130115

382996BV00004B/30/P